The Executor's Guide

The Executor's Guide

How to Administer
an Estate under a Will

Linda D. Kirby

Westport, Connecticut
London

Library of Congress Cataloging-in-Publication Data

Kirby, Linda D., 1950–
 The executor's guide : how to administer an estate under a will / Linda D.
 Kirby.
  p. cm.
 Includes bibliographical references and index.
 ISBN 0–275–98203–3 (alk. paper)
  1. Executors and administrators—United States. 2. Wills—United
States. 3. Decedents' estates—United States. I. Title.
 KF778.K57 2004
 346.7305′2—dc22   2003068723

British Library Cataloguing in Publication Data is available.

Library of Congress Catalog Card Number: 2003068723
ISBN: 0–275–98203–3

First published in 2004

Praeger Publishers, 88 Post Road West, Westport, CT 06881
An imprint of Greenwood Publishing Group, Inc.
www.praeger.com

Printed in the United States of America

The paper used in this book complies with the
Permanent Paper Standard issued by the National
Information Standards Organization (Z39.48–1984).

10 9 8 7 6 5 4 3 2 1

Contents

Acknowledgments

There are four groups of people to whom I would like to express my gratitude: First, there are my sons who have been variously patient and supportive throughout the process of my writing and whose needs for the essentials and niceties of life provide the primary motivation for all my work; second, there are my many clients who over the years have shared with me as their attorney the real-life experiences that made me see the necessity of this book; third, Harold Vogt, Ph.D., surrogate father, friend, and consistently wise counselor, who has taught me to see what is more important than being right; and most recently, Nick Philipson and Hilary Claggett at Praeger Publishing, whose energy and vision have made this book possible. Thank you all.

Introduction

If you have been named as Executor in a Will, this *Executor's Guide* is your step-by-step guide to administration of the estate. Administration of an estate is a complex and demanding task for reasons that are perhaps not apparent at first glance. When the ownership of property is ended by death, many people have competing interests in taking that property. A Will is not a document of title. The creditors, the state and federal taxing authorities, as well as the spouse, the children, other heirs, and those named in the Will have legitimate interests in the property. Those interests are protected by strict laws. In order to transfer the property to the new legitimate owner, all these competing claims must be cleared. The probate laws of each state give stringent instructions that must be followed in order to clear these claims. The responsibility to comply with these laws falls directly on the Executor. The *Executor's Guide* gives the Executor specific instructions to accomplish the tasks necessary to administer the estate of a Decedent who left a Will.

The *Executor's Guide* is not intended to replace competent legal counsel. The transfer of property at the time of death is the subject of extensive and complex law. Because the Executor owes a fiduciary duty to the estate and because the liability for mistakes can be considerable, the Executor is advised to consult an estate attorney at appropriate times. A competent probate attorney will be familiar with the specific laws of the state where the Will is probated and can guide the Executor surely and quickly through the required procedures.

If you are reading the *Executor's Guide* for the first time in an attempt to administer the estate of a loved one, you are undertaking many new and difficult tasks at a time when you are suffering a tremendous loss.

Every step you take will necessarily bring that loss to mind. Remember that grief is experienced in very different ways by different people, but everyone who suffers a loss grieves. Be gentle with yourself. Take the time you need to complete these tasks. Although there is much to do, you will accomplish it in good time.

The *Executor's Guide* gives instruction for the administration of an estate where the Decedent left a valid Will. When there is no Will, the probate proceeding is called an intestate proceeding and the property is distributed under the laws of inheritance or intestate succession. The person in charge of settling an estate without a Will is called the Administrator.

Superscript numbers in the text correspond to "Questions to Ask Your Attorney," which appears in Appendix VI.

Introduction to the Duties of the Executor

LEGAL LANGUAGE

The legal language used in statutes and legal documents is often unfamiliar to the Executor. Trying to understand unfamiliar legal terms can be frustrating, but in the same way that a mathematical formula or a recipe ensures a certain predictable result, the exact repetition of a legal phrase assures a consistent and reliable outcome. The Executor is well advised to learn and use these terms. A clear understanding of the proper meanings of the words will help reduce confusion.

The person who wrote and signed the **Will** is called the **Testator**. The Will is the written instructions of the Testator that deal with the Testator's property at death. The Will is signed at the bottom of the document by the Testator and must be properly witnessed under the state laws. In this book, the word "Will" is capitalized when it refers to this document. Once the Testator has died, he or she is called the **Decedent**. The words "property" and "assets" are used to describe everything the Decedent owned at death, not just the real estate. The word **estate** is often misunderstood. The probate estate[1.1] is the real estate and personal property owned by the Decedent solely and is subject to the Will and probate administration. The Decedent's taxable estate[1.2] consists of the probate estate plus all of the **non-probate property** owned by the Decedent at death, including property owned with others as joint tenants, insurance, annuities, retirement plans, trusts, or trusts with beneficiary designations, pay-on-death bank accounts, and transfer-on-death mutual funds accounts. This non-probate property is not controlled by the Will, but is part of the taxable estate. Those who are given real estate in a Will are called **devisees**, and the gift of real estate is called a **devise**. Those who are given personal property in the Will are called **legatees**, and the personal property they are given is called a **bequest** or **legacy**.

Other legal words will be defined throughout the *Guide* when the term is first used, and a glossary is located at the back. (Terms that appear in bold print in the text can be found in the Glossary.)

THE RESPONSIBILITIES OF THE EXECUTOR

The **Executor**[1.3] is the individual who is named by the Testator in the Will to execute or carry out the instructions in the Will. Once appointed by the court, the Executor has the primary legal responsibility for the **administration** of the estate of the Decedent.[1.4] The Executor's responsibilities include gathering, protecting, and managing the assets of the estate; assuring that all interested parties are given notice of the legal proceedings of the estate; selling personal property and real estate; making all required reports to courts and to the state and federal governments; paying all debts and taxes from the funds available; and finally, distributing the balance of the estate to those entitled to it.

Upon being appointed, the Executor has the same power over title to the property of the estate that an absolute owner would have, except the Executor holds the property for the benefit of those who ultimately take that property. Because of this power, the Executor has a special duty, called a "**fiduciary** duty,"[1.5] which is created when the Executor accepts the appointment as Executor. Bound by this fiduciary duty, the Executor's actions in administering the estate are judged by a standard of conduct much higher than mere honesty.

FIDUCIARY DUTY

Fiduciary duty is the duty the Executor owes to those entitled to the estate, including the surviving spouse, children, creditors, devisees, and legatees. The components of fiduciary duty are a list of virtues: care, diligence, prudence, loyalty, confidentiality, honesty, discretion, and intelligence. If the Executor fails to meet these standards, interested persons may bring legal action and the Executor may be liable personally for losses and penalties.

The Executor must exercise care, diligence, and prudence to preserve and protect the assets of the estate. The common law and statutory rule known as "the prudent person rule" requires that the Executor exercise the level of care and skill that a prudent person would exercise in handling the property of another. This level of care includes obtaining expert advice and assistance when necessary. If the Executor has some special skill or expertise, the Executor will be held to the standard of care and skill that a prudent expert with that skill or expertise would exercise in dealing with the property of another. The duty of *diligence* requires that the Executor act with reasonable promptness in the administration of the estate.

The duties of loyalty and confidentiality require that the Executor's conduct be faithful to the interests of those to whom the property ultimately will be distributed. In handling the estate, the Executor must keep the estate property separate from all other property. In management of estate property, the Executor must exercise prudence, discretion, and intelligence, first to protect principal and, second, to make the property reasonably productive. The Executor may not hold property that is setting idle or not earning income unless the Will gives the specific power and authority to retain nonproductive property.

Ultimately, honesty is the touchstone of fiduciary duty. To be honest means not only to behave with honor and with the highest integrity in the financial dealings with the estate's assets, but to be truthful and trustworthy in all matters. The Executor is required to be truthful, dependable, candid, open, and undisguised (known in today's jargon as transparent) to all who are owed the duty of honesty.

However, the Executor is not responsible for any decline in the market value of the estate assets so long as the decision to purchase and the ongoing decision to retain the asset was reasonable and prudent at the time each decision was made. Under the law it is the conduct of the Executor that is judged, not the performance of the investments. Both the law and common sense require that the Executor keep careful records of all transactions and the supporting documents for all required reports and **accountings**.

The Executor cannot delegate fiduciary responsibility. The major decision-making responsibility that requires judgment and discretion falls squarely on the Executor. However, the Executor can (and is well advised to) employ agents including attorneys, accountants, and investment advisors and, thus, delegate ministerial or clerical duties. The Executor has a duty to supervise these agents. Co-Executors must also pay careful attention to the actions of the other Co-Executors and must use reasonable care to prevent other Co-Executors from breaching fiduciary duties.

Unless waived by the Will, the Executor has a duty to avoid self-dealing.[1.6] Because the Executor has unfettered control of the estate of the Decedent but must act only for the benefit of the estate and those entitled to it, any act taken to benefit the Executor is seen as a conflict of interest. Except for the fee the Executor takes, the Executor can take no action with the estate's assets that would benefit the Executor or the Executor's family. This duty to avoid self-dealing is burdensome to families where the Executor is also a primary beneficiary as is so often the case. Where the Executor or a member of the Executor's family expects to be able to purchase the Decedent's real estate or personal property for a favorable price from the estate, the duty to avoid self-dealing is often disregarded to the Executor's later regret. The best remedy is a Will that waives the duty to avoid self-dealing. In the absence of a waiver in the Will, the Executor may seek court approval in advance of all acts that would be seen as self-dealing. The Executor may also seek consent of all interested persons before the action is taken. This consent may be included in a Settlement Agreement[1.7] as part of a plan for disposition of the estate. (For a discussion of Settlement Agreements see Chapter 11.) Although the Executor may seek a release of liability after the action is taken, it is very unwise to act and expect the interested persons to agree later.

LIABILITY OF EXECUTOR FOR BREACH OF FIDUCIARY DUTY

If the Executor fails to perform a fiduciary duty or performs an action that breaches a fiduciary duty and there is a loss that can be traced to that failure to act or to the act in breach, the Executor will be personally liable for that loss. The Executor will have to reimburse all those who are harmed from his or her own personal funds. In addition to actual damages for losses, the Executor may have to pay a penalty or surcharge for breach of fiduciary duty.[1.8] This penalty can be as much as 100 percent of the loss. Each state's statutes set the standards of conduct for the Executor and the penalties for a breach. The Executor should read the state statutes carefully. A copy of those statutes can be obtained from the estate attorney or local law library.

CO-EXECUTORS

Many times the Testator will name Co-Executors to administer the Will. The Testator's untutored belief is that two Executors can cut the work in half or that the dual appointment will be more fair. Instead, the administration of the estate by Co-Executors adds to the complexity of administration. If Co-Executors are named and appointed, each decision must be agreed upon by both Co-Executors and each legal document will require the signature of both Co-Executors. This requirement of consulting with two individuals increases the contact time with the estate attorney and increases probate costs.

Any disagreement between the Co-Executors concerning administration of the estate that cannot be resolved with informal mediation will require a court hearing for resolution. The estate attorney does not have a tie-breaking vote. Resolving these conflicts is time-consuming, which also adds to the cost of administration.

Often the Testator names two Co-Executors to assure that no one person has to do all the work. The work that the Testator often has in mind is the cleaning, sorting, and boxing of personal items; repairing and painting; moving and selling property; and completing the paperwork. It is true that all this work must be accomplished, but being named as a Co-Executor is not a guarantee that the Co-Executor will actually bend his or her back to the tasks. There is no requirement that a sole Executor must do the work alone. An Executor has the authority to hire help for any of these tasks. It is often advisable to employ professionals to do the work. Also, family and friends are often called upon to help.

The other primary motivation expressed by Testators who appoint Co-Executors is to allow the Co-Executors to watch each other to prevent unfairness. It is rare that the two individuals who are named as the Co-Executors have any experience working together cooperatively. The more usual connection is that the two who are named represent the competing interests in the family whose differences are undiminished after the death. Requiring two family members to work together under the stress of a death in the family promotes conflict rather than eases it. Co-Executors are not necessary to protect the estate. Through the court proceedings, any interested person can monitor the administration of the estate, protect his or her interests. and assure that all actions taken by the Executor are reasonable and prudent.

Personal liability of the Executor has a special twist where Co-Executors serve. Each Co-Executor has a potential liability for acts taken by the other Co-Executor and for duties the other Co-Executor neglects.[1.9] The responsibilities of each Co-Executor include the responsibility to monitor the actions of the other Co-Executor to assure that the estate is being administered for the benefit of those to whom the estate will be distributed, including creditors. Anyone named as Co-Executor should carefully consider declining to serve if serving will greatly increase probate costs or if the potential for conflict or liability is significant.

OUT-OF-STATE EXECUTOR OR OUT-OF-AREA EXECUTOR

Administration of an estate when the Executor lives out-of-state or out-of-area has become more and more common as our society becomes more mobile and technology makes long-distance administration easier.[1.10] Conferences with the estate attorney, accountant, real estate agents, and other professionals and service providers can be held conveniently over the telephone. The U.S. Post Office and other postal services permit prompt delivery of important original documents. Facsimile (FAX) machines found in offices everywhere and for public use at printing companies transmit information easily and quickly. Computer e-mail is rapidly becoming a useful means of long-distance communication. There are few tasks that actually require the Executor to be physically present, and most of these tasks can be delegated.[1.11] The estate attorney will know of local individuals or companies who can conduct real estate and estate sales, auctions, and appraisals; make repairs; do cleaning; and provide other necessary services.

An Executor who lives out-of-state must appoint an in-state agent, called a resident agent, to provide all interested parties with a name and address where legal notices can be properly sent within state.[1.12] This agent must be an in-state person with an in-state address to comply with state laws. The estate attorney is often chosen to be this agent. The appointment of the resident agent must be filed with the court. Also, in a few states, the court may require an out-of-state Executor to be bonded, even though the Will waives the bonding requirement. Check with your estate attorney for the state law requirement.

EXECUTOR CAN DECLINE TO SERVE

Any person named as Executor can decline to be appointed by the court or, after being appointed, withdraw, with the court's permission, at any time during the administration of the estate.[1.13] The person the Testator has named as Executor is often one of the people who will be most affected by the death. In each and every case, the Executor's ability to perform will be impaired by that loss. The normal reactions to the death of a loved one, including shock, mental disorganization, depression, anger, guilt, resentment, volatile emotions, and loneliness, will be experienced by each Executor to a greater or lesser degree. These should be expected. However, until the actual death, it is difficult to predict the level of disruption the Executor will experience. Administration of an estate is very difficult for a person whose experience of the loss has made attention to detail and careful organization difficult. Natural anger or resentment hinders disinterested, detached decision-making. The named Executor must carefully consider whether the tasks will be too difficult to perform under the circumstances.

In addition to the disruption caused by grief, there are a number of other reasons the Executor may decline to serve. The personal circumstances of the Executor, such as declining health, involvement in a divorce, or a very demanding job, are very good reasons to decline. The fact that the Executor no longer lives near the Decedent's domicile often compels the Executor to choose not to serve. When evaluating whether to decline to serve, the Executor should be aware that the tasks of administering an estate may take from six months to a year to complete. Finally, the Executor should carefully consider the risk of personal liability before taking on the responsibility of administering an estate. The Executor is not protected personally for errors he or she might make in administering the estate or for required tasks that he or she may fail to complete. There is no errors and omissions insurance available for noncorporate fiduciaries.

If an Executor declines to serve, the court will appoint the successor or alternate Executor named in the Will to serve as Executor. If no alternate or successor Executor is named or the successor is unable to serve, the court will appoint an Administrator *Cum Testamento Annexo* (C.T.A.) to administer the estate.[1.14] This Administrator C.T.A. will act in all regards as directed by the Will to carry out its instructions. The Administrator C.T.A. can be nominated by a legally interested party. Each state's statutes set the requirements for who can be an Administrator C.T.A.

EXECUTOR'S FEES AND EXPENSES

Executor's expenses and Executor's fees are separate items that need to be distinguished and explained. All expenses of the Executor should be reimbursed by the estate whether or not the Executor takes a fee.[1.15] Expenses include the cost of this book, paper, supplies, mileage, telephone charges, copy costs, and all other reasonable expenses necessary to administer the estate. Expenses of the Executor are allowable as expenses of administration so long as they are reasonable and the estate has enough money to pay those expenses. The Executor should be careful not to incur expenses that the estate will not be able to pay. The Executor's expenses are allowable deductions of the estate and are reported on state inheritance and state and federal estate tax returns.

The Executor's fees are the compensation paid to the Executor for the work done to administer the estate.[1.16] If the Will does not make a specific provision for fees, the Executor is entitled to a reasonable fee for the services rendered. A reasonable fee will take into account not only the value of the estate but also the nature of the work involved, the time spent, the complexity of the problems, and the professional background and experience of the Executor. The Executor should keep a detailed record of time spent and tasks accomplished.

If the Will provides instructions for payment of Executor's fees, the court will be guided by the Will when awarding fees. Sometimes, however, the fee provided in the Will is not reasonable and does not cover the real costs in time and effort. Perhaps administration of the estate is not going to be as simple as the Testator thought it would be. Or perhaps the Will states that the Executor is to receive no fee because the Testator believed that the Executor would also be receiving money as a legatee, but the estate does not have enough assets to pay the other bequests and devises and the Executor will receive nothing as a legatee. If the Executor's fee set by the Will is inadequate, the Executor should petition the court for a larger fee before administering the estate or as soon as the facts are known that show that the fee is not adequate. The Executor must ask for a fee that is reasonable under the circumstances. Remember, however, that the Executor must pay state and federal income tax on all compensation paid as an Executor's fee. In some circumstances the Will provides a specific bequest "in lieu of Executor's fees." This is a specified amount given to the person who is named as Executor. That individual is given a specified amount whether or not he or she serves as the Executor, but the individual is clearly expected to serve. The benefit of such a bequest "in lieu of Executor's fees" is that the Executor will not have to pay income tax on money received as a bequest. The risk is that the named Executor will not serve and the bequest will still be paid to that person.

Commercial or corporate Executors, such as the trust departments of banks and independent trust companies, publish a fixed fee schedule for the administration of estates. This fixed fee usually includes an amount based on the value of the estate plus itemized charges for additional services. The court will order the fees paid according to that schedule.

NEGOTIATION OF EXECUTOR'S FEES

When an individual is acting as Executor, the best time to decide on Executor's fees is at the very beginning of administration of the estate when the heirs, devisees, and legatees are first made aware of the numerous time-consuming tasks that must be completed to administer the estate. The most common psychological perception at the beginning of administration is that the estate money belongs to the Decedent and Executor's fees are perceived as simply a cost of the administration to be deducted before the devisees and legatees calculate their inheritance. As time goes on, unless a fee is established, the devisees and legatees will calculate their inheritance as a portion of the entire estate and will perceive an Executor's fee established later in the administration as reducing their share and taking money directly from their pockets. Unfortunately, many Executors are reluctant to discuss fees at the beginning of administration of the estate for fear of appearing greedy or more concerned with money than with the deceased person's wishes. A clear understanding about fees at the beginning of administration will prevent misunderstandings that are potentially much more serious at a later time.

Executors who early in administration of the estate believe that they will not take a fee for their work should consider that the psychological orientation of the Executor generally changes over the period of the administration. This is a natural, healthy change. Immediately after the death, the Executor is focused on doing what the Decedent wished and honoring the memory of the deceased person. As the grief begins to heal and life goes on, it becomes apparent that the work the Executor is doing is more for the devisees and legatees and less for the Decedent. It is wise to anticipate and plan for fees to avoid confusion later. The Executor can always choose to forego fees at the end of administration of the estate.

Whether or not the Executor ultimately chooses to collect a fee for services, the Executor must keep a detailed record of the time spent, tasks accomplished, factors in the decisions reached, travel expenses, telephone calls, and other pertinent details to protect himself or herself from claims that might be filed. Grief has many expressions. The Executor is often the target of the devisees' and legatees' criticism and complaints, both deserved and undeserved. Any confusion about administration can easily become accusations of improper acts. Misunderstandings about the legal or financial processes carry the strong potential for faultfinding against the Executor. Accurate records are the best tool the Executor can have to protect himself or herself.

INCOME TAX ON EXECUTOR'S FEES

As mentioned earlier, state and federal income taxes must be paid on any fee that the Executor collects.[1.17] If the fee puts the Executor in a higher tax bracket, the higher bracket will affect only the portion of income that is above the bracket, and in no event will the Executor pay more in taxes than a percentage of the fee received. Even the Executor who pays income taxes in the highest tax bracket is still better off financially to take a fee and pay the income tax on that fee. The only exception to this rule occurs when the Executor is the sole legatee under the Will and all the money the Executor would take would come to him or her as the legatee of the estate without payment of any income tax. Again, only when the Executor is the sole legatee is it economically advantageous to refuse a fee. Estimated tax payments must be paid on Executor's fees in a timely manner in order to avoid penalties. Consult with the estate attorney or tax preparer for specific instructions on taxes for Executor's fees.

POWER OF ATTORNEY

Often a Decedent who has prepared a Will has also prepared a **Power of Attorney** for managing financial affairs during sickness or disability. Even though that Power of Attorney was "durable," the power to act on behalf of the individual ends at the death of the Decedent.[1.18] No one should attempt to use the Power of Attorney after the death of the Testator to transact any business of the Decedent or the Decedent's estate no matter how convenient it may seem at the time. If the bank or account representative is unaware of the death, or is simply trying to help, the Power of Attorney can be (mis)used to withdraw funds, open safe deposit boxes, or make changes in accounts. The use of the Power of Attorney after the death of the Testator by the Executor or any other agent named in the Power of Attorney who knows of the Decedent's death is improper and may constitute theft, embezzlement, or breach of fiduciary duty.

CHECKLIST: FIRST TASKS

In the confusion, shock, and turmoil that immediately follow a death, the seemingly endless details can be overwhelming. Some simple organization and prioritizing will bring things into perspective. While some tasks need immediate attention, others can wait. The following is a list of tasks that need to be accomplished as quickly as possible and cannot wait for the Executor to be appointed by the court. Consult the estate attorney for help where needed.

1. Assure that any minor, disabled, or incapacitated person cared for by the Decedent has proper attention.
2. Assure that all pets and livestock are tended, plants and yards are watered, and lawns are mowed.
3. Contact the estate attorney for advice and counsel for the immediate needs of the estate, information about funeral arrangements, especially who is entitled to make funeral arrangements,[1.19] advice about publishing an obituary, and so on. This early advice can help avoid future costly mistakes.
4. Dispose of perishables in Decedent's home. Clean refrigerator and cupboards, remove trash, and flush toilets.
5. Protect real estate against theft, water pipe freezing, and other physical damage.

6. Retain answering services for phones still in use. Alert local police that the property is vacant. Discontinue services such as newspaper, milk, bread, other food deliveries, and fuel oil deliveries. Examine residence and other buildings to assure that they are locked and in good repair. If necessary, change or install locks and repair roofs, broken glass, and plumbing.

7. Place personal property that requires immediate attention in a safe place. Important papers, jewelry, cash, art, negotiable papers, billfold or pocketbook, keepsakes, and other personal items, such as family pictures, can be placed in a safe deposit box under lock and key. Cars, boats, motor homes, motorcycles, and airplanes must be secured and the keys also put in safekeeping. Vehicles owned solely by the Decedent should not be used by the Executor, devisees, or legatees. (See Chapter 7, Management of Assets.)

8. Locate cell phones and pagers and curtail use.

9. Identify all family and friends of the Decedent and notify them of the Decedent's death. Be sure to keep a complete copy of all names, addresses, and phone numbers of those contacted.

10. Locate the original Will to be read for instructions for burial or funeral arrangements. It may be necessary to secure access to the Decedent's safe deposit box to obtain the Will. (Consult the estate attorney on how to obtain access to the safe deposit box.) Deliver the original Will to the estate attorney. Chapter 2 discusses the Will in detail.

11. Prepare information for the obituary. See Obituary Information worksheet in Appendix IV.

12. Make funeral arrangements. Follow the burial instructions in the Will, in a letter written by the Decedent, or in a plan with the funeral home. Locate the burial plot or mausoleum. See Cemetery and Funeral Worksheet in Appendix IV.

13. Arrange for security at the Decedent's and family members' homes during the funeral service.

14. If the home of the Decedent will be a gathering place for family and friends, take care to adequately secure all items that could easily be picked up as keepsakes. Consider the advisability of limiting the use of the telephone by removing the telephone sets from the jacks or by requesting that the phone company discontinue long-distance service to that phone line.

15. Locate all credit cards held by the Decedent. The Decedent's credit cards may not be used for any reason. The Executor should eliminate the risk that these cards may be stolen or misused. First, copy the front and back of each card for a record, cut each card in half, return to the issuer with notification of the date of

Decedent's death. Keep copies of all correspondence. If the Decedent held credit cards with a surviving spouse or another person, the Executor should notify the issuer of the death of Decedent immediately and comply with their instructions on how to change the account to the survivor's name alone.

16. Assure that no motor vehicle is used by anyone unless and until insurance coverage for liability and collision is obtained for the estate. The Decedent's insurance does not cover drivers after Decedent's death.

17. Arrange for a family interview with the estate attorney as soon as possible. During the days when the family is gathered to attend the funeral is usually the best time to get family members together for this interview. Obtain full names and addresses for legal notice. Use the Heirs Contact Worksheet and Legatees and Devisees Worksheet in Appendix IV.

The Will

The Will is the Decedent's legal instructions for the management and disposition of his or her estate after death.[2.1] The Will is classically said to "speak at the death of the Testator" and thus has no effect until the death of the Testator. A Will is not filed for probate and cannot be contested until the death of the Testator. A Will can be revoked or modified at any time prior to death so long as the Testator is competent. At death, however, the words of the Will strictly control the disposition of the estate of the Testator. Promises that are not written in the Will, a codicil, or authorized memorandum cannot be enforced. A well-written Will can increase the powers of the Executor far beyond the powers granted by state statutes. These increased powers can accomplish significant savings of time and money. The Executor must carefully read the Will to determine the powers granted.

Today, many have a revocable living trust in addition to a Will. The Will controls the administration of probate assets, whereas the administration of the trust assets is controlled by the Trust. If there are probate assets, the Will must be offered for probate and the probate estate administered under the Will.

TYPES OF WILLS

An Executor may be required to administer an estate under one of a number of different documents. Various types of Wills are recognized.

Codicils and personal property memoranda may exist as valid additions to a Will. A discussion of various types of Wills, codicils, and memoranda follows.

Formal Will

The most familiar form of a Will is the typewritten Formal Will written by an attorney after discussion with the Testator and upon the express instructions of the Testator. The Formal Will follows the statutory requirements of the state where the Testator is domiciled, that is, intends to be his or her primary residence.[2.2] The Formal Will is the Will of one person and is executed with all the **testamentary** formalities required by the state statutes. There are many kinds of Formal Wills, including a simple Will, a pour-over Will, tax sensitive or tax planning Will, and a Will with a testamentary trust. The Formal Will requires witnesses that actually heard the Testator state the intent to sign a Will and who determined for themselves that the Testator was competent, knew what he or she was signing, and that he or she was not being forced to sign. The policy behind the requirement of witnesses is to assure that the Will was, in fact, intended as the Testator's Last Will and Testament and signed willingly without undue influence or duress.

Foreign Will

A Will is called a Foreign Will if it was written and executed, that is, signed with testamentary formalities, in a state or country other than the one in which the Decedent is domiciled at death. For example, if the Testator wrote and signed a Will while living in Michigan, but moved to California, did not change the Will, and then died in California, the Will written in Michigan is a Foreign Will in California. In general, a Foreign Will is valid if it was executed according to the laws of the state in which probate proceedings are opened (in this example, California) or according to the laws of the state of the Testator's domicile at the time it was written and signed (in this example, Michigan).[2.3] Any type of Will discussed here might also be a Foreign Will. The estate attorney will evaluate the validity of a Foreign Will in the state where Decedent was domiciled at death.

Joint Will

A **Joint Will** is a Will that serves as the Will for two or more people. The Joint Will may or may not be contractual. The Joint Will serves as the Will for each person and must be filed with the court at the death of the first Testator to die even though there are no probate assets to administer. At the second death, the original Joint Will can be found in the probate court file under the name of the first Testator to die. When searching for an original Will, the Executor needs to consider the possibility that the Testator executed a Joint Will that is already filed with the court.

Joint Wills are not favored by estate attorneys because of the myriad difficulties that can arise when the Joint Will is not filed at the first death. The problems are compounded by the changes that occur later in the survivor's life, such as remarriage, death of a child or beneficiary, conflict with a legatee of the Joint Will. Families are further vexed by the fact that Joint Wills are often meant to be contractual when written and those contractual provisions are difficult to enforce after the death of the second party to the Joint Will. Contractual Wills are discussed in the next section.

Contractual Will

A Contractual Will is a Will in which the parties have mutually agreed to certain terms, usually agreements to give assets to certain survivors. If those terms are violated, or another Will is written that does not follow the agreement and replaces the contractual Will, then those who were to benefit by the original agreement can enforce the contractual Will like a contract. Contractual Wills can be either Joint or separate Wills. Estate attorneys do not favor Joint or Contractual Wills today, yet many do exist. If a Will is contractual, the surviving Testator is allowed to consume the assets but is not permitted to give away or waste assets after the first death. Any change in the Will of the survivor raises the question of whether the beneficiaries of the Contractual Will are entitled to recover the gifts from the estate of the last to die when the Contractual Will is violated. Resolution of an improper transfer of property during the life of the survivor often requires litigation. Joint and Contractual Wills should be avoided. The administration of an estate under a Joint Will or a Contractual Will requires the careful attention of an experienced estate attorney. Again, an estate attorney should be consulted if there are questions about a Joint or a Contractual Will.

Handwritten Will

Handwritten or **Holographic Wills** are often found. Holographic Wills are in the handwriting of the Testator and signed by the Testator, but do not have the necessary witnesses and other testamentary formalities that are required for Formal Wills. These Handwritten Wills are valid in only a few states and must meet strict requirements.[2.4] In most states, Handwritten Wills are not accepted as valid Wills. The estate attorney will evaluate the validity of the Handwritten or Holographic Will. Additional writings or amendments to the Will, which do not have the elements of a Formal Will, often are evaluated as Holographic Wills.

Oral Will

In some states an Oral Will,[2.5] also called a Nuncupative Will, spoken to witnesses in anticipation of immediate death, such as may occur on a battlefield, immediately after a car wreck, or during the last illness, is recognized to transfer personal property. Competent, disinterested witnesses must hear the Oral Will. The Testator must declare to the witnesses that the spoken statement is his or her Will and must call upon those present to witness the Oral Will. The Oral Will must then be written down within the time period, usually a certain number of days, specified by state statute and signed by those witnesses. This Oral Will must be presented to the court for probate. In most states, only the personal property of the Decedent may pass under an Oral Will. An Oral Will cannot pass real estate. Also, an Oral Will cannot modify or revoke a valid prior written Will.

Living Will

A Living Will[2.6] does not give instructions for the management and disposition of Decedent's assets after death. It is a written statement made by an individual concerning his or her health care, usually expressing a desire for the discontinuation of life support devices under certain circumstances.

ADDITIONS OR CHANGES TO THE WILL

Codicils

The Testator may have changed the Will with a **Codicil**.[2.7] So long as the Testator was competent, and competency is presumed, a Will may be changed at any time prior to death. Any change that is written on the Formal Will after it is signed, even if initialed and dated, but not witnessed, has no effect. However, marking through any writing on a Will can revoke that language or complete sections of the Will. A Codicil is a separate document that must be signed with the same testamentary formalities as the original Will. A Holographic Codicil must meet the same requirements as an original Holographic Will. The estate attorney will evaluate the Codicil and any markings on the Will for their legal effect. The Executor must look carefully for all Codicils to the original Will.

Letter or Memorandum Distributing Personal Property

Some states allow a separate letter that was prepared and signed by the Testator making specific gifts of tangible personal property to become a part of the Will when this letter is mentioned in the Will.[2.8] The signatures of witnesses are not required for this letter to be valid. When permitted by statute, this letter allows the Testator a great deal of flexibility for giving away personal items. Only tangible personal property may be given by this letter—for example, jewelry, antiques, and photographs. Real estate, money, stocks, bonds, or certificates of deposit may not be given in the letter. To be valid and enforceable, this letter must be dated, must mention the Will and the intention to give these personal assets after death, and must be signed at the bottom.

Self-Proving Clause

After death, the signatures of the witnesses must be authenticated by either an affidavit of the witnesses (a requirement that has some obvious drawbacks if witnesses have died or cannot be located) or a self-proving clause signed and notarized at the time the Will was signed. The addition of a self-proving clause to a Will is authorized by statute in most states[2.9] and provides a tremendous benefit to the estate by eliminating the requirement of finding witnesses to a Will after the death of the Testator. In states that provide for a self-proving clause, the notary is not a substitute for a witness, but is in addition to witnesses.

Consent to Will by Spouse

Each state provides that a spouse may not be excluded from taking the amount provided by statute from the Decedent's estate unless the surviving spouse has consented to the Will.[2.10] The surviving spouse's consent must be voluntary and reasonable under the circumstances.

CUSTODY OF THE ORIGINAL WILL

The original Will, not a copy, must be presented to the court for probate. Every reasonable effort should be made by the Executor to find the original Will, original Codicils, and the originals of any Memorandum or attachments to the Will. The law makes the presumption that if the originals cannot be found, the Testator must have intended to revoke the Will and other attachments before death.[2.11] The Will should be found as soon as possible after Decedent's death.

The original Will may be in the possession of the person who has been named Executor or a family member. If the Will has not been found, the

Executor must search the safe deposit boxes and home of the Decedent. The Executor must contact the attorney who prepared the Will to determine whether he or she retained the original. Also, the Executor should contact any bank or trust company with which the Decedent was known to do business or which the Decedent may have named as Executor or Trustee to determine whether the bank or trust company has retained the original Will in their vault. Some courts provide a service for storing original Wills for a small fee. The Executor should check with the court in the county in which the Decedent was living at the time he or she may have written a Will. Because it was not uncommon in the past for married couples to execute Joint Wills, the court records should be checked for the probate proceeding of a spouse who predeceased the Decedent to determine whether an original Joint Will was filed at the first death. That Joint Will, unless revoked, is also the Will of the Decedent. If the original Will cannot be found, but a copy of the original is found, consult with the estate attorney to proceed.

LOST WILL

The presumption that the Will was revoked may be overcome only if certain procedures are followed and legally credible proof is offered to prove the contents of the lost Will and to prove that the Will was not revoked. It is not enough to say a Will is lost because it cannot be found. There also must be enough proof that the Decedent did not intend to revoke the Will to overcome the presumption that the Will was revoked. This is a heavy burden. The requirements for offering a copy or some other evidence of the contents of a Will in the place of an original Will varies from state to state and must be dealt with by the estate attorney.[2.12]

STALE WILL

In some states, if the Will was not offered for probate within a certain period of time, the Will cannot be offered for probate.[2.13] In most cases, if the Will was withheld and there is proof that the Will was withheld, an interested party who did not withhold the Will may offer the Will for a limited period of time.[2.14] A Will that is simply not found within the time limit is not a withheld Will. Check with the estate attorney for the state laws on stale wills.

WITHHOLDING THE WILL

If there is reason to believe that someone is withholding the original Will, Codicils, or attachments, the law provides stern and very effective measures to cause that person to produce those documents.[2.15] Implementation of these measures varies by state and requires direct orders of the court. Anyone who withholds a Will may be liable for losses to the estate and other interested parties and also may not be permitted to benefit from the later filed Will. The estate attorney must seek appropriate orders of the supervising court to force production of the Will.

If the Will does not provide as much to a person as the laws of inheritance would allot (and there is no requirement that it must), then there is an incentive for someone to withhold the Will and force the property to pass by the laws of inheritance. The state laws of inheritance usually provide that, in the absence of a Will, the surviving spouse and the children share the Decedent's estate. The inheritance laws provide equal shares to the children. Remember, if a Will cannot be found, the Testator is presumed to have revoked it.

In the current environment where successive marriages are common, there is often a strong incentive to withhold certain Wills. Some Decedents write a Will to give only an income interest to the surviving spouse and, at the death of the surviving spouse, give all the principal to the children of the Decedent. The surviving spouse's children get nothing. If this Will is successfully withheld, the surviving spouse will take a spousal allowance plus an intestate share, usually one-half of the rest of the estate, which he or she can later give to his or her own children. In another variation of this example, the Decedent's Will provides that his wife is to receive only an income interest for her life and instructs that the remainder is to go to charity at his wife's death. The Decedent has no children and his Joint Will was consented to by his wife at the time it was signed. The wife would benefit significantly (although illegally) from withholding the Will and taking all of his estate by intestate succession. Any time the laws of intestate succession benefit a person more than the provisions in a Will, there is a financial incentive to withhold a Will. In some circumstances, it may be advisable for a Will to be held for an independent party prior to Testator's death.

EVALUATION OF THE WILL

The legal sufficiency and validity of the Will, Codicils, and any attachments must be evaluated by the estate attorney before the Will is offered for probate. Without trying to catalog all the possible sources of a contest or conflict, the following are examples of some of the concerns that the estate attorney must evaluate under the laws of the state:

1. *Proper Jurisdiction*—In what state and county (or parish) must the Will be offered for probate? Must the Will be offered for an ancil-

lary probate in another state? Must other legal papers be filed in another county or state?

2. *Sufficiency*—Does the Will meet the requirements of a Will under the statutes? Is the Will written in the correct form for the state in which it is required to be probated? Was the Will executed properly under the laws of that state? Is the Testator's signature properly subscribed?

3. *Witnesses*—Is the Will properly witnessed? Are the witnesses legally competent and qualified to witness? Is the Will self-proving or do witnesses have to be found?

4. *Validity of Gifts*—Are the gifts given in the Will permitted under state law or are they in violation of public policy? Do the gifts given violate the **rule against perpetuities** (basically a rule that requires property to be given to someone who has the right to sell it to assure that the property remains in the economic mainstream) and other statutory limits to gifts? Have the gifts been given prior to death?[2.16]

5. *Revoked Will*—Has the Will been revoked by state law because of divorce or marriage or birth of a child? Did the Testator revoke the Will by a later writing?

6. *Capacity*—Is there evidence that the Testator did not have sufficient mental capacity at the time the Will was written?

7. *Duress*—Is there any evidence of undue influence, duress, coercion, fraud, or forgery?

The evaluation of the Will is the responsibility of the estate attorney. Because of the fiduciary duty owed to those who are ultimately to receive the estate, any irregularity or question of validity of the Will must be carefully considered and resolved. In cases where a conflict is not able to be resolved among the interested persons, the Executor must rely on the supervising court for a decision and an order that protects the interested persons and the Executor alike.

APPLICATION OF STATE LAW AND INTERPRETATION OF THE WILL

Surviving Spouse's and Minors' Rights

Once it is determined that the Will is valid and in the proper court, the estate attorney must determine whether the laws of the state apply to distribute a portion of the estate to the Decedent's spouse and minor children. The rights of the surviving spouse and **minor** children override anything written in the Will and most creditors' rights. In most states, the surviving spouse is entitled to homestead rights, certain spousal allowances, and other rights in the property of the Decedent regardless of what the Will says unless the surviving spouse has waived these rights. Minor children also have statutory rights of homestead and allowances for support that have priority over the instructions in the Will. (See Chapter 9, Claims and Demands on Decedent's Estate.) The estate attorney must be consulted to determine who is entitled to, the nature of, and the extent of these rights. The estate attorney must petition for and the court must order enforcement of these rights.

Creditors' Rights

Secured debt is satisfied from the property that secures the debt. If the value of the property is less than the debt, any balance that is due is treated the same as money due other unsecured creditors. After the rights of the surviving spouse and minor children have been determined, the assets of the estate next go to pay the funeral bill, expenses of last illness, and expenses of administrating the estate—and in some states, reimbursement for payments made from Medicaid for the benefit of the Decedent.[2.17] (See Chapter 9, Claims and Demands on Decedent's Estate.) If there is not enough value in the estate to pay these expenses in full, the court will allocate payment from the available funds. If some of the assets given to certain people in the Will must be sold to pay creditors, the statutes give instructions on which assets are required to be sold to pay the creditors.

Legatees' and Devisees' Rights

Only after surviving spouse's and minors' rights have been established and debts and expenses paid are the gifts that are given in the Will considered. The estate attorney will interpret the Will, Codicils, and attachments according to the state law to determine what gifts are given. If assets were left to someone who died before the Testator, the state statutory or case law will provide guidance for distribution of those assets.[2.18] (See "Lapse" in Chapter 12.) If the estate has too few assets to pay all the gifts, the law provides for a reduction or abatement of gifts in a certain order.[2.19] (See "Schedule of Abatement" in Chapter 9.) The estate attorney must be consulted for interpretation of the state law with regard to abatement.

POWERS GRANTED IN THE WILL

The Executor must read the Will carefully to determine what powers the Will authorizes. The Executor can be granted powers in the Will far beyond those granted by statute. These increased powers can significantly reduce the cost of probate administration. These powers can include, but are not limited to, the power to avoid bond, sell personal property and real estate without court supervision, distribute tangible personal property by memorandum, retain an asset that is not producing income, borrow money to make improvements or repairs, settle legal claims, avoid Conservatorships (see Chapter 5, Guardians, Conservators, Custodians, and Trustees) for minors or disabled adults, and make tax elections. Without the specific grant of power in the Will, the Executor not only must post a bond but must also seek court orders to accomplish many common tasks of administration.

READING OF THE WILL AND THE FAMILY INTERVIEW

Although a formal reading of the Will is not a legal requirement, the tradition of reading the Will serves many important purposes. The Executor may request a formal reading if the attorney does not suggest it. The legal heirs and devisees and legatees should gather to read the Will as soon as possible after the death to help minimize confusion and conflict. All legal **heirs**, devisees and legatees should be notified of the reading of the Will, and the Executor should schedule the reading to permit as many as possible to attend. It is highly recommended that only the legal heirs, devisees, and legatees attend the reading. Participation of spouses, in-laws, and friends not named in the Will can greatly hinder a free discussion of sometimes very private family issues. The heirs, devisees, and legatees are the only persons with authority to consent to settlement agreements. The smaller the decision-making group, the more likely essential decisions will be reached.

The meeting to read the Will provides the opportunity for the estate attorney to explain unfamiliar probate procedures to all of the interested persons. A clear understanding of what to expect will help the Executor deal with the questions and demands of family members, devisees, and legatees later. In addition to explaining the probate procedures, the estate attorney and the Executor can use this meeting to raise difficult issues that must be resolved to settle the estate. Some examples include:

- If a family member owed the Decedent money but no promissory note was signed, that family member can acknowledge and agree to repay the debt. Without such an agreement, the matter would have to be litigated at the estate's expense and, without the promissory note, the claim might not be upheld.
- At the reading of the Will, the method the devisees and legatees wish to use to distribute the personal property, such as whether

property should be liquidated in the estate or distributed in-kind, can be discussed and possibly agreed upon.

- If the Will is unfair and the devisees and legatees want to change the distributions, together they can agree to modify the Will and sign a Settlement Agreement.

Psychologically, the face-to-face meeting, usually after the funeral, is the time that most people feel most strongly that they want to "do what is right" and to "honor the Decedent." Many varied problems that plague estate administration can be solved with the participation of all the interested parties. This first meeting is often the best time to solve these problems. Careful consideration of problems and possible solutions by the Executor and the estate attorney before the reading of the Will serves to make the meeting the most productive.

CHECKLIST: NEXT TO DO

After the initial rush of activity, there are tasks that need to be accomplished to begin the legal administration of the estate.

1. File a change of address card with the U.S. Post Office to change the mailing address of the Decedent to a post office box or to the Executor's residence.
2. Collect the information about the Decedent needed to file the petition to begin probate proceedings.
3. Assist the Trustee in beginning to administer assets held in trust.
4. Take appropriate measures to protect the plumbing, air conditioning, and other mechanical installations in homes and other real estate from damage during periods of disuse.
5. Terminate all unnecessary utility services. Transfer necessary services into the name of the estate or the new occupant. Consider the necessity of certain services to protect the property from damage (e.g., gas and electric to prevent pipes from freezing). Be sure to ask for final bills and refunds where appropriate.
   _____ electricity
   _____ gas
   _____ telephone
   _____ trash
   _____ water
   _____ cable television
   _____ Internet
   _____ cell phone and pager
   _____ other

Remember, payment of current utilities is an expense of the estate and may be made if the estate has sufficient money. Payment of debts of the Decedent, including utility bills due at Decedent's death, requires a court order for payment.

6. Assure that any business that was actively managed by the Decedent is adequately maintained and managed (especially assure that wages are paid to employees and taxes are paid). Hire professional management where necessary.

7. Assure that any property managed by the Decedent such as farm and rental property is properly maintained.

8. Evaluate the Will. Consult with estate attorney about the following questions. Also see the Will Evaluation Worksheet in Appendix IV.

Is the original Will available?

Does the Will have a Self-Proving Clause?

Are the original Codicils available?

Is the Spouse's Consent to Will and Consent to any Codicils available?

Is there a Personal Property Memoranda?

What type of Will is this?

Does the Will meet the state's statutory requirements?

Is the Will properly witnessed?

Is there any evidence that the Testator was incompetent or under duress when the Will was signed?

Is there any evidence that the Will was forged or that the Testator was coerced to sign the Will?

Has the Will been revoked by a later writing, a divorce, or a marriage?

What powers are granted to the Executor in the Will?

In what state and county must the probate proceedings be filed?

What rights do the spouse and minors have?

Are the gifts given in the Will permitted under the law?

Opening Court Proceedings

WHY PROBATE IS NECESSARY

Probate administration of the Will is necessary to ensure careful, supervised administration of the estate; to pay funeral costs, expenses, and debts; to file income and death tax returns; to pay taxes; to clear title to real property; and to allocate and transfer assets to legatees and devisees under the Will. Many estates without a Will, including trust estates, are neglected because there is little or no pressure to administer the assets and no court-enforced guidelines to follow. When there is no probate administration, property is often not properly transferred. Many times debts and expenses, including funeral expenses, are left unpaid or are paid by only one family member instead of shared among all those who received assets. Probate administration has developed over the years to deal with the unlimited combinations of circumstances individuals leave when they die. The most important answers to the question of why probate is necessary are discussed in the following paragraphs.

To Prove the Will

A Will is legally binding only when filed with and approved by the court. The Will must be presented to the court for probate or proving.[3.1] Without court approval of the Will, no one is legally bound to follow the Will.

To Appoint the Executor

The person named as Executor does not have the legal authority to administer the Decedent's estate unless and until the court specifically appoints that person as the Executor.[3.2] The statement in the Will that an individual is named the Executor is merely a nomination. The court will honor that nomination unless some interested person comes forward and shows the court that the named person is unfit to serve as Executor. Although such a contest is rare, the family and other interested persons are entitled to notice and a hearing to raise the question of fitness before the Executor is appointed. In fact, the Executor cannot be appointed until all interested persons have had this opportunity under the laws of the state.[3.3] When the Executor is appointed, the court will issue **Letters Testamentary**. Only when the Executor has possession of these Letters Testamentary will he or she have the legal authority and responsibility to handle the estate, to sign tax returns and deeds, and to carry out the instructions of the Will.

Power of the Executor before Letters Testamentary Are Granted

No matter what the Will says or what the Decedent instructed before death, until a court order specifically appoints the Executor, the Executor-nominee has no authority to distribute any property, not even personal and household items, to legatees. In some states the Executor has limited powers to protect and preserve the estate and pay funeral bills before Letters Testamentary are granted.[3.4]

If there is some reason to believe that estate assets will be lost or damaged, the Executor-nominee may act to preserve the assets. However, the Executor-nominee should seek the advice and counsel of the estate attorney before proceeding. Also, the Executor-nominee must consult with the estate attorney before paying any bills of the Decedent before Letters Testamentary are granted.

To Grant Letters Testamentary

Upon the granting of Letters Testamentary by the court, the Executor is authorized to act for the estate.[3.5] Letters Testamentary are signed by the judge of the probate court and certified by the clerk of that court. The Letters Testamentary document is proof of the Executor's appointment and authority. A number of individuals and companies will require a copy of Letters Testamentary to transact business for the estate. The estate attorney will instruct the Executor in how to obtain certified copies of Letters Testamentary.

To Protect Interested Persons

Probate legal procedures protect those interested in the estate. The statutes for Will administration are very clear and well settled. The statutory rules allow all interested persons to exercise their rights without special knowledge. In an estate that is not probated, for example, where a trust or pay-on-death beneficiary designation is used to transfer assets, independent action is required to protect assets for a spouse and to prevent waste or misuse of funds. Often, if there is no probate administration, an interested person does not know what action is necessary to protect his or her interest and loses rights through ignorance.

To Pay Debts and Expenses

Unless and until the court appoints an Executor or Administrator, no one has the legal responsibility for paying the Decedent's creditors. The creditors may not be informed of a death in an estate that is not administered through probate. Creditors that know of the death have the legal right to begin probate proceedings themselves to assure payment of their claims.[3.6]

To Transfer Property

No property, real or personal, in the estate of the Decedent will be transferred under the Will unless the Will is administered through the probate proceeding under the laws of the state.[3.7] A common misunderstanding is that if the Will says that the property is to be given to a named person, that named person owns that property without any further proceedings. The Will is not a document of title but merely instructions to the court for the disposition of the estate assets. The court must order that those instructions be carried out fully and in compliance with the laws of the state before those named in the Will actually own their bequests and devises.

To Sign Tax Returns

Only the court appointed Executor has the authority to sign income tax returns and handle other tax business on behalf of the Decedent.

To Allow the Executor to Take Legal Actions on Behalf of Decedent

The Executor (or **Administrator**, if there is no Will) is the only person who has the legal authority to act on behalf of the Decedent's estate in prosecuting, defending against, or settling legal action. The surviving spouse, children, and other **next of kin** may also have statutory rights to sue on their own behalf for the death of the Decedent, if the death was caused by the negligent or intentional act of another.

To Allocate Assets among Creditors

Often the estate does not have enough assets to pay all the debts of the Decedent. Special care must be taken by the Executor to allocate the estate assets among the creditors according to classification of the expenses, taxes, and debts as provided by state law.[3.8] If an Executor pays one creditor in full and another creditor of equal classification is paid nothing because the money is spent, the Executor may be personally liable to the unpaid creditor to the extent that assets were not properly allocated. The clear instructions of the estate attorney and careful adherence to state law and court orders are the Executor's best protection from liability when paying creditors.

To Allocate Assets among Legatees and Devisees

Even if the creditors are paid, many times the estate does not have enough money left to pay in full all the bequests and devises written in the Will, so the Testator's instructions cannot be followed as they are written. In such cases, the state law provides strict directions for overriding the instructions written in a Will.[3.9] The person who does not receive what is clearly written in the Will might be confused and angry. An understanding of the controlling rules can help clear up any confusion. The Executor must rely on the estate attorney for interpretation of the statutes to request distribution upon court orders.

CHOICE OF PROBATE PROCEEDINGS

The choice of administration proceeding is dictated by the facts of each individual estate and not by the whim of the Executor or estate attorney. A Will cannot be filed for administration or interpretation until the death of the Testator. The type of probate administration proceeding is controlled by the type and value of assets in the Decedent's probate estate; the extent of the liabilities of the Decedent; whether the heirs, devisees, and legatees are competent persons; the potential for conflict; the need for the enforcement authority of the court; the goals of the heirs, devisees, and legatees; and finally, the provisions made in each state's statutes for probate of estates. Most states' statutes provide several types of probate proceedings in which a Will may be presented to the court.

If There Are No Probate Assets

Often at the death of the spouse, all the assets of the couple pass by joint tenancy with rights of survivorship or by beneficiary designations to the survivor. Although the personal property of the Decedent does not technically pass to the surviving spouse without probate administration, as a practical matter, if a probate proceeding were opened, then all household goods would be reserved to the surviving spouse under some form of a spousal allowance. Many surviving spouses choose not to file the Will with the probate court at the first death when there are apparently no assets to distribute. There is a danger here.

In those states where the Will must be filed with the court within a certain period of time, if the surviving spouse withholds the Will, he or she may not later offer the Will. If any asset was not properly titled in the survivor's name at the death of the spouse, that asset will be required to pass through an **intestate** or descent proceeding and be distributed according to the laws of intestate succession, which may be dramatically different than the Will's provisions. An example will help illustrate this too common occurrence.

> In this example, the deed to the residence and bonds in the safe deposit box are titled in the name of the deceased husband. Because the Will clearly gives his widow all his assets and no one informed her of the need to transfer the title to the home or the bonds, she believes that they all "belong to her." She did not offer the Will for probate. After several years pass, her son files for divorce from his wife and the son's wife includes the bonds and the home as part of the marital assets subject to division by the divorce court. The state where these people live (and the Decedent died) has a time limit for filing a Will and the opportunity to file the husband's Will has passed. Under the intestate succession laws of the state, the widow is entitled to only the intestate share of probate assets, which is usually not more than one-half. The son is also entitled to a share of his father's real estate and bonds. State constitutional homestead rights and spousal allowance rights may provide some relief to the surviving wife, but part of these assets will be determined to be marital property and will be divided by the divorce court between the son and the wife he is divorcing.

When someone who holds a Will chooses not to file that Will with the court, that person has violated a state statute. All states have statutory provisions that require a Will to be offered for probate by anyone having possession or knowing the whereabouts of that Will.[3.10] The penalty for failure to file the Will varies from state to state. At a minimum, the person who has possession of the Will and fails to file it, or knows its whereabouts and does not divulge this information, is liable to anyone harmed by the failure to file the Will and reasonable attorney's fees for bringing the matter to court. Even if there are apparently no assets in the estate, the Will can be filed to preserve it. Most states have an inexpensive procedure to preserve the Will of a Decedent when there are apparently no assets to administer.[3.11] If the Executor has possession of the Will and fails to file the Will (even upon the instruction of the surviving widow), liability for losses caused by that failure to file the Will fall on the Executor personally.

An attorney should not advise an Executor to act contrary to the statutory law of the state, and there should be concern if such advice is given. Filing a Will to preserve it gives a genuine benefit and protection for devisees, legatees, and the Executor. If an asset is discovered later and the Will has not been preserved, then whoever failed to file the Will is legally responsible for the harm done to the devisees and legatees who would have benefited under the Will. Another example will illustrate. A surviving spouse is given the Decedent's property under the Will. However, all bank accounts, investments, and IRAs pass to the surviving spouse outside of probate by beneficiary designations. The residence passes to the surviving spouse as a joint tenant. Only farmland is owned by the Decedent alone. The tenant farmer begins to pay rent directly to the surviving spouse after the spouse's death. Believing that "everything was taken care of," the surviving spouse told the Executor there was no need to spend the money on an attorney to file the Will. The Executor did not file the Will in his possession. Several years later when a child of the Decedent owed the IRS money, the farmland was attached to pay the debt. The Will could not be filed after the time limit for filing had expired. Through descent proceedings, a portion of the farmland was transferred to the Decedent's child and the farmland was partitioned and sold to pay the IRS. Had the Will been filed, the surviving spouse could have protected the farmland from the child's debt to the IRS. The benefit of filing the Will where there are no known probate assets is that if assets are later discovered to be probate assets, the Will will be available to control the distribution of the Decedent's assets according to the Decedent's written instructions.

Probate Estate Is Small and Does Not Include Real Estate

Most states have enacted statutes that allow a summary probate procedure or a simple affidavit for estates that do not include real estate and that are below a certain value ($10,000 is a common limit) so long as all of the Decedent's debts and taxes and the expenses of administering the estate are paid.[3.12] The affidavit procedure does not allow the Executor to invoke the power and authority of the court if a problem arises in the administration. Neither is the affidavit or summary procedure appropriate where there are creditors that are not paid. The Executor and the estate attorney must evaluate whether this estate complies with the requirements for the summary procedure or if a more complete procedure is necessary.

Beginning an administration proceeding as a simplified or summary proceeding and then transferring the administration to a full probate proceeding adds to the cost. Careful analysis of the estate before beginning any probate proceeding will help minimize these costs. The Executor and the estate attorney must carefully analyze the value and type of assets and the debts of the Decedent's estate to determine the best choice of proceedings under the circumstances.

Estates Where Real Estate Is Involved

Most states require that the full authority of the court be brought to bear on estates where real estate is part of the Decedent's estate. The payment of debts, taxes, and the expenses of administration from estate assets is necessary. The power of the state statutes and the court is used to organize and supervise that procedure.

Full administration of the Decedent's estate, as opposed to summary disposition, offers some significant benefits to the heirs, devisees, and legatees. Full administration establishes the legal right of certain persons to take the property against the claims of others and protects those who receive the property and the Executor from claims. The claims of all creditors are terminated if their claims are not presented within the period of limitations under the statutes. If the estate does not have sufficient assets to pay all the debts, taxes, and expenses, the court will order payment of these claims, bequests, and final distribution according to the actual priority of the rights of the interested persons. All persons who are legally interested in the estate are entitled to legal notice of these proceedings.

Full administration authorizes the method of selling assets through public and private sales during the probate proceedings and the distribution of the proceeds to pay creditors, legatees, and devisees. Full administration renders real estate titles merchantable and therefore able to be sold much sooner than they otherwise might be. The transfer of stocks, bonds, and other investments, by either liquidation or distribution, can be authorized in full administration. Administration in accordance with the state probate code extends the court's protection to the Executor who manages the affairs of the Decedent's estate and distributes the Decedent's property in accordance with court orders. Full administration provides heirs, legatees, devisees, creditors, and the Executor with the opportunity to participate and the assurance that the estate has been fully administered under the laws of the state.

Ancillary Probate

If the Decedent's estate includes real estate or tangible personal property in another state, the Executor, with the advice and aid of the estate attorney, must initiate probate proceedings in that state to transfer those assets. These proceedings are in addition, or ancillary, to probate proceedings in the Decedent's domicile. Requirements for ancillary proceedings vary from state to state. A second attorney must be employed who is licensed to practice in the state where the ancillary proceedings are to be opened.

Recording Proceeding in Another County

In order to properly record the transfer of real estate located in a different county (but the same state) as the Decedent's original probate proceeding, it is necessary to file a certified copy of the final court order of distribution in the county where the real estate is located. Similarly, if real estate is located in a different county (but the same state) as an ancillary proceeding, a certified copy of the final court order of distribution from the ancillary proceeding must be filed in the county where the real estate is located.

ESTATE ATTORNEY

As is evident by now, the probate administration of a Will is a legal process that always requires court proceedings. Money and property are the subject of these proceedings. The complexity of a Decedent's estate is determined not only by the value of the estate, but also by the types of property and the relationships of the interested persons. Detailed legal procedures exist for all different circumstances. There are three related reasons that the Executor must engage an estate attorney to perform the tasks required of an attorney. First, the Executor is not acting for himself or herself personally, but as a fiduciary for someone else, the estate and the estate's interested persons. Unless the Executor is an attorney licensed to practice in the state where the probate proceeding is filed, if the Executor acts in the place of the attorney the Executor would be engaging in the unauthorized practice of law. Second, as a fiduciary, the Executor is required to take all reasonable care under the circumstances to ensure that the estate is properly administered. This standard of "reasonable care" under the circumstances of a probate proceeding will require that the Executor hire a qualified attorney to handle legal matters. Third, the knowledge of an attorney who practices regularly in estate administration and in the probate court in the state where the Will is being offered is the Executor's best protection from personal liability. If the proper procedures are not followed and the Executor distributes money or property to the wrong persons, or if debts and taxes are not properly paid, the law will hold the Executor responsible from the Executor's own personal assets up to the amount improperly distributed. The involvement of an estate attorney is essential to guide the Executor through the detailed legal procedures.

Court clerks and staff members are instructed not to give legal advice on probate matters. Without a thorough knowledge of all the facts and circumstances of a particular case and a broad-based understanding of the law involved, any directions or information a court employee gives might be incorrect and create a serious problem. Court employees will advise that they are not authorized to practice law and will suggest contacting an attorney.

Other professionals, such as insurance agents and stockbrokers who deal with some aspects of Decedents' estates, are sometimes more generous with their advice. Put this advice into perspective. The formal training of sales staff is in sales of their own products and not legal probate administration. Their experiences with other clients may fit this estate, or there may be significant differences of which they are not aware. If their advice is wrong, they have no liability. Be sure to verify any advice you get with your estate attorney before acting upon it.

Estate administration is a highly technical area of the law requiring knowledge about taxes, property, and probate law and court procedure. Because fiduciary duty requires that the Executor make all reasonable efforts and take all reasonable precautions to protect the estate, the Executor will be required to seek competent legal assistance. However, not all attorneys are familiar with probate procedure or estate administration. The attorneys who practice primarily in this area will have an in-depth knowledge of this specialty. The Executor is not required to hire the attorney who prepared the Will to also be the estate attorney.

To find a qualified estate attorney, obtain a list of members from the National Academy of Elder Law Attorneys, ask the local bar association for their probate practice committee list, or obtain the attorney membership roster of regional estate planning councils. The yellow pages and advertisements will also identify attorneys who practice in the estate and probate area. Most serious and reliable estate attorneys belong to one or more of these organizations and advertise their specialty. But beware—being on the list does not guarantee that the attorney is qualified; it only guarantees that he or she paid the dues or advertising costs. The Executor must research the qualifications of a prospective estate attorney. This small effort is well worth the time. Ask attorneys who work in other areas and other professionals who deal with finances and investments for recommendations. An initial interview with an attorney should include a discussion of the attorney's involvement in the practice of probate law, the years of experience, the level at which the attorney expects the Executor to be involved, and a clear understanding about fees. The Executor and the estate attorney should agree upon the method of calculating the attorney's fees and have a clear written fee agreement.

After the estate attorney has been employed, if the Executor has any reason to believe that the estate attorney is not doing what is required, the Executor must deal with the problem immediately! The Executor has a fiduciary duty to supervise agents—and the estate attorney is one of those agents.

ATTORNEY'S FEES

The primary responsibilities of the attorney are evaluating and interpreting the Will and any codicils or attachments; determining the proper court procedure; preparing required legal documents; identifying legal heirs, devisees, and legatees; sending legal notice to all interested persons; counseling the Executor; preparing court documents; supervising preparation of tax returns and accountings; resolving legal issues; and interacting with the court, staff, and the judge. If there is a contest or an unusual or complex legal issue is raised, the attorney will be responsible for those matters. The estate will be billed for the time to prepare and complete litigation or settlement proceedings. Although some assets pass outside the probate estate, including assets held in joint tenancy with rights of survivorship or insurance proceeds with a named beneficiary, there is still work that the attorney must do in regard to these assets including preparing the inventory and tax returns, clearing the title, making spousal elective share claims, transfers, and assignments. That work will be taken into account in arriving at a fee.

Many essential tasks of administering the estate are primarily the responsibility of the Executor. However, if the Executor is not able or chooses not to perform these tasks, the attorney will assure that the tasks are completed satisfactorily and within a reasonable period of time. These tasks often require the attorney to be out of the office and are usually time-consuming. If the estate attorney performs the tasks of the Executor, the attorney's fees will reflect those additional burdens. One major added expense is additional attorney's fees required to be paid to the estate attorney for performing the duties of the Executor.

Attorney's fees are usually paid from the estate assets. If the estate does not have sufficient assets to pay the fees, the persons who are interested in having the estate administered must pay the attorney's fees personally. The attorney's fees can be determined on the basis of the actual time spent working on matters related to the probate administration of the Decedent's estate, by a percentage of the estate, or by some other method agreeable to the Executor and the estate attorney.

IS A BOND NECESSARY?

The Executor must post a bond before the court will grant Letters Testamentary unless the Will waives the bond. Some states may allow all interested persons to waive bond if certain conditions are met.[3.13] The amount of the bond is determined by statute and is calculated as a percentage of the value of the personal property plus the income in the estate.[3.14] The bond assures the full and faithful performance by the Executor of the fiduciary duties and protects the beneficiaries from mistakes, fraud, and embezzlement. The estate attorney will know of insurance companies that offer fiduciary bonds in the state where the Will is being probated.

DECEDENT'S NAME

The Decedent may have used more than one name in her or his lifetime, including a maiden name, a married name, an adopted name, a name with only a first or middle initial, a name with the middle name spelled out, a name with no middle initial, or a nickname. When assets are registered in a name, the transfer of that asset to the estate or to a new owner will require that the precise name on that asset be shown in the probate proceeding. This is accomplished very easily by including the additional names in the legal documents in the following manner: Mary Ann Jones a/k/a Mary Ann Smith a/k/a Mary A. Smith a/k/a Skip Smith. The abbreviation "a/k/a" stands for "also known as." Transfer of an asset registered in a name that is not included in the legal documents will require additional effort and paperwork. The Executor must provide the estate attorney with the information about additional names by which the Decedent was known. The Executor and the estate attorney also must carefully review the ownership records of all assets to assure that the name in which each asset is registered is included in the probate documents.

PROBATE TIMETABLE

The completion schedule for probate administration is controlled by the probate procedure chosen, the types of assets, the speed with which sales of assets can be closed, the problems of administration, and the quickness with which tasks are accomplished by the Executor and the estate attorney. The essential time points are shown on the timetables in Appendix I and Appendix II. The timetables can be used to discuss with the estate attorney the probate proceedings required in the Decedent's state of domicile.

CHECKLIST: OPENING COURT PROCEEDING

After the family interview and after the most pressing tasks have been carried out, complete the tasks that follow. These are important but can be completed in less of a hurry. The estate attorney will need to be consulted in regard to most of these tasks.

1. Obtain complete information about the Decedent, including legal name and all aliases used, date of birth, date of death, legal domicile at death, last residence, marital status, legal heirs, and the other pertinent information asked for in the Information about Decedent Worksheet in Appendix IV.

2. Determine the proper probate proceeding with estate attorney. File the original Will with court even if no probate assets are known.

3. Discuss with the estate attorney the basis of attorney and executor's fees, estimated costs of administration, and time required for administration.

4. Complete the timetable for the estate by inserting important dates as they become known.

5. Determine all interested persons (see Chapter 4, Identifying All Interested Persons); obtain correct legal addresses and social security numbers of all devisees and legatees. E-mail addresses can be obtained for informal communication. However, e-mail is not acceptable for legal notice procedures.

6. To speed administration, discuss with the heirs, devisees, and legatees the possibility of signing Waivers of Notice for the Hearing on the Petition to Admit the Will and to Appoint the Executor.

7. The estate attorney must advise the surviving spouse and dependents of homestead rights, spousal and children's allowances, the right of election against the Will, spousal share laws, and Q-TIP election for federal estate tax purposes.

8. Obtain complete information about assets, including complete legal descriptions, account numbers, CUSIP (Committee for Uniform Security Identification Procedure) numbers, names of owners, names of beneficiaries, where assets are held, insurance on the asset, and so on. (See Chapter 6, Inventory and Valuation of Assets, for detailed information on asset inventory.)

9. Obtain name, address, and account numbers on any debts owed by the Decedent. (See Chapter 9, Claims and Demands on Decedent's Estate.)
10. With the estate attorney, determine whether the estate is solvent or if the assets must be allocated among creditors according to state abatement statutes. Make decisions about payment of the Decedent's bills, including utility bills, credit cards, medical bills, and the like.
11. Determine which assets must be sold to raise cash to pay bills. (See Chapter 8, Sale of Assets.)
12. Discuss purchase of a grave marker. Have attorney request permission of the court to purchase the grave marker with estate assets. The grave marker is not part of the allowed funeral expense but is a claim against the estate that is like that of an unsecured creditor.

Identifying All Interested Persons

INTERESTED PERSONS

The primary guarantee of probate administration is that all the people who are interested in the estate are given the opportunity to fully participate in the probate proceedings. All interested persons have legally protected rights. An interested person is defined by state statute and varies from state to state (although not very much).[4.1] Interested persons include not only those named in the Will, the devisees and legatees, but also the heirs who would inherit in the event the Will were to be found invalid. Usually the surviving spouse and children, if any, are the heirs-at-law. If there is no spouse or children, the surviving parents are the heirs of the Decedent. In the event that there is no surviving spouse, child, or parent, the brothers and sisters are then the rightful heirs of the Decedent. Each state's statutes provide a precise list of heirs for various combinations of living relatives. Consult with the estate attorney for the heirs under the state law for the state in which the Will is being probated. Creditors are also considered interested persons and are entitled to notice of the proceeding. Those who have no legal interest as heir, devisee, legatee, or creditor do not have "standing" to be involved in the proceedings, are not entitled to notice, and cannot appear before the court.

The estate attorney and the Executor must determine who are the legally interested persons for the state where the Will is being administered. The Executor must search out the names, addresses, and other necessary information about all interested persons. A well-written Will should include the names of all heirs as well as the devisees and legatees. The estate attorney will advise the Executor regarding what procedures must be followed if the information cannot be found.

LEGAL PROCEEDINGS TO DETERMINE HEIRS AND BENEFICIARIES

If there are any questions as to the identity of the heirs under the state statutes, or legatees and devisees under the Will, the estate attorney must determine whether legal proceedings are necessary to resolve these questions. The questions that may arise include: Who are the descendants of a deceased beneficiary? Are children who have been adopted-out to new adoptive parents legal heirs of their biological parents under the statutes of the state? Does the state statute, case law, or the Will include children conceived before but born after the death of the Testator as heirs? Does the state statute, case law, or Will include children born out-of-wedlock or adopted children as heirs, devisees, or legatees? Proper legal notice to all interested persons is an essential requirement for administration. The identification of these interested persons is absolutely necessary.

MINORS, DISABLED PERSONS, AND BENEFICIARIES IN MILITARY SERVICE

In the event an interested person is not legally competent, the court will appoint a legal representative. This legal representative is called a **Guardian** *ad litem*. The sole purpose and duty of the Guardian *ad litem* is to protect the legal interests of the person who is not legally competent in the probate proceeding. The Decedent's estate will pay the attorney's fees of the Guardian *ad litem*.

A person who is a minor is considered legally incompetent. The age of majority—that is, when a person is no longer a minor—varies from state to state from age 18 to age 21. The court may appoint a Guardian *ad litem* if the court believes it is necessary to protect the minor's interest. When a devisee, legatee, or heir is on active military duty and unable to adequately participate in the probate proceedings, a Guardian *ad litem* will be appointed by the court to protect his or her interests. Any interested person who has been declared disabled or **incompetent** by a court is not legally competent and must be represented in the probate administration.

The Executor faces a more difficult question when an heir, devisee, or legatee is, in the opinion of the Executor, perhaps incompetent and unable to adequately participate in the probate proceedings but has not been determined to be disabled by a court or diagnosed by a physician. The decision to request that a Guardian *ad litem* be appointed for such a person needs to be made with the following principle in mind. The full administration of the estate and the release of the Executor from liability rest on the full and active participation of all interested parties in the probate proceedings. If there is a potential that the interests of any person will not be fully protected, then a request for the appointment of a Guardian *ad litem* will be the best protection for that person, the estate, and the Executor.

LEGAL NOTICE REQUIRED

A common question is whether certain people have to be informed about the contents of the Will when they will not be receiving anything under the Will. For example, must the child of a previous marriage be given notice when the stepmother has been given the entire estate? Or is notice required to be given to a brother of the Decedent, the Decedent's closest living relative, who has not been heard from in years when the Will instructs that the entire estate will go to charity? The answer in all cases is a resounding *YES!* The notice to all interested parties is strictly required by state statute. Proper legal notice is the best protection for the Executor and for those who will ultimately receive the estate to ensure that any contest to the Will is resolved, challenges to the administration are met, and the gifts given in the Will are upheld under the law.

WHEN IS LEGAL NOTICE REQUIRED?

Legal notice must be given to the interested persons at several critical points in the administration of the estate. Legal notice is the formal announcement by mail and, at certain times, by **publication** in a newspaper, of the date, time, and place of the hearing. A copy of the petition that carefully describes the issues that are to be presented to the court for determination must be sent with the notices that are sent by mail. The estate attorney must send legal notice in the proper form at the proper time. To comply with these strict notice requirements in a complex or difficult case, the estate attorney may need to request instruction from the court. Notice by publication is discussed in the last section of this chapter. A detailed discussion of the hearings that require specific notice follows.

Hearing to Open Estate and Appoint Executor

The first regular hearing for which interested persons are entitled to notice is the hearing that appoints the Executor and admits the Will to probate.[4.2] All interested persons must receive a copy of both the petition filed with the court and the Will. These interested persons are entitled to contest the validity of the Will and the appointment of the Executor if they have any reasonable legal grounds. Unless and until all interested persons have been given that opportunity, the court will neither admit the Will to probate nor appoint the Executor. Those who have a legal interest can direct questions about procedures, interpretations, or positions taken on probate administration matters first to the Executor, then to the estate attorney. The estate attorney will explain the legal position or interpretation. If there is a fundamental conflict—for example, a contest of the Will—which cannot be resolved outside of court, the interested person must employ independent legal counsel. If the interested person is successful in his or her contest, the court may order that the estate pay the costs of the contest. Generally, however, the Decedent's estate is not required to finance unsuccessful attacks on the Will or on the fitness of the named Executor.

Hearing on Creditors' Claims

The second regular hearing for which interested persons are entitled to notice is the hearing on creditors' claims if one is held.[4.3] When creditors file claims with the court for payment, the Executor, legatees, devisees, and other creditors may contest the validity of those claims. When there are insufficient assets to pay all the debts, taxes, and expenses of the estate, the Executor may be required to ask the court to order only partial payment of the claims. All these interested persons are entitled to notice of the hearing on creditors' claims and a copy of the petitions concerning those claims.

Hearing on Sale of Assets

If the Will does not waive court supervision of the sale of estate assets, the Executor will be required to seek court orders for permission to sell, for a determination of sales price, and for approval of the sale. Legatees, devisees, and creditors are entitled to notice of these hearings and the details concerning the sale of property.[4.4]

Other Hearings

There are numerous other court orders that the Executor may request to fully administer the estate. Each request for an order will be heard by the court. Some of the hearings on these requests can be held without notice to the legatees, devisees, and creditors who continue to have a legal interest in the estate if the court determines that their interests will not be impaired. Any request for an order that might impair the rights of the interested persons will require proper legal notice to the interested persons of the hearing on that request.

Final Distribution of the Estate

The last regular hearing to which interested persons (legatees, devisees, and creditors who have not yet been paid in full) are entitled to notice is the request for an order on the final **distribution** of the estate.[4.5] The petition for final settlement sets forth the precise distribution of the estate assets that is proposed and requests the court to order that distribution. An attached accounting sets out the income of the estate and distributions of estate assets during administration. This hearing offers the best and last opportunity for the interested persons to object to the actions of the Executor or to improper distributions.

Interestingly enough, although the inventory of the estate is required to be filed with the court and is open to the public for inspection, not all states require the Executor to send a copy of the inventory to the interested persons.[4.6] Anyone (even those who have no legal interest in the estate) may obtain a copy of the court file, including the inventory, from the court clerk.

While the state and federal taxing authority will file a letter stating that the necessary estate or inheritance taxes have been paid, estate and inheritance tax returns are not a part of the court records. A complete list of the Decedent's assets including all probate and all non-probate property is required to be listed in the death tax returns. Only those persons who can show both a legal interest and a legitimate need will be able to obtain those death tax returns.

WAIVERS OF NOTICE

After a petition is filed in the court, there is a required waiting period of approximately two to four weeks before most hearings. The period of time from filing of a petition until the hearing is intended to give all interested persons adequate time to research the matters raised, seek the advice of legal counsel, and prepare for the hearing. If there is no contest or objection, this delay is unnecessary. By a signed document, the heirs, legatees, and devisees can waive notice of the hearing and the matter can be set for immediate hearing. Before signing a waiver of notice, an interested person must receive a copy of the petition that has been presented to the court for decision and must determine that he or she does not wish to contest any matter in that petition. In fact, the person signing the waiver has actual notice of the hearing, but says, in effect, there is no need to wait the required period of time for a hearing because he or she does not object. The use of waivers of notice of hearing can greatly speed court proceedings. However, each and every devisee, legatee, and when necessary, heir must sign the waiver. Any one person who delays, refuses, or simply neglects to sign prevents the use of waivers of notice and may delay the court proceedings even further. The Executor should discuss the use of waivers of notice with the estate attorney.

PUBLICATION OF NOTICE

In addition to the written notice mailed to interested persons, legal notice by publication is required when a Will is filed with the court to give notice to creditors and other interested persons, such as heirs, not known to the Executor. Additional publication of notice may be required when an estate sells real estate or at final distribution if the estate is distributing real estate. This notice must be published in a newspaper approved by the court. Usually several separate publications of the notice spaced a week apart are required. The estate attorney must send these notices to the publisher in a form that complies with state law. The publisher will send proof of publication to the court and to the estate attorney after payment is made. Proof of publication is required to be filed with the court before the court will hear a petition that requires publication notice. Careful attention to all notice requirements will prevent continuance of the hearing and additional delays and costs.

CHECKLIST: IDENTIFY AND NOTIFY

The identification of all those who have a legal interest in the estate is essential. The following tasks must be accomplished in order to properly administer the estate.

1. Determine who are the legal heirs of the Decedent. Are these heirs competent? Obtain full legal names, birth dates, and addresses of all heirs and, if any is not competent, his or her legal representative. (See Appendix IV, Worksheets and Forms: Heirs Contact Worksheet.)
2. Determine who are the devisees and legatees of Decedent's Will. Are these persons living and competent? Do they wish to disclaim a gift? (See Chapter 11, Special Considerations.) Obtain full legal

names, birth dates, addresses, and social security numbers of all devisees and legatees. If any is not competent, obtain the name and address of his or her legal representative. (See Appendix IV, Worksheets and Forms: Legatees and Devisees Worksheet.)

3. Confirm that the estate attorney has sent the required written legal notice for all hearings or obtained waivers of notice from all interested persons for each hearing.
4. Confirm that the required notice has been published and proof of publication sent to the court.
5. Notify the Social Security Administration, Railroad Retirement Board, Veteran's Administration, and other agencies paying benefits that the Decedent has died.
6. Notify all clubs, organizations, and activities in which the Decedent participated of Decedent's death. Request refunds where appropriate. Return club property.

Guardians, Conservators, Custodians, and Trustees

The purpose of this chapter is to focus on the special issues that the Executor must face when a minor or disabled or incapacitated adult is involved in the Decedent's estate. The Executor must take special care in administering the assets when those assets must be distributed to a minor or a disabled or incapacitated adult, when the Will appoints a **Guardian** of a minor, and when the Decedent was the Guardian of a minor or disabled or incapacitated adult. This chapter does not discuss the details of applying for and administering a Conservatorship or Guardianship. Guardianship and Conservatorship proceedings are quite involved because of the strict safeguards that are necessary to protect the individual whose person and property are ordered into the care of another. The estate attorney will provide guidance in those proceedings. This chapter addresses the questions of who needs a Guardian or a Conservator and what are the duties of a Guardian or a Conservator. This chapter also discusses two methods, other than Conservatorship, that a Will can use to direct management of assets given to those who do not have legal capacity to own or manage property for themselves. Those two methods, the appointment of a Custodian under the **Uniform Transfers to Minors Act (UTMA)** and the appointment of a Trustee in a trust, are frequently used to avoid the cost and ongoing, restrictive, and expensive intervention of the court that is necessary with a Conservatorship.

WHO NEEDS A GUARDIAN?

A minor child who does not have a living natural or adoptive parent needs a Guardian. And any disabled, incapacitated, or impaired adult needs a Guardian. A minor child is a person who is under legal age. In most states, the legal age is eighteen (18).[5.1] A disabled, incapacitated, or impaired adult is a person of legal age who is unable to care for himself or herself or his or her property.[5.2] When a Guardian is appointed, the minor or the disabled, incapacitated, or impaired adult is called the **Ward**.

For a disabled, incapacitated, or impaired adult there is a circumstance where a Guardian may not be necessary. If, before he or she became disabled, the disabled adult had appointed an attorney-in-fact under a durable Power of Attorney for Health and Personal Care, that attorney-in-fact has legal authority to care for the disabled adult without being appointed as Guardian by the court.[5.3] The Power of Attorney must deal specifically with health and personal care issues to substitute for a guardianship. A Power of Attorney that deals with financial issues do not necessarily give authority for health or personal care decisions. The Power of Attorney for Health and Personal Care must detail each and every power the person wishes the attorney-in-fact to exercise, including the power to withhold medical treatment, nutrition, and hydration and to remove life support equipment if those are desired.

APPOINTMENT OF A GUARDIAN
FOR A MINOR CHILD

If the Decedent is survived by a minor child and is also survived by the other natural or adoptive parent of that minor child, the natural or adoptive parent is the natural Guardian for the minor child (unless parental rights have been legally terminated). The court will not appoint a legal Guardian. This is true even if the Decedent named someone else to be the child's Guardian in the Will. It is also true even if the child has not lived with the surviving natural or adoptive parent. The surviving natural or adoptive parent has the legal right to custody of the child. The protection of a child from an unfit parent is beyond the scope of this *Guide*. Those seeking to protect a child after a custodial parent's death should consult with child protective services in the state where the child resides or seek independent legal counsel.

Only when the minor child has no surviving natural or adoptive parent will the state court appoint a Guardian for the minor child. (Some state statutes call this Guardian a "Guardian of the person" of the minor child.) This Guardian will have custody and control of the minor child but not necessarily control of the property of the minor. In determining who should be appointed as the Guardian, the court will usually confirm the nomination made by the Decedent in his or her Will. If the Will is silent with regard to the appointment of a Guardian, the court is required to follow the state statutory guidelines for choosing and appointing a Guardian.[5.4] A minor over the age of 14 may have some right to nominate his or her own Guardian.[5.5] In making its decision, the court will consider, among other factors, the fitness of the person nominated, the workload that the appointment will impose, and the religious tradition of the minor and the nominee. Guardians are entitled to reimbursement of expenses and a reasonable fee from the estate of the minor child.

The Guardian of a minor child is entitled to receive any social security benefits payable for the support of the child. The payments are required to be used for the minor child only, and the Guardian is required to account for these payments to the Social Security Administration on an annual basis. If the Decedent's Will gives assets to the minor child, careful provisions need to be made in the Will to coordinate the use of these assets with the social security support payments and to provide for distribution to a Trustee or Conservator.

APPOINTMENT OF A GUARDIAN FOR
A DISABLED ADULT

The Executor has no responsibility (as Executor) to seek appointment of a Guardian for a disabled, incapacitated, or impaired adult. If the Decedent's Will nominates a Guardian or Successor Guardian for such an adult, the Executor should notify the nominee immediately so that independent Guardianship proceedings can be initiated.

The Guardian of a disabled, incapacitated, or impaired adult is entitled to receive the social security benefits payable for the support of the disabled adult. The law requires the payments to be used for the disabled adult only, and the Guardian is required to account to the Social Security Administration for these payments on an annual basis. Careful provisions need to be made to coordinate the use of other assets of the disabled adult with these social security payments. Guardians are entitled to reimbursement of expenses and a reasonable fee from the estate of the disabled person.

For a disabled, incapacitated, or impaired adult there is a circumstance where a Conservator may not be necessary. If, before he or she became disabled, the disabled adult had appointed an attorney-in-fact under a durable Power of Attorney for financial affairs, that attorney-in-fact can manage the disabled adult's financial affairs without being appointed as Conservator by the court. The Power of Attorney must detail each power the disabled adult wishes the attorney-in-fact to exercise. The Power of Attorney for financial affairs must deal specifically with financial issues and must authorize the attorney-in-fact to receive assets from an estate, beneficiary designation, or trust distribution. A Power of Attorney that deals with healthcare issues will not automatically give authority for comprehensive financial decisions.

WHEN DECEDENT WAS GUARDIAN OF ANOTHER PERSON

If the Decedent was the court-appointed Guardian of a minor child or a disabled, incapacitated, or impaired adult, the court that appointed the Guardian must be notified of the death. Although care of the minor child or disabled adult must be assured, the Executor is not responsible, as Executor, for giving that care. As a practical matter, the Executor may be involved as a family member or as a compassionate bystander but has no legal duty to take over the Guardianship. The Executor should contact the estate attorney immediately for guidance. The procedures for appointing a successor Guardian are part of an independent court proceeding for Guardianship and are not part of the Decedent's probate proceeding. The Will of the Decedent may nominate a successor and that nomination will be considered by the court but is not controlling.

DUTIES OF THE GUARDIAN

The Guardian of a minor child or a disabled, incapacitated, or impaired adult is subject to the control and direction of the court at all times and in all things. It is the duty of the Guardian to carry out the specific duties and powers assigned by the court. The Guardian must assure that the personal, civil, and human rights of the minor child or disabled adult are protected. The Guardian will have custody and control of the minor child or the disabled adult and must provide for care, medical treatment, living accommodations, education, support, and maintenance.

The Guardian is required to ensure that the Ward lives in the least restrictive setting that is reasonably available. The Guardian must obtain court approval to place the Ward in a facility or institution, remove organs, amputate a limb, undergo psychosurgery, consent to or withhold life-saving medical procedures, or consent to any biomedical or behavioral experiment or sterilization. The Guardian may not, on behalf of the Ward, consent to termination of parental rights, and the Guardian may not prohibit the Ward's marriage or divorce. The Guardian is not obligated to use his or her own financial resources to support the Ward unless the Ward is the spouse of the Guardian.

WHO NEEDS A CONSERVATOR?

While a Guardian deals with the personal and healthcare decisions for a minor or disabled or incapacitated adult, a Conservator deals with the financial decisions. If the Decedent, through a Will, pay-on-death, or other **beneficiary** designation gave assets to a minor child or a disabled adult and no trust was created or other provision made in the Will for distributing those assets for the benefit of the child or the disabled adult, the Executor must ask the court to appoint a **Conservator** (known in some states as the "Guardian of the estate") to receive the assets. Without special provisions in the will, the Executor cannot deliver the assets directly to the child or disabled, incapacitated, or impaired person.[5.6] The minor child or disabled adult is called the **Conservatee** when a Conservator has been appointed.

In many states, there is a statutory exception to the rule that a minor's property must be distributed to a Conservator. When the assets that are to be distributed are below a certain minimal value ($5,000 is customary), some states allow these assets to be distributed to the parent or Guardian of a minor under a Uniform Transfers to Minors Act or some similar provision without creating a Conservatorship, without further court intervention, and without posting bond.[5.7]

APPOINTMENT OF A CONSERVATOR FOR A MINOR CHILD OR DISABLED ADULT

In most cases, the court must name a Conservator to hold, manage, and distribute the assets of a minor or disabled, incapacitated, or impaired adult. If the Decedent named a Conservator in the Will, the court will appoint the named person unless that person is shown to be unfit. The natural or adoptive parent of the minor child, although the natural Guardian of the child, is not necessarily entitled to be appointed as Conservator. However, if the Will does not name someone else to be the Conservator, the child's parent may have priority in the state statutory scheme.[5.8] Some states may require appointment of a Conservator who is a resident of the state in order to confer jurisdiction of the court over the individual.[5.9] A trust company or bank trust department can be appointed as the Conservator, instead of an individual, to obtain independent, professional management of the assets.

Bond Required for the Conservator Unless Waived by Will

Unless waived by the Will, the Conservator will be required to post a fiduciary bond.[5.10] This bond ensures the proper performance of the Conservator with regard to the minor child's or disabled person's estate. The Executor should be aware that the cost of the bond is paid from the estate of the minor child or disabled person on a yearly basis and can be quite expensive. The estate attorney will know the state's bonding requirements and the sources for bonds; and, if a bond company refuses to bond the named Conservator, the attorney will be able to discuss alternatives. For example, the appointment of a trust company as Conservator may provide a special economic advantage: A trust company is bonded as an institution, and the Conservatee's estate does not have to purchase a separate bond.

DUTIES OF A CONSERVATOR

The Conservator is a fiduciary and is held accountable by the court for all acts undertaken in that fiduciary capacity. The fiduciary duty required of the Executor, discussed in Chapter 1, applies to Conservators as well. Generally, the Conservator is empowered to do the following:

1. Possess and manage the estate of the Conservatee
2. Pay for necessities, such as food, shelter, and medical care, for the Conservatee
3. Pay Conservatee's debts
4. Invest Conservatee's funds in approved investments
5. Sell assets of the Conservatee's estate
6. Prosecute and defend legal cases for the Conservatee

Any significant nonroutine actions the Conservator believes should be taken in the best interest of the Conservatee may require court approval. These actions may include sale of a residence, major changes in investments, and purchase of a car for a minor. In most states an annual inventory and accounting of the estate of the minor or the disabled person must be filed and approved by the court.

DISTRIBUTION TO AN ADULT WHO HAS NOT PREVIOUSLY BEEN JUDGED DISABLED

In the case where there has been no court determination of disability but there is clear evidence that the adult is disabled, incapacitated, or impaired, the Executor is faced with a particularly delicate problem. If the Executor distributes assets to that disabled or incapacitated person, the disabled adult may lose those assets. Possibly the Executor will be accused later of being responsible for the improper distribution. Common sense cautions that money should not be given to someone who cannot handle it. But initiation of proceedings for the determination of disability may be outside the Executor's duty and authority. However, the Executor, through the estate attorney, may petition the court for the appointment of a Guardian *ad litem* to protect the interests of the person believed to be disabled. The participation of the Guardian ad litem is sufficient legal protection for the potentially disabled person. The Executor should feel more comfortable following the orders of the court for distribution when the Guardian *ad litem* has participated in the proceedings on behalf of the potentially disabled person.

CUSTODIAN UNDER THE UNIFORM TRANSFERS TO MINORS ACT

A Will can instruct the Executor to transfer assets to a Custodian under a Uniform Transfers to Minors Act (UTMA) for the benefit of a minor as an alternative to a court appointed Conservator.[5.11] The Testator may name whomever he or she wishes to be the Custodian. There is no requirement that a parent be named as the Custodian. The Custodian is not required to be bonded. Generally, the Uniform Transfers to Minors Act provides that the Custodian shall have control of the assets and collect, hold, manage, and invest them for the benefit of the minor. The state's Uniform Transfers to Minors Act controls distribution of those assets to the minor. Without court supervision, the Custodian may pay for the minor's benefit so much of the assets as the Custodian considers advisable. A Custodian is entitled to be reimbursed for reasonable expenses incurred in his or her duties as Custodian. In addition to the reimbursement for expenses, the Custodian is entitled to a reasonable compensation for his or her services.

If the Decedent was a Custodian of an asset that is held under the Uniform Transfers to Minors Act, a successor Custodian must be appointed and the assets re-titled into the name of the new Custodian. If the document that originally created the Custodianship names a successor Custodian, that person will be named. If it does not, a successor may be nominated. The estate attorney must petition the court to appoint a successor Custodian.

TRUSTS FOR MINORS AND DISABLED ADULTS

The Testator may, by Will, direct the Executor to distribute the share of a minor or a disabled person to a **Trust** that has been created previously or is created in the Will. A Trust is an excellent method of protecting and conserving a legacy and controlling the distributions to a minor or a disabled adult over an extended period of time. The Testator may waive the requirement of a bond for the **Trustee** in the Will.

Assets may be held in Trust for a child's entire life or until the child reaches some age determined by the Testator. For example, the Trust can be written to manage the child's money until the child reaches age 45 and then the Trustee is instructed to distribute the balance to the child. The Trustee can be instructed to distribute all or part of the income and principal of the Trust to pay for education, healthcare, or support of the child. Or, the Trustee can be instructed to distribute all of the income to the child for life. Trusts can be written to address a number of specific problems or concerns. The Trust may be created by the Decedent before death, in the Will after death, or by another person before death or in a Will. The Trust must be created before the Executor distributes the assets to the Trustee.

CHECKLIST: GUARDIANS, CONSERVATORS, CUSTODIANS, AND TRUSTEES

Review the following questions to determine whether further action is necessary.

1. _____ Did the Decedent's death leave a minor child without a surviving parent? If yes:
   _____ Does Decedent's Will nominate a Guardian?
   _____ If the minor child is age 14 or older, does the child wish to nominate a Guardian?
   _____ Have estate attorney file a Petition to appoint a Guardian for the minor child.
2. _____ Was the Decedent the court-appointed Guardian or Conservator for a minor child or a disabled adult? If yes:
   _____ The court must be asked to appoint a successor.
   _____ Final accounting and report on the condition of the Ward must be prepared and filed with the court for approval.
3. _____ Did the Decedent by a Will, Trust, or beneficiary designation leave assets to a minor child or a disabled, incapacitated, or impaired adult? If yes:
   _____ Executor must distribute those assets to a Conservator or, if authorized by Will or statute, to a Custodian under the Uniform Transfer to Minors Act (UTMA) or to a Trustee under a Trust.
4. _____ Was the Decedent a Custodian for assets of an underage child under the UTMA? If yes:

Estate attorney must petition the court for appointment of a new Custodian.

5. ____ Was Decedent a Trustee for a Trust that holds assets for another person? If yes:

____ The Trust document must be consulted to determine the successor Trustee.

____ An accounting must be prepared and submitted to those entitled. Executor may wish to seek court approval of accounting.

If no successor Trustee is named the court must be asked to appoint a successor Trustee.

6. ____ Is Decedent survived by a disabled spouse or other disabled interested person?

If yes:

____ The Executor must inform the estate attorney to assure proper notice and protection is given to those disabled persons.

Inventory and Valuation of Assets

INTRODUCTION TO IDENTIFYING ASSETS

The probate code in each state requires the Executor to make a complete and accurate **inventory** of all real estate and tangible personal property owned by the Decedent in the state of domicile at death and of all intangible property owned by the Decedent wherever that property is located.[6.1] The foundation of estate administration is this complete and accurate list of all the Decedent's property correctly valued as of the time of death. Obtaining the necessary information about what the Decedent owned and determining the value of those assets is discussed in detail in this chapter.

DISCOVERY OF ASSETS

The task is to discover all the items of value the Decedent owned at death (whether or not they are probate assets) and all items of value given away by the Decedent in the three-year period before death. These items of value are called assets. A complete list of these assets must be prepared for several purposes. A complete list is necessary to organize the proper care and management of every asset. A portion of this list must be reported to the court as the probate estate and made a part of the court record shortly after Letters Testamentary are granted. The entire list of assets must be reported on the **inheritance** or other **death tax** return and on the state and federal estate tax returns, if these are required to be filed. Each asset must be evaluated to determine what income must be reported on behalf of the estate or the beneficiaries. Lastly, the disposition of each asset must be carefully accounted for in the final settlement of the estate.

WHERE TO LOOK FOR ASSETS

The Executor must diligently search for all the assets of the Decedent. A bit of sleuthing is necessary in many cases. Fiduciary duty requires the Executor to make all reasonable efforts to discover assets. This standard requires that at least the Executor must look carefully for evidence of assets in the following locations.

Testator's Inventory

A list of assets, compiled by the Testator before death, is an invaluable aid in finding assets. This list is such an enormous help that it would be wise for a person named as Executor in a Will to encourage the Testator to compile this list when the Will is written and to update it on a regular basis. Many times a careful attorney, financial planner, or accountant will make an informal inventory before a Will is written or when an estate or financial plan is undertaken. The Executor should ask these professionals for such an inventory. If the Decedent used a personal computer, check his or her personal computer files for asset lists, especially those programs that provide investment tracking and asset record keeping capabilities.

Personal Papers

The Decedent's personal papers are an important place to look for information about assets. The Executor must find the personal papers of the Decedent and put them in a safe place. Important personal papers are often kept in unexpected places. All desks, file cabinets, safes, lock boxes, purses, billfolds, briefcases, drawers, and boxes of papers must be searched. In some instances, a search of the following may be fruitful: contents of a freezer, refrigerator, in canned goods with hidden compartments, in books on the shelf, behind pictures, in closets, in spaces in the walls, in hiding places in furniture, under linens, in boxes, in basements, and in the glove box and trunk of the automobile.

The papers should be sorted as the search progresses. Some papers have actual value and need to be placed in safekeeping. These valuable papers include cash, stock certificates, bonds, certificates of deposit (CDs), and promissory notes. However, most papers are only records and are useful to help locate actual assets. (For a more detailed discussion of protecting valuable papers, see Chapter 7, Management of Assets.)

Often, in searching through personal papers, there is some clue to an asset—for example, a notice that an insurance policy has been canceled or that a bank account has been closed. In order to fulfill the responsibility to make all reasonable efforts to discover assets, the Executor must contact that insurance company and the bank to inquire whether the Decedent had purchased a replacement policy or had transferred the bank account to another account in the same bank.

Bank Records

The checking account records will contain valuable information about sources of income and debts. A deposit of an oil royalty check and a payment to a loan company are evidence of an asset and a debt. The check records for the past few years should be carefully examined to uncover clues to these assets and debts. If the bank records are not among the Decedent's papers, the Executor can request those records from the bank. The bank will ask to see the Letters Testamentary before releasing the Decedent's records.

Safe Deposit Box of Decedent

Any safe deposit box that the Decedent owned, either solely or as a joint tenant with anyone else, must be opened and its contents inventoried. Even if the box was considered to be the property of another person and the Decedent's name was on the box only as a convenience, the Executor has the duty to open and inventory the box for the estate. If the Executor is denied access to the box by the bank for any reason, the estate attorney should be consulted and will obtain entry either by a statutory procedure or by court order. If a safe deposit box cannot be located, the Executor should inquire at each bank where Decedent held an account whether Decedent rented a box at that bank.

Safe Deposit Boxes and Safes of Others

Often the Decedent has given papers and valuables to others for safekeeping, and those may be held in the safe deposit box, safe, or files of someone else. A bank or trust company may hold valuables in their vault. The Executor must ask likely persons whether they hold documents or property for the Decedent, either in a safe deposit box, a home safe, or any other place.

Tax Returns

The Executor must obtain the Decedent's income tax returns for at least the two previous years. These income tax returns will list the sources of taxable income. The Executor must then determine whether the assets which produced the income remain in the estate at the date of death.

Unclaimed Property

Banks, companies, and governments lose track of owners because of death, misspelled names, changes of address, post office mistakes, companies that go out of business, forgotten bank accounts, uncashed checks, and utility, rent, and security deposits that are never collected. The Executor should check for unclaimed funds with the unclaimed property depositories in the states where property is likely to be located. The Executor can search for unclaimed property nationally on the Internet at sites such as www.unclaimed.org and www.missingmoney.com.

Mail

The Executor must gather, open, and read the mail of the Decedent for evidence of assets and debts. Monthly, quarterly, and yearly account statements from bank, savings and loan, credit union, stock, bond, and mutual fund accounts show where assets are located. Payments of dividends or interest and statements of taxable income will reveal the assets that are the source of those payments. Real estate tax bills and safe deposit rental renewal statements which arrive quarterly, biannually, or annually will disclose the location of land and safe deposit boxes. Income reported on IRS Form 1099 and the state income report sent after the first of the year will show sources of income in the year of Decedent's death. Clubs and organizations to which the Decedent belonged will send literature on a monthly basis and a dues statement annually. Refunds of membership dues are estate assets. Monthly and quarterly magazine, music, and book club literature will signal potential debts and possible refunds. Storage bills, vehicle tag renewal notices, and royalty checks alert the Executor to assets and debts of the Decedent. It is prudent to monitor the Decedent's mail for a full year to discover assets even though most of the estate assets may be distributed before a full year has passed.

Agents and Representatives

Those people who represented the Decedent will have pertinent information about the Decedent's assets. These agents may include lawyers, attorneys-in-fact, accountants, bankers, stockbrokers and investment account representatives, insurance agents, and financial planners. The Executor must request information, preferably in writing, from all known agents and representatives. The Executor must request a copy of all information known to the agent or representative that shows assets of the Decedent's estate or that would lead to discovery of assets of the estate. Even if the Executor believes that all the information is previously known, it is essential to request the information from each and every agent and representative of the Decedent to assure that no stone is left unturned.

Family and Friends

The Executor must ask the friends and family members about any assets that the Decedent owned at death. It is especially important to ask about assets that passed by joint tenancy or pay-on-death beneficiary designation—for example, a certificate of deposit that has a family member's name on it as a joint tenant. The family member who is entitled to the gift may not especially wish that anyone else know about the gift and may believe (incorrectly) that secrecy will avoid taxation of that asset. The Executor is responsible for reporting all assets transferred at the Decedent's death on any necessary tax returns and must make reasonable efforts to discover those assets. The Executor must ask if the family members have received any assets from the Decedent outside of probate and make reasonable efforts to discover the value of those assets.

The Executor must also ask family and friends if money was owed to the Decedent. Debts of family members and friends that are evidenced by a promissory note are clearly assets of the estate. The Executor may not choose to forgive or ignore those debts. The promissory note is the legal evidence of the debt and should be placed in safekeeping. If money is owed that is not evidenced by a promissory note or other signed evidence of the debt, the Executor should consult with the estate attorney for guidance.

Other Sources of Information about Assets

There are many other sources of information about the Decedent's assets. Insurance records may list assets owned by the Decedent that were covered by an insurance policy. If the Decedent had applied for credit, the lender frequently will have required a complete report of the borrower's financial status including a net worth statement. That net worth statement may contain helpful information about the Decedent's assets. If the Decedent or the Decedent's spouse had applied for governmental assistance through Medicaid or a similar program, the application for assistance requires a complete statement of assets and may contain valuable information.

CONFIRMATION OF ASSET OWNERSHIP, ASSET DESCRIPTION, AND VALUE

Discovering the assets is only the beginning. As part of the responsibility for inventorying and valuing assets, the Executor is required to confirm the description, the legal ownership, and the value of the asset. Confirmation of this information by a written statement is strongly recommended. A telephone conversation about an asset, although extremely useful in tracking down an asset, is not sufficient to confirm the information. A written statement protects the Executor and gives the best possible information if the estate is audited. If this information is collected as assets are discovered, there is seldom a need to retrace steps to confirm the description, ownership, and value. The technical task of confirming the description, ownership, and value is often assigned to the estate attorney. Discuss the requirements of confirmation with the estate attorney.

OWNERSHIP MODES

Property can be owned in a number of different modes. It is essential for the Executor to understand the modes of ownership for two reasons. First, the mode of ownership dictates the Executor's responsibilities for that asset. Second, the mode of ownership of each asset is a critical part of the legal description on the inventory and the required tax returns.

Possible ownership modes include sole ownership, joint tenancy with rights of survivorship, tenancy by the entireties, tenancy in common, life estate, remainder interest, reversionary interest, and trust ownership. The Executor must fully administer all assets in the probate estate that are solely owned or owned as tenants in common. The Executor is responsible for reporting property held in joint tenancy with rights of survivorship on inheritance, **estate tax,** and other death tax returns and to the probate court if a surviving spouse makes a claim for a spousal share from jointly owned property. The Executor must discover whether the Decedent owned a remainder interest in property for which another person's life estate has not expired, and the remainder interest must be administered with the other solely owned property in the probate estate. Consult with the estate attorney for all questions relating to the mode of ownership. The following discussion briefly describes the possible modes of ownership.

Sole Ownership

Sole ownership is ownership in the Decedent's name alone with no other owner. If no beneficiary is named, assets owned solely by the Decedent are part of the probate estate. Assets owned by the Decedent as sole owner often have a beneficiary named. If a beneficiary is named, the asset will pass directly to that beneficiary. Though an asset with a beneficiary is not part of the probate estate, it is part of the Decedent's taxable estate. The Executor and the estate attorney must determine whether the solely owned asset is part of the probate estate.

Joint Tenancy with Rights of Survivorship

Joint tenancy with rights of survivorship is co-ownership with one or more other persons. At death, the property held in joint tenancy with rights of survivorship passes by operation of law to the surviving joint tenants. It does not matter that the Decedent put all the money into the joint account or bought the joint real estate with his or her own money. The joint asset belongs to the surviving joint tenants and is not part of the private estate. A Will cannot change that result. The only exceptions to this rule are convenience accounts and the state statutory schemes that allow a surviving spouse to claim a share from the property held by the Decedent with someone other than the surviving spouse. Convenience accounts are accounts that are set up as joint tenancy accounts solely for the purpose of providing the convenience of allowing the joint owner to use the account for the benefit of the genuine owner. (See the discussion in Chapter 7 concerning joint tenancy bank accounts.) The joint tenancy convenience account is sometimes used as a substitute for a power of attorney with unexpected and unfortunate results. It is a poor substitute for proper estate planning. The surviving joint owner must relinquish the account ownership of a joint tenancy convenience account to return the account to the Decedent's estate. For estate tax purposes, there are special rules for including jointly owned property in the Decedent's taxable estate.[6.2]

Tenancy by the Entirety

Tenancy by the entirety is very similar to joint tenancy with rights of survivorship in that the surviving tenant owns all the property at Decedent's death by operation of law. However, only married couples may own property as tenants by the entirety and neither spouse may sever or end the tenancy during life without the consent of the other. Tenancy by entirety is recognized only in certain states.[6.3]

Tenancy in Common

Tenancy in Common refers to "joint owners" too. These joint owners also co-own property with one or more other persons. However, at death, property held by tenants in common does not pass to the surviving joint tenants. Instead the Decedent's proportionate share of the property belongs to the Decedent's estate and, after all the expenses, debts, and taxes are paid, passes under the Decedent's Will to the devisees or legatees. Many states favor tenancy in common over joint tenancy with rights of survivorship as a mode of owning property. These states require that the intent to own property with rights of survivorship be very clearly set out in the deed or title.[6.4]

Life Estate, Remainder, and Reversion

A **life estate** is the full ownership of property but only for the period of time measured by someone's life. The life that measures the length of the estate can be either the life of the life estate owner or the life of another person. At the death of the person whose life measures the estate, the full ownership of the property passes immediately to the **remainderman,** if a remander is given. The **remainder** interest in property can be granted in a deed, a Will, or a trust after a life estate. If there is no remainder given, the interest that is left after the death of the person whose life measures the life estate is called a reversion and returns to the estate of **Grantor** of the life estate. Life estates that end at Decedent's death are common in Trusts and, in some states, for farm and ranch land ownership. The life estate on the life of another, the remainder interest, and the reversionary interest may be includable in the Decedent's **taxable estate** and, in a few instances, the probate estate.

Term of Years

An interest in an asset for a term of years is full ownership of the asset but only for a specific period of time measured by days, weeks, months, or years. Ownership for a term of years usually applies to real estate, and the time period of the interest is written on the deed. A term of years interest can have a specific value and may be part of both the probate and taxable estate. If the Decedent had the right to own the property after the term of years expired, that **future interest** is an asset, has value, and can be part of the probate and the taxable estate.

Trust Ownership

A Trustee is the legal owner of the assets held in trust for the benefit of another. If the Decedent was the Trustee, a new Trustee or successor will take over according to the Trust instrument, or, if there is no successor Trustee named in the Will or Trust, the court will appoint a successor. When the Decedent Trustee was not a beneficiary of the trust and held no ownership interest, the trust assets are not a part of the Descendent Trustee's estate.

If the estate of the Decedent is the beneficiary of a Trust, that beneficial interest may be subject to probate administration. The rights of the beneficiary in the Trust estate are controlled by the terms of the Trust document and by state law. Commonly, a Trust will make provisions for an alternate or contingent beneficiary instead of naming the Decedent's estate as beneficiary. The estate attorney will evaluate the Trust to determine the proper beneficiary and whether any interest in the Trust is includable in the Decedent's probate or taxable estate.

Beneficiary Designation

The Decedent may have owned assets for which he or she named a beneficiary. A person, a Trust, or the estate may be named the beneficiary. That beneficiary will receive the assets directly. The asset with a designated beneficiary is not probate property unless the estate is the beneficiary. In most states, bank accounts, insurance policies, stocks, bonds, mutual fund accounts, annuities, IRAs, 401(k)s, other retirement programs, and Trusts may have named beneficiaries. In some states, a beneficiary may be named for motor vehicles and real estate. There is no readily available procedure for naming a beneficiary of tangible personal property, such as personal and household items, that has no title or registration unless that personal property is placed in Trust and a Trust beneficiary is named. The Executor must report the value of assets that pass by beneficiary designation on any **federal estate tax** or state death tax returns.

VALUATION AND APPRAISAL

The complete inventory of the Decedent's property must include not only an accurate legal description and statement of ownership of each asset but also its correct date-of-death value. This concept of the value on the date of death is very important. Because the value of assets can fluctuate on a daily basis and income can increase the value of an account, valuation of an estate can be confusing. It is very helpful to imagine taking a snapshot of the financial picture of the Decedent's estate on the date of death so that only what was owned at that moment and its value at that time is considered. Whether the value of the assets goes up or down, the date-of-death value is the key value for completing the probate inventory and for inheritance (succession) and estate tax returns. These fluctuations in value become important when the estate is distributed. (See Chapter 12, Final Settlement, Distribution and Closing the Estate.)

For purposes of the estate tax returns, there is a second date that is sometimes used to value an estate. This date is called the **alternate valuation date** and is exactly six months after the Decedent's date of death. The value of all the assets on the date six months after the date of death is compared to the value of all the assets on the date of death. If the total value of all the assets is less on the alternate valuation date than on the date of death, that lower value may be used for estate tax purposes.[6.5] For the estate tax return, all the assets must be valued either on the date of death or on the day exactly six months after the date of death. The federal tax law does not allow some assets to be valued on the date of death and other assets to be valued on the alternate valuation date.

Fair Market Value

The value that must be used in all valuations is the **fair market value**. The IRS defines the fair market value as follows:

> The fair market value is the price at which the property would change hands between a willing buyer and a willing seller, neither being under any compulsion to buy or sell and both having knowledge of relevant facts.[6.6]

Determining the full and fair market value is easy in some instances, more difficult in others. If property is sold at arms length before tax returns are prepared, the actual sales price will be conclusive evidence of the fair market value of the asset. Valuation of some assets will require a formal appraisal. Other assets may be informally appraised or valued by reference to a stock exchange price on the date of death. The balance shown in records of the company for the account on the date of death will value accounts. Refer to the Summary of Assets in Appendix V for instructions concerning valuation of specific assets.

Appraisal

An appraisal is conducted by an independent third party who has an appraiser's license and special qualifications. These licensed appraisers are also sometimes called qualified appraisers, and the valuation they give is called a qualified appraisal. In some instances, informal valuation of property by a dealer is sufficient. Whether a qualified appraisal or informal valuation is required depends upon the circumstances in the estate and the type of asset. Because the qualified appraisal can be expensive, the Executor and the estate attorney should carefully consider whether there is a need for this appraisal. The estate attorney can provide guidance to the Executor to determine when a qualified appraisal is necessary and which appraisers or dealers are most appropriate to value each type of asset. The types of assets that commonly require a qualified appraisal include real estate and interests in real estate, tangible personal property including art collections, coins, and stamps, and intellectual property such as copyrights, patents, and trademarks.[6,7] The closely held business interests, partnership interests, inventories, equipment used in business, and accounts receivable are examples of assets that may require special valuation techniques. An informal valuation of an asset may be sufficient in some cases. Someone who deals in the type of asset that is being valued may make this informal valuation. For example, a coin dealer or jeweler may provide an adequate informal valuation of a coin collection or jewelry. The estate attorney can assist the Executor in obtaining names of experienced dealers and appraisers.

ORGANIZING INFORMATION ABOUT ASSETS

The information discovered about each asset must be organized in a way that will allow the Executor to complete all reports and tax returns as easily as possible, preserve the information that supports those reports and returns, and allow the Executor to create a plan to manage and transfer each asset. The Asset Evaluation Form shown in Appendix IV should be completed for each asset in the Decedent's estate.

CHECKLIST: INVENTORY AND VALUATION

1. Discover Decedent's assets. Search the following:
   ____ Testator's inventory
   ____ Personal computer files
   ____ Financial advisors' work papers
   ____ Personal papers
   ____ Bank records
   ____ Safe deposit box
   ____ Tax returns
   ____ Mail
   ____ E-Mail and Internet Web sites of the Decedent
   ____ Agents and representatives
   ____ Family and friends

    ____ Financial statements made to obtain loans or to qualify for assistance

    ____ State and national lists of unclaimed property

    ____ List of assets covered by insurance policies

    ____ Bank or trust company vault

2. Confirm asset description.
3. Confirm asset ownership.
4. Confirm any beneficiary and pay-on-death designation for each asset.
5. Confirm asset value on date of death.
6. Provide information to estate attorney to prepare the probate inventory for the court.
7. Review and sign the inventory.
8. Confirm asset value on alternate valuation date six months after date of death.
9. When necessary, have attorney prepare an amended inventory to correct any mistakes in the original and to include assets discovered after the original inventory was filed.
10. When necessary, amend or correct estate, inheritance, or succession tax returns to correct any mistakes in the originals and to include assets discovered after the original returns were filed.

Management of Assets

MANAGEMENT PLAN

The management of the assets of the estate is the responsibility of the Executor from the time the Executor is appointed until those assets are distributed. Management can be as simple as writing checks for utility bills or as complex as managing an investment portfolio or running a business. Management can also include contracting to have maintenance and repairs made on estate assets, leasing or renting estate property, borrowing money to pay a payroll for a business, and hiring a bookkeeper to write checks and keep records. Fiduciary duty requires the Executor to take all necessary and reasonable measures to protect the estate's assets from loss, damage, or theft. This obligation to use all reasonable measures to protect assets creates the obligation to employ experts to assist in management when the Executor does not possess the necessary experience, expertise, or time to accomplish the tasks.

The Executor must ensure that assets are not damaged or lost because of a failure to act. The Executor should meet with the estate attorney and other professionals as needed to plan specifically for the management and protection of each of the estate assets. A written plan for management should include what actions are necessary for each asset and who is to accomplish each task.

NEED FOR IMMEDIATE ACTION

Certain management issues demand immediate attention. These include providing shelter, food, water, and medical care for pets and livestock; disposal of perishable goods; cultivation and harvest of crops in the ground; and management of any ongoing business that was owned by the Decedent. The person who is named as Executor in the Will, but who has not yet been appointed by the court, has the authority by statute in some states to act to preserve the estate assets.[7.1] The powers authorized by these state statutes may include making arrangements to protect the assets needing immediate care. All states provide a summary procedure for the appointment of a special administrator to act to preserve assets that need immediate attention. All assets that need immediate attention should be discussed with the estate attorney, and a plan should be formulated to address all needs as soon as possible.

USE AND OCCUPANCY OF ESTATE ASSETS

Family members or beneficiaries often ask the Executor to approve the use of the Decedent's automobile or residence before those assets are properly distributed. Many ask the Executor for permission to take personal items even before the funeral is over. The Executor has no authority to approve the use or distribution of estate property before the court appoints the Executor. After the Executor is appointed, the duty of the Executor is to protect and preserve the estate assets and distribute those assets only according to court order. The Executor takes a serious risk of personal liability for any loss that results from the use of the residence or the car or allowing personal items to be taken before the court orders distribution. To avoid liability and to be sure to treat all legatees properly, it is safest to allow no distribution until the court orders it.

SECURE PERSONAL ITEMS

The Executor can secure the items that might easily be removed from the Decedent's residence. Jewelry, billfold or purse, credit cards, cash, photos and albums, important papers, cash, decorative pieces including wall decorations, silver, crystal, china, knickknacks, antiques, tools, guns, stamp and coin collections, electronic and computer equipment, computer programs, and all other items that could easily be removed should be gathered, placed in a locked box, suitcase, or storage facility and secured. The Executor can visit the Decedent's home and/or office to determine what is valuable and what is movable. There often is reluctance or a taboo that hinders an Executor's moving the property of the Decedent soon after a death. However, the Executor's responsibility to protect property requires that this property be stored in a secure place. A failure to act may result in the loss of assets or an improper distribution to family and friends.

Safe deposit boxes and rented storage units are appropriate places to store valuables. Insurance should be purchased on the assets in storage. Often a family member or friend will offer to store items in their home or garage to save money. This is not a wise idea. Storage with the family members places the risk of loss on the Executor, not on the person who is storing the items, and the Executor cannot insure those assets. The loss of property owned by the Decedent's estate is not covered by the friend's or family member's insurance because they did not own the asset. A written inventory of all stored items should be prepared immediately and kept for future reference. This list is very important for the Executor's protection and for insurance purposes.

THE OBITUARY

The obituary in the local paper announces to the world who the Decedent was, where he or she lived, who the close family members are, where they live, especially who lived with the Decedent and who lives out of town, and the dates and times the house will be empty because the family will be attending the funeral. Even if the obituary does not mention all these particulars, anyone who knows the name of the Decedent can call the funeral home to ask the date and time of the funeral services and find the address in the telephone book, from directory assistance, or on the Internet.

Steps can be taken to ensure the security of the residence and its contents. Some of the most effective steps include carefully wording the obituary to minimize the information a burglar might use, hiring security to occupy the residence during the funeral services, installing a permanent security system in the house, and removing valuables and placing them in a secure place. Long after the funeral is over, the fact that the house is empty or that an elderly person or a single woman is in the house alone is evident from the obituary.

INSURANCE TO PROTECT ESTATE ASSETS

The Executor's duty to protect and preserve the estate assets includes assuring that assets are adequately insured. The Executor must purchase insurance to protect real property against loss from fire, flood (if needed), vandalism, theft, and liability as soon as possible after being appointed. The insurance coverage that the Decedent had purchased may not cover the full value of the assets in the estate. The Executor must evaluate the insurance coverage to be sure that the assets are fully insured.

The Executor should be aware that many homeowner's policies require that the residence be owner occupied in order for any claim to be paid. This is true even if the Decedent had paid the premiums for coverage far in advance. If the house is broken into when the Decedent is no longer occupying the residence, the insurance adjusters for many companies can and will decline to pay the claim. The Executor should ask the insurance company to extend the policies to cover the unoccupied house for a grace period and get any agreements to do so in writing. Or, if the company will not extend the coverage on the residence and contents to the estate as a courtesy, the Executor must obtain a rider, or an addition to the policy, that will cover any losses to the building and contents after Decedent's death. The name of the insurance agent, the name of the company, the amount of coverage, type of coverage, a copy of the policy, the policy number, and any restrictions of the policy must be kept by the Executor.

Insurance on automobiles may not cover drivers of the automobile after the policy owner is deceased. The state law that requires all vehicles to have liability insurance applies to automobiles owned by the estate of a Decedent. In the event of an accident, the Executor's failure to have obtained insurance covering new drivers may create a personal liability for the Executor as well as liability for the estate of the Decedent. It is not enough to know that the Decedent's premiums have been paid. The Executor must contact the insurance agent to obtain written assurance that the automobile is fully insured for anyone who might be driving it after the Decedent's death. If the automobile is not insured, then the Executor must not permit anyone, including the Executor, to drive it.

Insurance on personal property located in the residence or in storage also may be required. The Executor must contact the insurance agent to obtain written assurance that the coverage on household contents is in effect.

In addition to considering the liability and casualty insurance needs of the estate, the Executor must cancel all unnecessary policies, request refunds of premiums, and change ownership of the insurance policies to the estate where necessary.

SAFE DEPOSIT BOX

The Executor must close the Decedent's safe deposit box and open one in the name of the estate to hold only estate assets. If the Decedent's safe deposit box is held with another person, the Executor will need to notify the bank in writing that the Decedent is no longer responsible for rental payments on the box. The bank may require that the other joint tenants obtain a new safe deposit box and sign a new contract. The Executor should obtain a refund for safe deposit rental due to the Decedent.

PROTECTION OF VALUABLE PAPERS

A significant amount of time will be spent going through the Decedent's personal papers. Careful review, organization, and storage of these papers will make the Executor's tasks much easier. Papers that belong to others should be returned to their rightful owners.

Legal Papers

The Executor is well advised to lease a safe deposit box at a local bank or savings and loan in the name of the estate for the safekeeping of the Decedent's valuable papers and other personal property. The following papers should be found and placed in safekeeping:

_____ Birth certificates

_____ Communion and confirmation

_____ Adoption records

_____ Naturalization papers

_____ Military records and discharge papers

_____ Marriage certificates

_____ Judgments

_____ Divorce decrees and property settlements

_____ Annulments

_____ Death certificates

Keys, Combinations, and Codes

Keys and combinations to locks should be secured as soon as possible. If there is a doubt that someone who should no longer have access has a key or if a key cannot be found, the Executor must act promptly to replace the lock and secure the new key.

_____ Keys or combinations to safes

_____ Keys to safe deposit boxes

_____ Keys to home and other buildings

_____ Keys to cars

_____ Keys to gun trigger guards

_____ Keys to files, freezers, desks

_____ Keys to luggage

_____ Keys to jewelry boxes

_____ Other keys or combinations

_____ Codes for garage door openers and entry

_____ Passwords and pass codes for access to computer files

Agreements, Contracts, and Investments

Certain documents must be presented in the original to be effectively enforced. The originals of these documents must be carefully preserved. A safe deposit box is the best place to keep them.

_____ Promissory notes

_____ Mortgages

_____ Loan agreements

_____ Installment agreements

_____ Contracts

_____ Pre-nuptial (pre-marital) agreements

_____ Post-nuptial agreements

_____ Partnership agreements

_____ Buy-sell agreements

_____ Assignments

_____ Stocks

_____ Bonds

_____ Options

_____ Certificates of deposit

_____ Leases

_____ Deeds to real estate

_____ Conveyances of mineral interests

_____ Division orders

_____ Insurance policies

_____ Annuity policies

_____ Vehicle titles

_____ Cemetery deeds

_____ Funeral and burial contracts

_____ Receipts for items under warranty

Records

The originals of the following papers can be replaced with some effort. These valuable papers can be kept in a secure file or case.

Signed and dated tax records

_____ Income tax returns for past three (3) years

_____ Prior gift tax returns

_____ Employer tax returns and records

_____ Current income tax reports

_____ Current W-2s, 1099s, and state income reports

_____ Receipts for purchase of assets to establish cost basis (see Chapter 10 for a discussion on basis)

_____ Personal property and real estate tax records

Statements of accounts

_____ Bank account records

_____ Canceled checks

_____ Brokerage account records

_____ Stock margin accounts

_____ Retirement plans (401(k), 403(b), IRA, pension, etc.)

_____ Annuities

Records

_____ Credit card account numbers

_____ Family health records

_____ Health insurance records

_____ Employment records

_____ Education information

_____ Appraisals

_____ Appliance manuals

_____ Organization affiliations and memberships

_____ Subscriptions

_____ Baptismal, Communion, and Confirmation records

Bills

There is yet another group of papers that must be kept. These are the
bills that were either owed by the Decedent at death or incurred after
death in the administration of the estate. These bills must be collected
in order to give proper legal notice to all those who were owed money
at the Decedent's death and to pay those expenses owed in the administration of the estate.

Rent and Utilities

____ Electric

____ Gas, coal, or oil

____ Water

____ Trash

____ Cable television

____ Telephone

____ Long-distance telephone

____ Cellular phone and pager

____ Internet service

____ Rent

Services

____ Sprinkler

____ Lawn services

____ Exterminator

____ Pool services

____ Security

Credit Card Accounts

Card Name	Account Number

Loans

Lender	Account Number

Mortgages

Mortgage Lender	Account Number

Medical

Doctor's Name	Patient Account Number

Hospital   Patient Number

_____   _____

Emergency Medical Services   Date of Service

_____   _____

Pharmacy   Account Number

_____   _____

Optometrist   Patient Account Number
_____

PAYMENT OF BILLS

The decision of which bills to pay, if any, and when to pay those bills
is an important part of the Executor's duties. The preservation of the
assets may require that utilities be left on to protect the property.
Payment of mortgage and loan payments may be necessary to prevent
default on a loan and repossession of an asset. And, as mentioned
earlier, insurance may be necessary for real estate, personal property,
and vehicles. When the estate does not have enough value, a well-in-
tentioned payment by the Executor of a legitimate bill may expose the
Executor to personal liability. Careful planning for payment of bills is
necessary. If the Executor suspects there may be more debts and expenses than assets, the Executor must contact the estate attorney before
paying a single claim. Read Chapter 9, Claims and Demands on
Decedent's Estate, for guidance on the payment of bills.

CASH REQUIREMENTS OF THE ESTATE

The estate will need money to pay the bills and the administration
expenses. In order to estimate the cash requirements of the estate during
administration, the Executor must look at the items that will need to be
paid over the course of the administration and determine when these
amounts will be required to be paid. This analysis will reveal also
whether the estate is insolvent.

If there is not enough cash to pay for the immediate expenses, but the
estate has assets of sufficient value to pay all the estate expenses once
those assets are sold, a sale of assets may be necessary to obtain the cash
to pay debts and expenses. If sale of assets is necessary, the Executor
must act to sell those assets as soon as possible. See Chapter 8 for the
discussion of the sale of assets and Chapter 9, Claims and Demands on
Decedent's Estate, for the discussion of which assets must be sold first
to pay debts and expenses. If the estate is insolvent—that is, the assets
are not worth enough to pay the debts—then a careful plan for administration of the estate must be made. You must proceed cautiously!

ESTATE CHECKING ACCOUNT

An estate checking account is essential in the management of the
estate. This account must be opened in the name of the estate and must

hold only estate funds. All the amounts received and spent will be recorded in this one account. Commingling of the funds of the estate with anyone's personal money is a breach of fiduciary duty.

The Executor may open the estate account only after the court appoints the Executor. The Executor will need Letters Testamentary to open the estate bank account. Any checks payable to the Decedent or the estate of the Decedent should be held in a safe place until the estate bank account can be opened and the check deposited directly into the estate account. As the estate's assets are liquidated, all the proceeds should be deposited into the estate checking account. All debts of the Decedent and the expenses and taxes of the estate must be paid from this account. If the deposit and expenditure information is carefully recorded at the time of each transaction, the accounting on closing will be quick and easy.

JOINT TENANCY ACCOUNTS USED TO PAY EXPENSES

A special word about joint tenancy accounts is necessary here. Many people anticipating death arrange to have cash available to pay immediate expenses, funeral costs, and other necessary items by creating an account that is held in joint tenancy with rights of survivorship with another person (often the Executor). The perception of the surviving joint tenant is often that the money belongs to the Decedent, not to the surviving joint tenant. The ownership of these accounts, by law and contract, passes immediately to the surviving joint tenant upon the Decedent's death. For purposes of the probate inventory and tax reporting, the cash in the account belongs to the surviving joint tenant. When the Executor is a surviving joint tenant and the money in the account was earmarked to pay debts and expenses, there is an almost insurmountable urge to commingle the joint account money and the estate money. The problem can be solved in several ways, but the situation needs some careful thought and one clear decision.

The surviving joint tenant can relinquish the ownership of the account to the estate by a signed writing. This writing will describe the account as a convenience account on which the surviving joint tenant's name was added merely for the convenience of the Testator and will state that the account was not intended to be a gift to the surviving joint tenant. The account then becomes part of the Decedent's probate estate and is available to pay expenses and debts. The money that remains after debts and expenses are paid will be distributed according to the Will.

Or, the surviving joint tenant may decide that he or she intends to keep the funds. If the surviving joint tenant decides to keep the funds, he or she is not obligated under the law to use those personal funds to pay the Decedent's debts or expenses—with a few very narrow exceptions. The exceptions include when the surviving joint tenant is personally liable for the debt and when the state spousal election laws make joint tenancy vulnerable to the claims of the surviving spouse if someone other than the surviving spouse is the joint tenant.

Or, if the surviving joint tenant wishes to pay the bills with that money, but intends to claim the account, he or she may make a loan of cash to the estate that is documented by a signed writing that includes the terms of repayment. The cash borrowed from the joint tenant should be removed from the old joint account and placed in the new estate account.

Or, the surviving joint tenant may pay the expenses, debts, and taxes directly from the joint account (which is now his or hers alone). The surviving joint tenant then becomes a creditor of the estate and must make a claim for reimbursement. If there is not enough money in the estate to pay all the bills or the amount paid was unreasonable, such as a funeral expense greatly in excess of the normal charge in the local area, the court might not approve the claim and the surviving joint tenant might not be fully reimbursed. Claims on the estate must be made within the nonclaim period, even by the Executor, or the right to reimbursement will be lost. (See Chapter 9, Claims and Demands on Decedent's Estate.)

The Executor or any other surviving joint tenant who has received the funds earmarked for payment of funeral bills and estate expenses should decide before using the funds whether the money belongs to the estate or to him or her. Once that decision is made, the proper handling of the funds is clear as described earlier.

ACCOUNTING

The Executor is responsible for keeping a complete and accurate record of the financial transactions that concern the estate. These records will be necessary for the preparation of tax returns and for filing the accounting with the court to eventually close the estate. If securities or other **income**-producing assets are specifically bequeathed giving beneficiaries income from those assets, the Executor must prepare a separate accounting for those assets.

In addition to a complete check register, a voucher system can be used to create a complete record of the financial transactions. As claims on the estate are paid, the Executor should complete the information relevant to each transaction on a separate voucher, attaching the statement and the receipt for payment. A copy of the check used to pay the claim is also attached directly onto the voucher. There should be one voucher for each check written. The vouchers are filed in check number order. The check register will serve as the index for the vouchers. An example of a voucher appears in Appendix IV.

EARLY DISTRIBUTION OF ASSETS

Legatees and devisees often ask to receive distributions immediately. Executors sometimes want to distribute at least part of the estate as quickly as possible. Sometimes, early distribution is advisable. Certain assets lend themselves to early distribution. For example, early distribution of an automobile will save insurance and maintenance costs and perhaps provide needed transportation. Early distribution of personal property is sometimes beneficial to the estate to avoid storage and insurance costs and to allow use by beneficiaries. There is a tax savings that can be achieved by an early distribution if the income from the estate exceeds the exemption amount. Also, early distribution of assets that carry out income may be advisable when an income tax savings can be achieved. Specific bequests can be paid early in order to avoid paying interest on these gifts. Special needs of the beneficiaries may require an early distribution. However, the court will make no early distribution order before the inventory is filed with the court, the creditors have been notified, and tax returns filed. Discuss the requirements and added costs of an early distribution with the estate attorney. In determining whether a partial distribution of assets is warranted, consider that a partial distribution is another court proceeding that will require extra work from the estate attorney, thus increasing the cost of administration.

DEATH CERTIFICATES

Death certificates are necessary to transact certain business of the estate. Usually the funeral home will order death certificates and deliver them to the surviving spouse, Executor, or a family member. If the funeral home does not order the death certificates, the estate attorney or the Executor can obtain them from the Department of Vital Statistics of the state.

How many certified death certificates are necessary? The following chart will help you determine how many are needed.

Death Certificates must be filed with the following:

_____ Estate Attorney (one)

_____ Social Security Administration (one)

_____ Federal Estate Tax Return (one)

_____ State Death Tax Returns (one for each state's return)

_____ Securities Transfer

> _____ Stocks (one for each transfer agent for stock held in certificate form and one for each brokerage account)

> _____ Bonds (one for each transfer agent for bonds held in certificate form and one for each brokerage account)

> _____ Treasury bills, notes, and bonds purchased directly from the Federal Reserve (one for each account)

> _____ Mutual Funds (one for each account or company)

_____ Transfer of Real Estate held in Joint Tenancy with Rights of Survivorship (one for each county where real estate is located)

_____ Transfer of Real Estate held in Tenancy in Common (one for each county where real estate is located)

_____ Transfer of Real Estate with Payable on Death Deed (one for each county where real estate is located)

_____ Life Insurance (one for each insurance company)

_____ Transfer of a motor vehicle title (one for each department of motor vehicles)

_____ Transfer of Deposit Account with Payable on Death Beneficiary (one for each bank, savings and loan, and credit union)

_____ Transfer of Annuity (one for each insurance company)

_____ Retirement Accounts (one for each pension, IRA, 401(k), 403(b), etc.)

_____ Transfer of Trusteeship to a Successor Trustee (one for each asset in Trust)

LETTERS TESTAMENTARY

All actions taken by the Executor that require proof of the Executor's authority will require a copy of the Letters Testamentary signed by the judge and properly certified by the court clerk. The Executor can obtain certified copies of Letters Testamentary from the estate attorney on an as needed basis. Because most companies require that the Letters Testamentary be certified within 30 to 60 days of the day the Executor seeks to exercise his or her authority, the Executor should obtain these certified Letters Testamentary only at the time they will be used. Stocking up on certified Letters Testamentary might result in Letters with certification dates that have expired before they can be used.

DECEDENT WAS A FIDUCIARY

If the Decedent was a fiduciary—that is, an attorney-in-fact for another person, the Executor or Administrator of another person's estate, a Trustee, a Custodian under a Unified Transfers to Minors Act, a Conservator, or a Guardian—the Executor has the responsibility to alert those involved of the Decedent's death and wind up all the financial affairs relating to the fiduciary relationship. The Executor must determine what position the Decedent held; notify the principal, the successor fiduciary, the beneficiaries, or the representatives of the beneficiaries of the Decedent's death and secure the Decedent's accounting records for that fiduciary relationship. The appointment of a successor fiduciary as soon as is reasonably possible should be encouraged by the Executor. The Executor must file the accounting of the Decedent's activities with the court or with those who were named to receive an accounting and obtain a discharge from liability for the Decedent's estate.

RETITLING ASSETS

In some states, the assets in an estate must be retitled into the name of the estate to await distribution to the devisees and legatees. However, the effort of retitling is often unnecessary, expensive, and burdensome. The Executor at the end of administration also may transfer the assets of the estate to the devisees and legatees directly out of the Decedent's name. Nonetheless there may be some assets that will require transfer to the estate for proper management. Discuss whether the assets should be transferred into the estate's name with the estate attorney.

INVESTMENT OF ESTATE ASSETS

There may be a large amount of cash that needs to be invested awaiting final distribution. If the Executor does not invest those funds, there will be a loss of income to the estate, a loss for which the Executor is potentially liable. The Executor must take great care to ensure that the funds are invested prudently. The standard for investment of estate funds is different from the standard an individual would use to invest his or her own funds. The Executor must be aware that state laws impose restrictions on investments.[7.2] The estate attorney will be able to provide a copy of those restrictions. The provisions of the Will may override some of these restrictions. The Executor must reread the Will carefully and examine the state law to determine the permitted investments.

Because the estate exists for a limited period of time, the risk of loss from inflation is minimal. The investment tactics that would be advisable for an individual over a longer period of time may not apply to investment of estate assets. The Executor is well advised to invest estate funds that will be used or distributed in a short time in accounts that have virtually no risk of loss and are easy to convert to cash, even though the return on the investment is not the best that can be found. These safe and liquid investments include savings accounts, short-term C.D.s, money market funds, and U.S. Treasury Bills.

INVESTMENTS PURCHASED BY DECEDENT

Duty to Make Assets Productive

Where the Decedent had previously invested in property that is unproductive (for example, a residence that is empty, farm land that is not being planted, or cash in a non–interest-bearing account) or underproductive (such as a low-interest checking account or rental property rented for less than market value), the Executor may be required to ensure that this property becomes fully productive as soon as possible. If the Executor fails to make this property productive, the Executor may have to pay for the loss personally. The Will can waive this requirement. But without the specific waiver in the Will or an agreement in writing from all interested persons, the Executor must make sure the property or asset is producing income. When this requirement will impair the value of the asset or hinder distribution, the Executor may seek instruction or permission from the court to leave the asset idle.

Duty to Diversify

Where the Decedent has previously invested an excessively large portion of his or her assets in one type of asset—for example, the stock of one company—the Executor may be required to diversify that investment. Diversification means to spread the risk of loss by spreading the investment into many different stocks or other assets. While the Executor is not usually liable for a drop in market price, the failure to diversify the investments within a reasonable time may cause the Executor to be liable for such a loss. Some state statutes give special protection to Executors who retain the investments that the Decedent had purchased prior to death.[7.3] The estate attorney will be aware of the laws of the state where the estate is being administered.

CHECKLIST: MANAGEMENT OF ASSETS

The management of each asset must be planned. The Summary of Assets in Appendix V of the *Executor's Guide* discusses the management of each type of asset. Refer to this Summary for specific instructions for each asset in the estate. The Management Instructions section of the Asset Evaluation Form in Chapter 6 should be completed for each estate asset. Make a list of the necessary actions for each asset and the person who will complete each task.

1. Secure Decedent's personal items.
2. Gather and sort valuable papers and place them in safekeeping.
3. Prohibit use of estate property before distribution.
4. Determine cash needed to pay debts and expenses of administration.
5. Determine whether estate is solvent or insolvent.
6. Discuss payment of funeral expenses and expenses of administration with estate attorney.
7. Complete Asset Evaluation Form in Chapter 6 for each asset. Make a complete management plan for each asset. List specifically what needs to be done for every asset and who is to do it. Hire help where appropriate.
8. Evaluate whether sale or early distribution of assets is advisable.
9. Insure real and personal property.
10. Open estate checking account.
11. If Decedent was a fiduciary, prepare accounting and secure discharge from liability for Decedent's estate.

8

Sale of Assets

Estate assets may need to be sold to raise cash to pay bills or taxes, to protect real estate or personal property from a falling market, or to divide the proceeds of the sale of an asset among several legatees or devisees. The Executor may need to consider sale of assets for other reasons as well. Certain stock can be sold back to the corporation that issued the stock (redeemed) to obtain a tax-favored distribution from that corporation.[8.1] The sale of estate property before final distribution by the Executor can be accomplished more quickly and conveniently than waiting to sell an asset after distribution to the ultimate owners. Sale by the Executor avoids the confusion of direct participation of all the devisees and legatees in the negotiations for a sale.

Any estate asset may be sold during the administration of an estate unless the Will prohibits sale or gives that asset as a specific gift. Sometimes assets must be sold even when sale is prohibited. The Executor should discuss with the estate attorney the need to sell assets when the Will prohibits sale or the asset is specifically devised or bequeathed. (See Chapter 9 for a discussion about ademption.)

The sale of personal property and real estate can be accomplished as soon as the Executor has proper authority. When the authority to sell is given expressly in the Will, the Executor may act to sell the property as soon as the Letters Testamentary have been granted. If the Executor is carrying out a sale without a specific order from the court, the Executor must be very careful to ensure that the Will properly authorizes the sale. The Will must expressly permit the Executor to sell the type of property that the Executor is seeking to sell. If personal property is to be sold, the Will must give specific authority to sell personal property. Likewise, if real estate is to be sold, the Will must give specific authority to sell real estate. The authority to sell real estate is not authority to sell personal property.

If the Will does not give express authority for the sale, the estate attorney must obtain a court order authorizing the sale of the property. In some states, if the Will does not specifically authorize sale, the Executor must show that the sale is necessary to pay debts, expenses, taxes, or legacies, or that the asset is a wasting asset (the value of the asset will be less as time goes by), or that the sale of the real estate is in the best interest of the estate for some other reason.[8.2] Even if there are no debts to pay and the value is not falling, all interested persons can agree that the sale is in the best interest of the estate and the court will order the sale. The estate attorney must prepare and file the proper legal documents for the sale and give necessary notice or obtain waivers of notice from all interested persons. All proceeds of a sale must be deposited into the estate account for administration and await the court's order of distribution.

DUTY TO NOT SELF-DEAL

For obvious reasons, the sale of estate property to a family member or friend of the Executor is prohibited by state statute whether the Executor has authority to sell property without court supervision or not.[8.3] This prohibition may be overcome if the duty not to self-deal is waived in the Will, if all interested parties approve before the sale, or if the court, with full knowledge of the relationship, approves of the buyer and the sale price before the sale.

ACCOUNTING FOR SALE

Even when the Will waives court supervision or approval of a sale, a complete accounting of the sale must be filed and approved by the court before the estate can be closed and the Executor discharged. The Executor must keep a copy of the contract for sale, the seller's closing statement, and the payment check to support the report of the sale.

MINIMUM SALE PRICE

State statutes control the minimum sale price for both personal and real property.[8.4] This required price is usually a percentage, for example 80 percent, of the appraised value or of the value reported in the probate inventory. The estate attorney must be consulted before any asset is sold to ensure that the sale price complies with the minimum price. If there are no buyers at the required minimum price, the Executor must seek court authority to reduce the sale price, and the probate inventory must be amended to reflect the change in value.

HOW TO SET THE PRICE

Setting the sale price is the responsibility of the Executor. The advice of the estate attorney and a realtor for real estate or dealer in personal property will be a helpful guide, but the Executor has the final decision. Although the Executor should attempt to get the best possible price, it is also important to complete the sale within a reasonable period of time. Maintenance of the property, taxes, insurance, and utilities are all expenses that cannot be recovered. A prompt sale removes these expenses from the estate.

The Executor is controlled in the minimum price only by the statutory limit. But how high should the Executor set the price? Real estate buyers expect to offer something less than the asking price, so pricing the real estate above the lowest acceptable price is prudent. However, pricing the real estate too high can prevent potential buyers from looking at a property that is clearly outside of their budget. The Executor must also consider that when a property has been too long on the market because of an inflated price, the property becomes stale. Part of the information available to any potential real estate buyer is the original listing date. The buying public wonders what is wrong with property when it is on the market too long. Asking for an amount that is slightly above the amount that the Executor expects the real estate to bring is ideal to promote a quick sale. Setting the price for personal property requires a similar analysis.

SALE OF PERSONAL PROPERTY

The sale of the Decedent's personal and household effects in an estate sale is often attempted by an Executor or family member who has perhaps been successful with personal garage sales in the past. However, an estate sale conducted by a professional is recommended. The Executor is encouraged to bear in mind that the sale of the deceased person's estate and a garage sale differ in several important ways.

1. The other duties of the Executor are demanding and time-consuming, and in most instances, they involve dealing with estate assets other than the personal property. The value of these assets can far

exceed any amount that will be generated by the sale of the personal property.

2. The Executor, in most cases, is grieving. The necessary contact with the personal items of the Decedent will be a constant reminder of the loss and can create an intense emotional reaction. A natural tendency is unconsciously to avoid these painful reminders. This avoidance too often causes the sale to be delayed. Professionals are not emotionally involved with the property.

3. An estate sale is the sale of an entire household, an undertaking of far greater scope than a personal garage sale. The Executor often seriously underestimates the magnitude of the task.

4. The Executor's personal knowledge concerning the proper pricing of assets is restricted to the Executor's own limited personal experience. Professionals know the price that the items will bring in the area where the sale will be held.

5. Professionals know how to schedule and advertise the sale for the best attendance. Professionals know how to display and present the items to obtain the best price. When professionals conduct the sale, the unsold property remaining after the sale will be sold to an auctioneer. Professionals will clear out the remaining items after the sale and clean up.

6. Fiduciary duty requires the Executor to make reasonable business decisions about the sale of estate property. The good intentions of the Executor may not be enough if the sale is delayed or improperly handled. The Executor's duty is to ensure that the sale of the personal property is accomplished as soon as possible and that the highest value is received.

DISTRIBUTION OF PERSONAL PROPERTY TO FAMILY MEMBERS

Sometimes the distribution of personal property to the family is attempted by a sale to only family members for cash, with the cash then divided among the family members participating in the sale. Technically, it is legal to distribute personal property this way so long as all the family members are legatees and entitled to an equal share of the personal property. However, this method has several significant problems and should be avoided. First, such a sale is not a bona fide sale because it is not open to the general public where the price is the best that can be obtained. Instead the sale is limited by the finances of those limited number of people involved where some will undoubtedly have more available cash than others. Second, it is not a sale authorized by a will or ordered by the court. Third, and most complained of, even though the proceeds are ultimately distributed among the buyers, serious offense often is taken when a child has to buy her mother's crystal or a son has to buy his dad's fishing tackle box. The psychological perception of buying a loved one's personal items and the disparity of financial resources among family members make this method of distribution of personal property unsatisfactory. See Distribution of Personal Property in Chapter 12 for more appropriate methods for distribution of personal property.

SALE OF REAL ESTATE

As discussed in the introduction to this chapter, if the Will gives proper authority, the Executor can sell real estate without court approval. If the Will does not expressly grant authority to sell real estate, the Executor must request authority to sell from the court. The estate attorney must be consulted in each instance to ensure that the price meets the state statutory requirements for a minimum price.

Whether the sale is accomplished by private sale, by a realtor, or by auction, the Executor should make no warranties or statements of the condition of the property to the buyers, even if the Executor installed the new roof or the central air-conditioning system himself or herself. The Executor will be sorely tempted to promote the property to the buyer by describing what he or she believes is known about the condition of the property—for example, when the roof was installed and when the plumbing and electrical system were brought up to city code. This is an area of potentially serious personal liability for the Executor as well as for the estate. The statements of the Executor may be considered by the buyer as a warranty of the condition of the property. If these statements prove to be incorrect, the buyers may make a claim against the estate and against the Executor personally. Estate property should be sold "as is," and the buyers must be required to inspect the property for themselves or to hire professional inspectors to inspect for them. Requests for repairs made by the buyers can be dealt with as those requests are made.

Sale of Real Estate at a Private Sale

Sale of real estate by a private sale has the advantage of saving from 3 percent to 7 percent of the sale price as commission to the realtor. Sale by private sale assures that control of who buys the property remains with the Executor. Caution dictates that when real estate is sold to someone related to the Executor or other interested person, unless permitted specifically in the Will, the court must approve prior to the sale.

When real estate is sold by private sale, whether for all cash or with a mortgage, a sales contract must be prepared and signed by all parties. This contract is necessary for the buyer to obtain financing, for the closing company to close the sale, and especially to protect the Executor. A sales contract should be signed by all parties and state, in detail, the terms of the sale including purchase price, closing date, provisions for earnest money, and how the condition of the property is to be determined. The estate attorney should prepare this contract for a private sale. At closing—that is, at the execution of all the terms of the sales contract—the Executor will receive the proceeds and deliver possession of the property to the buyer. An Executor's Deed will be prepared by the estate attorney for the Executor's signature.

It is extremely unwise for the Executor to agree that the estate will carry the note for the buyer. Carrying a note is actually loaning the money to the buyer. If the potential buyer cannot obtain sufficient credit from an established savings and loan company or a bank, then loaning the buyer money from the estate is not prudent and the Executor may be violating his or her fiduciary duty to the estate.

Sale of Real Estate by a Realtor

The Executor can have real estate sold by a realtor in virtually the identical manner as an individual would have real estate sold by a realtor. However, the Executor's conduct, as always, must meet the fiduciary standards. The Executor should avoid hiring close friends or relatives in the business of real estate because the objectivity that is necessary for the Executor to supervise the realtor is compromised. A real estate broker provides the valuable services of advertising, showing the property, and assisting in the negotiation of a contract. The majority of the time, employing a realtor to sell real estate is the most reliable way to offer the real estate to the largest number of potential buyers and to obtain the best price quickly. It is wise for the Executor to contact several well-established and reputable realtors to discuss the sale of the property. The Executor should pay special attention to the listing price suggested by the realtor, the realtor's plans to promote the property, the length of time the estate will be under contract with the realtor, and the percentage of the commission. In any listing agreement with a realtor, there should be a provision for sale without commission to persons who have already expressed an interest in the property.

Sale of Real Estate at Auction

The real estate can be sold at auction for a quick sale to avoid the continuing costs of maintenance, utilities, taxes, and insurance. The

Executor should contact several reputable auction companies to discuss timing of the sale, sales cost, reserved bids, and advertising. The auctioneer must provide a receipt for the amount of the proceeds. The sale of the real estate to an auctioneer, even when there is to be a later auction, is still a sale of real estate by a private sale and requires court approval unless the Will waives such approval.

CHECKLIST: SALE OF ASSETS

_____ Is the sale necessary to pay funeral bill, expenses, taxes, or debts? If yes, check order of Abatement. (See Chapter 9 for a discussion on abatement.)

_____ Is the sale necessary to avoid loss in a falling market or to avoid ongoing costs of taxes, insurance, maintenance, and upkeep?

_____ Is the sale necessary to distribute the asset? (Would "in-kind" distribution be more advantageous?)

_____ Is the sale in the best interest of the estate for some other reason?

_____ Is the sale price high enough under the state statutes? If no, adjust price or petition for a reduction in value and amend the inventory.

_____ Is the sale permitted to these buyers without court approval? If the buyers are related to the Executor—get court approval!

_____ Does the Executor have authority in the Will to sell assets without court authority? If no, petition the court for approval of sale.

_____ Retain listing contract and sales contract.

9

Claims and Demands on Decedent's Estate

After the assets of the Decedent's estate have been gathered and inventoried and the immediate needs for management of the assets have been taken care of, the next major task of the Executor is to determine and pay the valid claims and demands against the estate. These claims and demands include any claim for **homestead**; spousal and minors' support allowances; the expenses of the funeral, last illness, and administration of the estate; Medicaid reimbursement and demands for debts owed by the Decedent at death. Only those demands that are legally enforceable and that are made to the court in the probate proceeding within the time allowed by law may be paid. It is not enough that the Executor knows money is due. The Executor does not have the authority to pay a demand or claim unless the claim or demand is properly filed within the time allowed and ordered paid by the court. Claims for taxes are the exception to this rule. See the discussion on taxes in this chapter.

NOTICE TO CREDITORS

Whether or not the estate is solvent—that is, able to pay all its debts—all known creditors must be notified in writing of the Decedent's death and of the opening of the probate proceeding. In addition, notice of the Decedent's death and the probate proceeding must be published in a newspaper approved by the probate court. These notices must fulfill the requirements of the state statutes and include the date, time, and court in which the creditors must make their demands against the estate. The estate attorney will know the requirements for these notices.

Written Notice Must Be Mailed to All Known Creditors

The estate attorney must mail written legal notice to all known creditors of the estate. Written notice to all known creditors is a requirement of federal constitutional law as well as state law.[9.1] All creditors who are known or could reasonably have been discovered by the Executor are entitled to written notice before their claims are barred— that is, no longer legally valid. This puts a heavy burden on the Executor for identifying creditors.

In order to properly notify known creditors, it is essential that the Executor compile an accurate list of all creditors, including family and friends who are owed money, complete with the name and address of each creditor and any account numbers. It is important to distinguish between the debts of the Decedent before the death and the expenses of administration incurred after the death. The Executor is expected to make a complete list of all debts owed by the Decedent at the Decedent's date of death, whether or not those debts have since been paid. If someone—for example, a family member—has paid the debt or expense, that person becomes a creditor of the estate. These debts are deductions for the estate and can lower inheritance taxes, income taxes, and estate taxes if the court approves the payment.

Discovering the creditors is a challenge in the administration of an estate. The Executor will have access to the Decedent's mail. Most creditors will inform a debtor at least monthly that some amount is due. It is advisable to wait for a full billing cycle to determine all the known creditors.

Notice Must Be Published

Within a certain number of days after the filing of the petition for probate of the Will, notice to creditors of the estate must be published in a newspaper as required by the state's statute. The estate attorney must request the proper form of notice in a publication authorized by the court. This publication of notice informs creditors that they must exhibit their demands against the estate within a certain number of days from the first published notice, and that if their demands are not exhibited, they shall be forever barred from collection. "Exhibited" means that the claim for a certain amount is made in the proper form and filed with the court in the probate proceeding. This period of time from the first publication of notice to the date that all claims are barred if not exhibited is called the **nonclaim period**.[9.2]

Family Creditors

If anyone has loaned money to the estate, perhaps to pay for the funeral or an overdue mortgage payment to the loan company, it is essential for that person to file a claim in the probate court for that debt within the time limit for filing claims. If this claim is not filed in the time period allowed, it may not be allowed even though a family member made the payment and even though the Executor and others are aware of the claim.

ALL CLAIMS MUST BE EXHIBITED BY CREDITORS

All claims that money is owed to creditors, including claims of the state, must be exhibited. The creditors exhibit their claims and demands for payment by filing a petition for allowance of their claim in the probate court within the given period of time (the nonclaim period). Claims of persons under disability, including incompetents and minors, must also meet these requirements. However, when debts are due to the United States government, such as taxes, it is not necessary for the federal government to file a demand for payment in the probate proceeding. It is the Executor's responsibility to assure that nothing is due to the federal government.

APPROVAL AND PAYMENTS OF CLAIMS

When the time period for making claims has passed, the attorney must ask the court for approval of uncontested claims and demands. Uncontested, or admitted, claims and demands are approved without a hearing in some states. If there is a hearing, that hearing is ordinarily an informal one without witnesses or argument. If a claim is contested, the Executor or the creditor may request that the court hear evidence. Notice of the hearing on contested claims and demands is given to other creditors as well as heirs and beneficiaries of the estate so that these other creditors may participate.

Before paying any bill, the Executor must be sure that the proper petition has been filed with the court by the creditor, that an order has been issued by the court authorizing payment, and that a receipt for payment is received.

One theme bears repeating: All the claims must be exhibited by the creditors and ordered paid by the court before that claim may be paid.

If the creditor fails to properly or timely exhibit the claim, the Executor may not pay the debt. Debts that are not properly exhibited are no longer collectable or valid. The Executor must not pay such debts or he or she will be personally liable to the estate.

TYPES OF CLAIMS AND DEMANDS ON ESTATE

The claims against the estate of the Decedent are separated into several types or classes. Each class of claims has a different priority for payment under the state statutes. This hierarchy of claims controls which creditor gets paid from an estate that does not have enough in value to pay all the creditors.

Secured Creditors

When estate assets secure a debt, the court will order that debt paid at least to the extent of the value of the asset. If there are sufficient assets to pay all creditors, then any amount remaining on the debt over the value of the estate asset that secures the debt will be ordered paid from other assets along with the claims of other unsecured creditors.

Homestead and Spousal and Minors' Allowances

The strong public policy to avoid impoverishing a surviving spouse and minor children is expressed in the states' laws that guarantee a homestead right and spousal or dependent allowance from the Decedent's estate before any other unsecured claim on the estate is paid.[9.3] The only claims that supersede these spousal and minors' rights are the mortgage and purchase money liens on assets. Homestead and support allowances must be formally requested, approved, and specifically ordered by the court.

Funeral Expense

Assuring the burial of the Decedent's body is also of great importance. This public policy is expressed by the state law making the payment of funeral expenses next in priority for payment just after secured creditors, homestead, and the support of the surviving spouse and minor children.[9.4] However, the purchase of a headstone or other grave marker is not considered part of the essential funeral expense. Instead, the headstone is considered an expense to be paid after the claims of unsecured creditors.

Medicaid Reimbursement

Many states have enacted laws that provide that any money spent for medical assistance paid by the government for long-term care of the Decedent or the Decedent's spouse may be recovered from the Decedent's estate or the estate of the Decedent's spouse after the death of the last one to die. The priority for payment of this expense varies by state.[9.5]

Expenses of Last Illness

If the debts of the patient (soon to be Decedent) were too great, medical care facilities might question the ability of the patient to pay and the patient might not receive adequate medical care in his or her last illness.[9.6] To assure that no one is denied medical care in his or her last illness because of previous debts, state law makes the expenses of last illness a priority claim after secured claims, homestead and support claims, reimbursement of medical assistance, and funeral expenses.

Expenses of Administration of the Estate

Assuring that the Decedent's estate is administered is ranked next in importance. The expenses of administration are paid after the secured claims; homestead, spousal and minor support allowances; funeral expenses; reimbursement of medical assistance; and expenses of last illness.[9.7] The expenses of administration must be reasonable and ordered paid by the court. Expenses of administration include costs of maintaining estate property and expenses associated with the probate of the Will, including attorney, accounting, and Executor's fees.

Taxes

Debts owed to the state and federal government for taxes have priority over the other claims against the estate according to the law of the state in which the estate is being administered.[9.8] In some states, the homestead, spousal and minor support, funeral expenses, expenses of last illness, and the expenses of administration of the estate have priority and may be paid before taxes. In other state, taxes have priority. The Executor must check with the estate attorney for specific instructions concerning payment of taxes if the estate does not have enough value to pay all the demands and claims. In all states, taxes have priority over the unsecured claims of creditors.

Judgments and Liens

Judgments for claims made against the Decedent and general judgments and **liens** against the Decedent's property are paid before the unsecured creditors.[9.9]

Unsecured Creditors

All other creditors who are owed money by the Decedent at death are paid only after the secured creditors' claims, homestead, spousal and minor support, funeral expenses, expenses of last illness, expenses of administration, Medicaid reimbursement, judgments, liens, and taxes are paid.[9.10]

A word of caution to the Executor who is pressured by a creditor to pay a debt before the priority of the debt is determined (in some states this is called classifying the claim), the schedule of abatement is applied, and the court orders payment. The law protects the Executor only if the Executor follows proper probate procedure. If a debt is improperly paid, the Executor may be personally liable for the amount improperly paid. It is essential that the Executor resist the aggressive tactics of a creditor who demands immediate payment. Direct the creditor to contact the estate attorney for information about debt payment.

INSOLVENT ESTATES

Many probate estates do not have sufficient probate assets to pay all the claims, expenses, and debts of the Decedent. When there are sufficient assets to pay all debts, taxes, and expenses of administration and give the full amount to each devisee and legatee, the Executor's job is straightforward. When there are not sufficient assets to pay the debts, taxes, and expenses, some beneficiaries will lose their gifts, while others may not. The Executor may incur personal liability for improper payment of some demands, expenses, or debts before others or for improper use of certain estate assets to pay the debts. The Executor should review each claim, expense, and debt with the estate attorney. The estate attorney will assist the Executor to determine whether the estate is insolvent and to order the claims and demands for payment according to the hierarchy in the state statutes. The estate attorney will advise the Executor on abatement of assets, if necessary, to determine which legatee or devisee is to lose all or part of his or her testamentary gifts.

SCHEDULE OF ABATEMENT

The payment of debts, taxes, and expenses from certain assets of the estate and not from others is perhaps the most difficult aspect of estate

administration to explain and the least understood by devisees, legatees, and Executors. But this understanding is critical to avoid making
mistakes and to avoid the liability that accompanies such mistakes.
Demands and claims are paid from the assets according to the instructions of the Testator in the Will or, if the Will does not include instructions, then the demands and claims are paid according the order set out
in the state statutes.[9.11] This is called the schedule of abatement. Simply
put, the statutes state that certain classes of gifts are used first to pay
allowances, funeral expenses, Medicaid reimbursement, expenses,
taxes, and debts before the next class of gifts is touched. Each state has
its own precise order of abatement. The classes listed here are arranged
in the most common pattern of abatement from the first class of legacy
and devise used to the last:

Residuary Devises are exhausted first.

Residuary Bequests are exhausted next.

General Devises are next.

General Bequests are next.

Demonstrative Devises are next.

Demonstrative Bequests are next.

Specific Devises are next.

Specific Bequests are the last to be used to pay claims and demands.

If the remaining debt will not exhaust all of one class of gift necessary
to pay the allowances, expenses, taxes, and debts, then the recipients of
that class will pay a proportionate share of the remaining debt.[9.12]

It is necessary to understand the classes of gifts given in a Will in
order to understand the state statutes that require payment from
certain classes of gifts and not from other classes. These classes of
gifts are important also in determining whether the income from a
gift goes with the gift or to the residuary legatee. This income aspect
is discussed in Chapter 12 under Estate Income. The classes of gifts
are distinguished by whether the gift is of personal property or real
estate and whether the gift is specific, general, or residuary. A bequest
is a gift of personal property, that is, anything that is not real estate.
The personal property given may be tangible, such as household
items, tools, jewelry, and furniture, or intangible, such as stock, bonds,
and patents. A devise is a gift of real estate. Real estate is land and
those things attached to it. These classes of gifts are discussed in
greater detail below.

Classes of Gifts

Specific Bequest. If the Testator describes the specific personal property that an individual is to receive, the Testator has made a specific bequest. Some examples of a specific bequest include "I give to my son, Sam Doe, my Winchester rifle serial number 12345678," "I give to my daughter, Sarah Jane Doe, my Series EE bond numbered A12345," "I give to my mother all the stocks in my Merrill Lynch Account number 456333," "I give to my friend, Joe Smith, the balance in the bank account number 123456 at the Second State Bank of Smalltown," and "I give to the Basic Christian Church my IRA account number 787878 at The Investment Company." These specific bequests are protected by state statutes and are used only as the last resort to pay the allowances, expenses, reimbursements, taxes, and debts.

Specific Devise. A specific devise is a gift of a specific piece of real estate. Examples include: "To my son, Robby Roy, I give the family farm located in Small County," "I give my residence located at 123 N. Palm to my friend, Mary Kales," "To my cousin, Slim Boyd, I give my mineral interests located in Butler County, Kansas, on the property described as Section 1, Township 2, Range 3 West of the 6th Prime Meridian." Specific devises are also protected by statute and are used to pay claims and demands only if all the other gifts, except specific bequests, are exhausted first.

Demonstrative Bequest. A demonstrative bequest is a gift of personal property that is intended to be given first from a certain fund but, if that fund is not available, then the gift is clearly meant to be paid from the general assets of the estate. An example of a demonstrative bequest is "I give to my nephew, James Wesley, $10,000 to be taken from my Second National Bank CD #0011999 if I own such CD at my death. If I do not own such CD at my death, then from my other assets." Thus, a demonstrative bequest is, in part, a specific bequest and, in part, a general bequest. Whether, for the purpose of the abatement statute, the demonstrative bequest will be treated as a specific bequest or a general bequest is a matter of state law. If the Executor is required to use the abatement statute to determine which classes of assets are to be used to pay claims and demands, then the Executor must be aware that a possibility exists of a gift that is not clearly a specific gift and not clearly a general gift. The estate attorney may be required to seek a determination by of the court in classifying the gift.

Demonstrative Devise. A demonstrative devise is a gift of real estate intended to be given first from a certain parcel of real estate, but if that parcel is not available, then the gift is clearly meant to be given in the form of some other real estate. An example of a demonstrative gift of real estate may be worded "I give to my son, John Hawk, 480 acres of land to be taken from the land that we farm in Butler County if that land is in my estate at my death; if such land is not in my estate at my death then from any land that I own at my death." The demonstrative devise is a combination of a specific and a general devise. For the gift to be classified as a demonstrative gift the Testator must have intended to make an unconditional gift and the gift must be given from a primary source. If the Executor is required to use the abatement statute to determine which classes of assets are to be used to pay claims and demands, then the Executor must be aware that a possibility exists that this gift is not clearly a specific devise and not clearly a general devise. The estate attorney may be required to seek a determination by the court to classify the gift.

General Bequest. A general bequest is a gift of an amount or quantity that may be satisfied out of the general assets of the estate. For instance, a general bequest is "I give $50,000 dollars to George Simple," or "I give 20 shares of Telephone Company stock to Sarah Short."

General Devise. A general devise is a gift that may be satisfied out of the general assets of the estate. An example of a general devise is "All the real estate I hold in Kansas at the time of my death I give to Hannah Long." Claims and demands must be paid from these general bequests and devises before specific bequests and devises are used.

Residuary Bequest. The gift of all the "Rest and Residue of my Estate" is a residuary bequest. A simple statement that "I give the balance of my estate to my wife" is a residuary bequest. Specific and general bequests and devises require special language to create them. Residuary gifts do not. All assets that are not given as specific or general bequests or devises are given in the residuary. A residuary gift can include both personal property and real estate. The **residue** is used first to pay the claims and demands on the estate.

ACCOUNTING FOR PAYMENTS AND ABATEMENT

With the schedule of abatement in mind, the Executor can determine, with the help of the estate attorney, how much and which of the gifts given in the Will must be sold to pay creditors. The written accounting of the source of each payment to a creditor is an extremely important tool in explaining the final distribution of the estate to devisees and legatees. This tool is especially important when the assets given to one class of devisees or legatees in the Will are used to pay these claims and demands, but assets given to another class are fully distributed to those devisees and legatees without being reduced by payment of claims and demands.

WARNING ABOUT SPECIFIC GIFTS IN A WILL

A note of warning must be sounded about the use of specific devises and bequests. Many times a Will is written when the Testator has the most money the Testator will ever have, and the Will is written on the optimistic presumption that the amount of money will remain the same or increase until death. Testators often give a fixed amount of money to charities or to a favorite child based on this large amount of money, leaving a spouse who is dependent upon the "rest and Residue" of the estate. For example, the Testator wrote in a Will "I give $10,000 to the Humane Society, $20,000 to my church, $30,000 to my college, and all the rest and Residue of my estate to my beloved spouse." The spouse consented to this Will in writing. At the time of the execution of the Will and signing of the spouse's consent, the Testator had an estate of $300,000. However, fortunes shifted. The stock market plummeted, and nursing home expenses before the husband's death depleted the estate to $80,000. The Will was not changed, the gifts to the charities remained the same in spite of the changed circumstances. The spouse received what was left after the payment of $60,000 to the charities; the funeral bill; the debts; taxes, and expenses of administration of the estate. The spouse's share was less than $15,000 instead of the $240,000 she had expected to receive. If the Will had been carefully written, the spouse would have been protected from this change in fortune.

Creditors

The following is a list of potential creditors that the Executor must consider. No doubt there will be other creditors. Watch the Decedent's mail for

- Taxes
  - _____ State and federal income tax
  - _____ Personal property tax
  - _____ Real property tax
  - _____ Gift tax
  - _____ Intangible tax

- Rent and Utilities
  - _____ Electric
  - _____ Gas, coal, or oil
  - _____ Water
  - _____ Trash
  - _____ Cable television
  - _____ Telephone
  - _____ Long-distance telephone
  - _____ Cellular phone
  - _____ Internet service
  - _____ Association dues
  - _____ Rent

- Services
  - _____ Sprinkler
  - _____ Lawn services
  - _____ Exterminator
  - _____ Pool services
  - _____ Security

- Credit Card Accounts

Card Name	Account Number
_____	_____
_____	_____
_____	_____
_____	_____
_____	_____

- Margin accounts

Account Name	Account Number
_____	_____
_____	_____

- Loans, Mortgages, Installment Purchases

Lender	Account Number
_____	_____
_____	_____
_____	_____

- Medical

Doctor's Name	Account Number
_____	_____
_____	_____
_____	_____

- Medicaid Reimbursement _____

- Hospital

_____   _____

- Emergency Medical Services

_____   _____

- Dentist

_____   _____

- Pharmacy

_____   _____

- Optometrist

_____   _____

CHECKLIST: CREDITORS

1. Pay no bill without a complete accounting of the financial status of the estate.
2. Collect the names and addresses of all known creditors. Determining the exact amount of the bill is not necessary to send the notices.
3. Assure that the estate attorney has notified the known creditors of the Decedent's death, of the time limit for making claims, and of the creditors' statutory rights.
4. Aid creditors in filing claims against estate, if appropriate.
5. Determine whether any family member or friend has a claim arising out of a courtesy to the Decedent or the estate. Help the family member or friend make that claim within the time period allowed.
6. Prepare a schedule for payment of all claims, paying careful attention to the hierarchy of claims and reserving sufficient funds for payment of future expenses of administration.
   - Hierarchy of Claims
     Secured Creditors

      Homestead and Spousal and Minors' Allowances
      Funeral Expense
      Medicaid Reimbursement
      Expenses of Last Illness
      Expenses of Administration of the Estate
      Taxes
      Judgments and Liens
      Unsecured Creditors

- Schedule of Abatement
  - Residuary Devise
  - Residuary Bequest
  - General Devise
  - General Bequest
  - Specific Devise
  - Specific Bequest

7. Investigate claims filed against the estate.
8. If contesting a claim, aid the estate attorney in preparing for the court hearing.
9. Consider early payment of high-priority claims, particularly funeral expenses, to claim a discount or to avoid interest.
10. Pay claims classified, allowed, and ordered by the court; obtain and file receipts for those payments.

Taxes

This chapter will give the Executor a general overview of the tax matters that must be considered for proper administration of the estate.[10.1]This discussion is intended only to aid in the decisions about what reports, forms, and tax returns are required to be filed. This chapter is not a substitute for competent tax advice and assistance. The Executor should be especially aware that there is a potential for personal liability associated with failure to properly report and pay taxes owed by the Decedent and the estate.

INCOME TAX FOR THE BENEFICIARIES, DEVISEES, AND LEGATEES

One of the first questions the Executor will be asked by anyone who receives property from an estate is whether income taxes have to be paid on the value of the property received. As a general rule, property received by the devisees and legatees is not required to be included in the taxable income of the recipient.[10.2] Only when the Decedent had taken advantage of provisions of federal law to defer payment of tax,[10.3] when the Decedent had earned income that had not been received before death,[10.4] and when the estate earns income after the Decedent's death is income tax payable by the recipient on that money. The use of federal laws to defer income tax is common. The Decedent's estate may include IRAs, 401(k)s, defined benefit plans, E and EE bonds, H bonds with interest rolled over from E and EE bonds, tax deferred annuities, and other federally qualified plans that generate taxable income to the estate or to the recipients. Many estates will be due salary or wages that the Decedent had earned but had not yet received.

Although most of the assets received from the Decedent's estate are not taxable, the income generated by the assets after the death of the Decedent, such as interest on bank accounts, dividends on stock, rent on real estate, or gain on the sale of any asset, is taxable as income to the estate or the recipient. Also, anyone who takes a fee for acting as the Executor or payment for doing work for the estate is required to report that money as income on his or her personal income tax return.[10.5] Reimbursement for expenses of the estate, however, is not income and is not taxable.

BASIS STEP-UP

The concept of taxable gain is an important concept to understand in the calculation of income tax for recipients of assets from the estate. When assets are sold or exchanged, the gain is taxed as income. Gain is calculated as the excess of the sale price over the basis. (Sale price minus basis equals gain.) Because the basis of the asset is used to determine the gain or income on the sale, calculating the basis is critical.

The basis is calculated in one of three ways. First, the original purchase price is the basis to the original buyer.[10.6] Second, a carry-over basis applies if the asset was given as a gift during the original purchaser's life.[10.7] The recipient of the gift takes the same basis the donor had in the property as the carry-over basis. Third, at the death of an owner the current tax laws permit a more taxpayer-friendly calculation of a stepped-up basis. The stepped-up basis is the value of the asset on the date of death.[10.8] The consequence of these three basis rules is that if an owner holds property that has greatly increased in value since it was purchased and the owner sells that property before death, income tax will be due on the difference between the basis and the sales price. If the owner gives the property away before death, the new owner will have the same basis as the original owner and will have to pay income taxes on the same gain as the original purchaser would have paid. If instead the original owner holds the property until death, the basis in the hands of the new owner is stepped-up to the date of death value. The new owner who takes the property after the Decedent's death pays no income tax because the basis and the sale price are the same and there is no gain.

An example will illustrate these three ways to calculate basis.

If an individual buys a classic car for $40,000 and sells that same car two years later for $60,000, he has realized a $20,000 gain or profit that he must declare as capital gain income. His basis was the purchase price for the classic car, the $40,000, and his sale price was $60,000.

If the individual had not sold the car but had given it to his daughter as a birthday gift, and two years later she sold it for $60,000, she too would realize a gain or profit of $20,000 that she must declare as capital gain income. She received the car as a gift with the same basis of $40,000 that her father had. Her basis is called a carry-over basis.

But suppose the individual died two years after he bought the car, having held the car until he died. If the car was given by a specific bequest to the daughter she would receive the car with the stepped-up date-of-death basis—in our example, $60,000. When the daughter now sells the car for $60,000, there is no gain and no income tax payable.

In 2001 a new law was passed, the EGTRRA of 2001, which replaces the stepped-up basis with a carry-over basis rule for the estates of those who die after December 31, 2009. There is an important exception to this new rule. Even after December 31, 2009, the basis of qualifying assets may be increased or stepped-up to $1,300,000 generally or up to $3,000,000 for property transferred to a surviving spouse. This exception will continue the current taxpayer-friendly basis step-up provisions for the majority of estates. Whether under the new law or current law, a new stepped-up basis is allowed whether or not the estate pays an estate tax. The property receives a stepped-up basis even though no federal estate tax return is filed. When no estate tax return is required to be filed, the valuation for the stepped-up basis is determined under the same tax laws and regulations as the valuation would have been for the estate tax return.[10.9]

FILING TAX RETURNS FOR THE DECEDENT AND THE ESTATE

The Executor has the authority and the responsibility to make all reasonable efforts to assure that the necessary tax returns and reports are properly completed and filed and that the taxes are paid to the extent the estate has funds. The tax returns that may be required include income tax returns (IRS Form 1040 and State Income Tax Return) for the Decedent for past and current years, income tax returns for the estate (IRS Form 1041 and State Income Tax Return), federal and state gift tax returns (IRS Form 709), state death tax returns (inheritance, succession, or estate tax), federal and state estate and generation-skipping transfer tax returns (IRS Form 706), and the "large transfers" report. The Executor also has the responsibility to file the Notice of Fiduciary Capacity

(IRS Form 56), which announces to the IRS that the Executor has been appointed and requests a separate tax identification number (EIN) for the estate (IRS form SS-4). A more detailed discussion of each of these returns and reports follows. (See also the list of returns and forms at the end of this chapter.)

Actual preparation of the returns by the Executor is not required. The Executor is well advised to seek competent, experienced help to prepare these returns. The Executor's primary task will be to gather the information required to complete the returns accurately. A number of determinations must be made from the information the Executor gathers, including which items must be included as income; which are exempt; what deductions, exclusions, and exemptions are allowable; and what tax rates are applicable for the estate. The Executor will be judged as a fiduciary on whether he or she took all reasonable care to assure that the returns were properly completed and filed. If the Executor knows or should know that he or she does not have enough experience to complete the returns properly, then fiduciary duty requires that the Executor obtain the necessary help to complete the returns properly and on time.

In the sections that follow, the tax forms and returns that may be required are discussed. The options available to the estate are also listed. The Executor should consider each item separately.

IRS FORMS SS-4 AND 56

The estate is a separate tax-paying entity and must have its own tax identification number (EIN). IRS Form SS-4 requests this number. The IRS is notified of the appointment of the Executor as the person responsible for the estate with Internal Revenue Service Form 56 Notice of Fiduciary Capacity. These forms are necessary to establish the proper foundation to clear the estate for final distribution.

DECEDENT'S INCOME TAX RETURNS

Federal and state tax laws require that income tax returns be filed annually for all individuals unless the income of the individual is below a certain income threshold. This means that the Executor must assure that the Decedent's last income tax return is filed on time and must be sure that previous years' returns have been filed. The Executor should obtain copies of the prior years' income tax returns for at least three (3) years before the Decedent's death. The date these returns are filed begins the running of the statute of limitations upon any claims the IRS may have against the estate of the Decedent for those tax years. These returns also contain information that is valuable to the Executor in discovering the assets of the estate.

The Executor must provide the tax return preparer with accurate information in ample time for the returns to be prepared and filed within the deadlines. The Executor's complete and confirmed inventory of estate assets at the date of death also is essential. Because the estate expenses and the Decedent's debts may be deductions that can reduce the income taxes, it is important that the Executor prepare a careful accounting of those expenses and debts. The Executor should ask the estate attorney, CPA, or return preparer to confirm the filing deadlines for each report and tax return to minimize the Executor's potential personal liability in this area.

The Decedent's last personal income tax return is due for the period beginning on the first day of the tax year in which death occurred (usually January 1 in the year of the death) and ending on the date of death. Final returns are required to be filed if the income during this short period exceeds the income limitations.[10.10] Even if the income of the Decedent does not exceed this limit, the Executor can choose to file this final return to close the Decedent's tax identification number—that is, the Social Security number—and to give a final return from which the period of limitations on income tax claims can begin to run. Although the return is filed for the period ending on the date of death, for the calendar year taxpayer, the last return is not due until April 15 of the year following the year of death.

The last income tax return of the Decedent must be filed by the Executor (or the surviving spouse, if any) using the standard forms for the individual, Federal Form 1040 or 1040A and State Form 40. The federal income tax return must be filed with the district director or the designated service center for the district where the legal residence of the Decedent was located. The Executor should consult the tax preparer, CPA, or the estate attorney for the address of the appropriate IRS Service Center.

Estimated Tax Payments

There is no requirement that a declaration of estimated tax be filed after the Decedent's death and no further payments need to be made on behalf of the Decedent after death on a declaration filed before the Decedent's death. If, however, husband and wife filed the declaration jointly, the survivor must continue to make payments unless the estimate is amended. The surviving spouse should consult a competent tax advisor for assistance regarding estimated tax reporting and payment.

Joint Income Tax Returns

One valuable option available to a surviving spouse is the right to file a joint income tax return with the Decedent for the year within which the Decedent died. This joint return is for the short tax year of the

Decedent ending on the date of death and for the full year for the surviving spouse. The joint return can be filed only if the Decedent and the surviving spouse were eligible to file joint returns at the time of Decedent's death and if the surviving spouse has not remarried prior to the end of the taxable year.

ESTATE'S INCOME TAX RETURNS

The estate is regarded as a taxable entity that is separate from the Decedent and beneficiaries of the estate. The estate files a separate return (IRS Form 1041 and State Estate Income Tax Return) called a fiduciary return, has its own taxable year, and is subject to tax on its income. A federal fiduciary tax return must be filed when the gross income of the estate for the taxable year is $600 or more or when any beneficiary of the estate is a nonresident alien. The federal fiduciary return is to be filed by the Executor with the district director or with the service center designated for the district where the Executor resides or has its principal place of business. The state fiduciary return must be filed with the Department of Revenue for the state.

Generally speaking, with certain important exceptions, the taxable income of the estate is computed and taxed in the same manner as the income of an individual, although the rates may vary. The three main exceptions are (1) an estate is not subject to self-employment tax; (2) certain expenses of the estate that are both necessary and reasonable and that were incurred and paid in administering the estate of the Decedent are allowed as deductions to reduce the income that is subject to tax; and (3) the estate operates as a conduit for determining the taxable income allocated to its beneficiaries.

One of the major features of estate income taxation is the deduction that the estate receives for distributions to the beneficiaries of the estate. The practical consequence of this distribution deduction is that all of the estate's income will be taxed either to the estate or to the beneficiaries, but not to both.

Assets of the estate will generate income. The income may be interest, dividends, gain, rent, or any other type of income that assets can generate. The Summary of Assets in Appendix V describes the type of income each asset is expected to generate. The Executor must also be aware of "income in respect of a Decedent" in determining the income of the estate. Generally, "income in respect of a Decedent" is income that was earned prior to the Decedent's death but not received until after death. Thus, interest on notes accrued to the date of death but not payable until after death, dividends declared on stock prior to death but payable after death, and wages earned prior to death but not payable until after death are all examples of "income in respect of a Decedent."

FEDERAL ESTATE TAX RETURN

To report the federal estate taxes, the Executor for the estate of every U.S. citizen or resident whose gross estate, plus adjusted taxable gifts and specific exemptions, is more than the Unified Estate and Gift Tax Credit amount must file Federal Estate Tax Form 706.[10.11] Sometimes it is advisable to file a federal estate tax return for estates that do not exceed the unified credit amount in order to establish the value of certain assets and avoid a challenge to the estate value later.

The Unified Gift and Estate Tax Credit and the tax rates were dramatically changed, and many "experts," including the IRS staff, have indicated that they anticipate further changes. The current rates and credits are set out in the following. However, consult the estate attorney, CPA, or tax preparer for the **Unified Tax Credit** and tax rate schedules for the year in which the Decedent died. The tax law that repealed the estate and generation-skipping taxes and greatly increased the exemptions is subject to a "sunset" provision that reinstates the prior law unless Congress acts prior to 2011.

The Executor must file Form 706 to report estate tax due, if any, within nine months after the date of Decedent's death unless an extension of time to file has been filed. The Executor must also pay any estate tax due within nine months after Decedent's death unless an extension to pay has been filed and granted. Interest is charged on late payments, and there are penalties for filing the return late and for paying the tax late. If the delay in filing was caused by the Executor's failure to act,

Unified Estate and Gift Tax Credit Chart

Year	Sheltered Amount	Credit Amount	Maximum Tax Rate
2001	675,000	220,550	55%
2002	1,000,000	345,800	50%
2003	1,000,000	345,800	49%
2004	1,500,000	555,800	48%
2005	1,500,000	555,800	47%
2006	2,000,000	780,800	46%
2007	2,000,000	780,800	45%
2008	2,000,000	780,800	45%
2009	3,500,000	1,565,800	45%
2010	Estate tax repeal	Estate tax repeal	0% estate tax/ 35% gift tax
2011	1,000,000	345,800	

the Executor is personally liable for those penalties. If a federal estate tax return was required, the federal estate tax closing letter must be filed with the court prior to the court hearing on the petition for final settlement of the estate.

The Executor will be required to file a tax return under the new law (IRC §6018) to report "large transfers" at death when the fair market value of property other than cash exceeds $1,300,000. This return will have to be filed with the Decedent's final income tax return. This return must contain, among other facts, a full description of the property, the adjusted basis in the hands of the Decedent, the fair market value on the date of death, the length of time the Decedent owned the property, the name and social security number of the new owner of the property, and the amount the basis was increased. The Executor can be fined $10,000 for failure to furnish the required information. There is a reasonable cause exception to this penalty; however, it should not be relied upon to avoid the penalty when the Executor could have discovered and furnished the information with reasonable effort.

GENERATION-SKIPPING TRANSFER TAX

If during life or at death the Decedent transferred more than the **Generation-Skipping Transfer Tax** Exemption to a skip person or persons while the intervening generation was still living, the amount transferred that is over the exemption is also subject to a generation-skipping transfer tax. The tax act that repealed the estate and generation-skipping taxes and greatly increased the exemptions is subject to a sunset provision that reinstates the prior law unless Congress acts prior to 2011.

A skip person is one who is two or more generations younger than the donor or Decedent if the intervening generation is still living. For example, a grandchild or the grandchild of a brother or sister is a skip

The Generation-Skipping Transfer Tax Exemption

2001		1,060,000
2002		1,060,000
2003		1,060,000
2004		1,500,000
2005		1,500,000
2006		2,000,000
2007		2,000,000
2008		2,000,000
2009		3,500,000
2010	Generation-skip tax repeal	no generation-skipping tax
2011		1,000,000

person if the child's parent is still living. This tax law is intended to tax wealth in each generation and to prevent gifts that skip a generation to avoid the estate tax in one or more generations. Federal Form 706 is used to report a generation-skipping transfer tax. Some states also require that a state generation-skipping transfer tax return be filed and a state generation-skipping transfer tax be paid.[10.12]

STATE INHERITANCE, SUCCESSION, OR ESTATE TAX RETURN

In states that impose a state death tax—that is, an estate, succession, or inheritance tax—the state death tax return may be required for the estate of a Decedent who died domiciled in the state, whether or not a tax is due.[10.13] A death tax return may also be required for a state where the Decedent owned real property or had significant tangible personal property. Customarily, the state death tax return must be filed within nine months of the date of Decedent's death or penalties and interest will be owed.[10.14] The inheritance, succession, or estate tax closing letter from the state director of taxation officially showing that all state death tax owed has been paid or that none is owed must be filed with the court prior to the hearing on the petition for final settlement of the estate. Contact the estate attorney, CPA, or tax preparer for information regarding the death tax law in the state in which the estate is being probated.

CONSENT TO TRANSFER

When the assets in the estate are to be transferred, stock agents, bond trustees, and other fiduciaries may require the assurance that all state death taxes have been paid. In some states, before the state department of revenue issues its closing letter, but after the estate or inheritance tax return has been filed and the taxes shown on that return have been paid, the Executor may request a Consent to Transfer. If a Consent to Transfer is required, consult the estate attorney for instructions to obtain one.

The State's Department of Revenue will eventually issue a tax closing letter or certificate of non-taxability that all state estate, succession, or inheritances taxes have been paid to the extent that the assets were reported on the return. Upon the order of final disposition, the court will find that all taxes have been paid. This court order, based on the tax closing letter and the statements of the Executor that all assets have been reported properly and all taxes paid, is the final assurance that the taxes are paid.

ELECTIONS AND OPTIONS

Throughout the administration of the estate, the Executor is required to make certain choices that significantly affect the estate and, ultimately, the beneficiaries. Some of these choices are elections that are set out in the Internal Revenue Code. Others are decisions that are presented in the state law or in the practical administration of the estate. The Executor's fiduciary duty requires that the Executor give careful consideration to the consequences of each of these elections and options. The Executor is cautioned that doing nothing is not acceptable when an election is available that would save the estate or a beneficiary some expense. This is another way of saying, "Ignorance is not an excuse." Failure to make certain elections may result in personal liability for the Executor.

If the Executor has given instructions for the elections and options in the Will, the Executor must follow those instructions or obtain court approval to vary those instructions. If the Will does not give instructions, the Executor must act in the best interest of the estate. The Executor must deal with all beneficiaries impartially. The Executor is advised to set out in writing the facts relevant to the election or option with a description of the consequences of that election for each beneficiary. The weighing of the factors that the Executor uses to make the decision should also be written. This will require the Executor to look at the facts and circumstances of each election and option and evaluate the choices. This written statement is the best evidence that the Executor used due care in coming to the decision.

Often the potential exists for saving taxes for one beneficiary at the expense of another beneficiary. In that case, the duty of impartiality and the duty to use reasonable care to achieve the greatest savings are in conflict. In situations where the correct decision is not clear, the written statement can be presented to those who will be affected for their written approval or to the court for a decision.

Two general types of elections are discussed here. The first are the elections that are presented in the Internal Revenue Code for individual and estate income tax, gift tax, and estate tax. The second are the other elections or options that are presented to the Executor in the administration of the estate that may have tax consequences.

ELECTIONS PRESENTED IN THE FEDERAL TAX CODE

_____ Whether to deduct medical expenses of the Decedent on the income tax return or the estate tax return.[10.15]

_____ Whether to deduct expenses of administration of the Decedent's estate on the Decedent's last income tax return or on the federal estate tax return.[10.16]

_____ Whether to file a joint individual income tax return with a surviving spouse or to file separately.[10.17]

_____ Whether to include the accumulated bond income on series E and EE government bonds on the Decedent's last income tax return or on the estate income tax return.[10.18]

_____ Whether to use gift splitting provisions that permit one spouse to give twice the amount of the exemption ($10,000) per person per year and have the other spouse split the gift as if he or she had made the gift, thereby doubling the amount that one spouse can give per person that is exempt from the federal estate and gift tax.[10.19]

_____ Whether, when given discretion in the Will, to deduct the value of property given to a surviving spouse on the Decedent's estate tax return.[10.20]

_____ Whether to value the property in the estate at the date of death or at the alternate valuation date, which is exactly six months after the date of death.[10.21]

_____ Whether to value real property in the estate at its fair market value or at the special use value, which is lower but limited by stringent rules.[10.22]

_____ Whether, when the value of a closely-held business is more than 35 percent of the value of the estate, to pay estate taxes in installments.[10.23]

_____ Whether, when the value of stock in an estate exceeds 35 percent of the value of the estate, to redeem stock at a tax-favored rate in an amount not exceeding death taxes and funeral and administration expenses.[10.24]

_____ Whether to request an immediate tax audit to relieve the Executor of liability.[10.25]

ELECTIONS AND OPTIONS NOT PRESENTED IN THE FEDERAL TAX CODE

The second type of election is not presented directly in the Internal Revenue Code but may have significant tax consequences. In making these elections, the Executor must consider many factors in addition to the tax consequences.

_____ When to open the estate.[10.26]

_____ Whether the financial records will be kept on a calendar year or on a fiscal year.[10.27]

_____ What investments will be made with estate assets.[10.28]

_____ Which administration expenses will be charged to income and which to principal.[10.29]

_____ Whether to allocate tax payments to Residue only or to allocate tax payments to legacies, devises, and Residue.[10.30]

_____ Whether to accumulate or make partial distributions of estate income before the estate is closed.

_____ Whether a beneficiary should be asked to renounce a power to invade principal in a charitable remainder trust in order to obtain a charitable deduction for the estate.[10.31]

_____ Whether a beneficiary should be advised that disclaiming certain property may permit the estate to take advantage of the estate and gift tax unified credit or the generation-skipping tax exemption.[10.32]

_____ Whether to pay federal estate tax with United States Treasury Bonds known as flower bonds.

_____ When to settle claims either against or in favor of the estate.

_____ Whether to distribute assets of the estate in cash or in-kind.

_____ What assets to allocate to different beneficiaries, especially with regard to the assets' likelihood to appreciate.[10.33]

_____ Whether to ask a beneficiary to take distribution of retirement benefits as something other than a lump sum.

_____ When to terminate the estate administration.

It is extremely important for the Executor to discuss these elections and options with the estate attorney and the CPA or the tax preparer to determine the best decisions to make for the estate. Where there is a written state or federal law that provides a choice for the Executor, the potential for personal liability if a decision is neglected is very high.

WHO PAYS THE TAXES?

Who has the obligation to pay the taxes

The determination of whose share of the estate must bear the cost of the taxes is extremely important for the devisees and legatees as well as personally important for the Executor. This is an area in which the Executor is exposed to personal liability if the payment is improper.

If the Will gives instructions regarding payment of taxes, those instructions must be followed. The most common provision requires payment of taxes from the Residue. Too often the Will does not address the fact that property of significant value is passed outside of probate by joint tenancy with rights of survivorship and by beneficiary designations. When the Will does not carefully provide for payment of taxes based on the amount each beneficiary receives, the results can be alarmingly unexpected. An example will illustrate: A widowed farmer whose estate was worth $1.5 million wanted to treat his three children equally. To his son who farmed with him he gave the farmland worth $500,000 by means of a Transfer on Death Deed. To his older daughter who had left home years ago, he left the proceeds of an insurance policy for $500,000 by naming her the beneficiary. And, to the younger daughter, his favorite, who had lived at home and cared for him in his old age, he left the balance of his estate in his Will. The Will was written with the customary language, "After payment of all just debts and taxes, I give all the rest and Residue of my estate to my faithful younger daughter." The farmer died believing that he had given each of his children $500,000 or an equal one-third of his estate.

The expenses of the funeral, payment of all the farmer's debts, medical expenses, the current year's income taxes, expenses of the estate administration, and the estate taxes on the entire $1.5 million dollar estate were paid from the Residue before the dutiful younger daughter got her share. The federal estate tax was owed on all the assets, including the farmland that went to the son and the insurance death benefit that went to the older daughter. The estate tax due was $280,000. The taxes, debts, and expenses were paid from the Residue of $500,000. The dutiful younger daughter received only about $200,000 of the old farmer's estate primarily because the Will instructed that the taxes were to be paid from the Residue.

If the Will instructs that the taxes are to be paid proportionately and that the Executor is to seek payment from the joint tenants and the beneficiaries, the Executor should consult with the estate attorney for guidance in this procedure. If there is no instruction in the Will, the state statutes will designate the source of the tax payments. If the source is the Residue and there are not enough funds to pay all taxes from the Residue, the state statutes set up a hierarchy of estate assets from which payment of taxes must be paid. See Chapters 9 and 12 for an explanation of the tax apportionment and abatement schedules.

Determine Whether Gifts Qualify for Charitable Gift Tax Treatment

If the Will makes a bequest to a charity, the Executor must consider several aspects of this gift carefully for tax consequences.[10.34] If the charity is not a qualified charity—that is, the charity is not registered as a tax-exempt entity with the IRS—the gift is not tax-exempt and the estate and inheritance taxes due on such a gift must be paid from the estate. (Churches when engaged in religious rather than money-making activities are not required to register as tax-exempt charities with the IRS, but are tax-exempt without registration.) If the charity is a qualified charity or a church, then the gift is exempt from paying estate and inheritance tax. The Executor must obtain a copy of the IRS letter from the charity showing the tax-exempt status before the distribution is made.

Next, the Executor must determine what property to give to the charity. If an asset is specifically bequeathed to the charity, that asset must be given. Ideally, the Testator will have directed those assets that will be taxed as income to the recipients—that is, 401(k), 403(b), IRAs, tax deferred annuities, and EE bonds—to be paid to the qualified charity. Assets with a low basis and a large gain are ideal gifts to charities before death because the gain will not be taxed as income to the charity. Because the charity is exempt from state and federal income tax, the gift of these types of assets permits more to go to the charity and less to pay taxes.

LIABILITY OF EXECUTOR FOR TAX DECISIONS

The Executor's duty is to make decisions concerning the administration of the estate, including filing of tax returns, claiming deductions, and making distributions that will result in the greatest overall benefit to the estate. The Executor must make proper payment of all debts, expenses, and taxes according to the Will or the state's statutory hierarchy for payment. An Executor who pays any part of a debt or expense before paying a tax claim that has a higher priority is liable for the improper payment. A word of caution is necessary here. The Executor may not rely on the IRS to claim the taxes in the probate proceeding. The federal government is not required to file a claim, object to the distributions, or make an appearance in the state court proceedings. The responsibility rests solely on the Executor to search out any tax debt. Another note of caution: The liability of the Executor is not confined to tax liabilities that accrue only during administration of the estate. The taxes due from the Decedent before death are also a tax debt that has the protection of these stringent state and federal laws.

Unfortunately, the Executor cannot simply pay the taxes first when other obligations, especially funeral bills, expenses of last illness, and costs of administration may have a superior claim under the law of that state. Fortunately, the responsibility of the Executor for unpaid taxes is limited to only the value of the assets of the estate that would have been properly available to pay the taxes. If the estate does not have enough total assets to pay the taxes, the Executor is not liable for the taxes that remain unpaid.

The Executor must take special care to limit personal liability for taxes owed because the Executor cannot escape liability for improper payment on the ground that a competent attorney or accountant advised the fiduciary in handling the estate.[10.35] And the Executor is not relieved of liability under the tax laws by receiving an order of final discharge from the state court.[10.36] Nevertheless, seeking competent legal and tax advice and obtaining the approval of the court remain the best means available to minimize personal liability and should be used when there is a contested issue. However, other means of avoiding personal liability such as the ones listed next should also be used.

Make All Reasonable Efforts to Discover the Tax Debts

First, the Executor must make all reasonable efforts to discover any unpaid tax debts. This is essential because, before the Executor is liable, the Executor must either know of the tax debt or must be aware of facts that would put the Executor on inquiry notice of the tax debt. (Inquiry notice means that the Executor has enough facts that he or she knows or should know to ask for more information.) The Executor must review all prior filed tax returns, file Form 56 to notify the IRS of the appointment of the Executor so that the IRS will send tax notices to the Executor, and make inquiry into the Decedent's financial situation with adequate follow-up on all potential tax issues that are raised. The Executor should give notice by a second Form 56 when the Executor is discharged.

Make Provisions for All Taxes before Distribution

Second, because the Executor is responsible only for payments or distributions out of the estate before tax liabilities are paid, the Executor should not distribute the estate without making adequate provision for the payment of all known or suspected tax liabilities. The Executor may need to delay some or all distributions until all tax debt issues are resolved. Distributions may also need to be delayed until all statutes of limitation have passed.

Determine Which Debts, Expenses, and Taxes Have Priority

The Executor should consult with the estate attorney to determine the hierarchy for payment of debts in the state in which the estate is being probated. The Executor can pay debts having a first and prior lien. In addition, some states' courts have ruled that an Executor may pay reasonable costs of estate administration, the Decedent's funeral expenses, the cost of a headstone, and the state's statutory surviving spouse's and minors' allowances without incurring personal liability. The Executor must not pay any debt or expense that does not have priority over debts to the United States or the state government.

Obtain a Receipt and Refunding Agreement before or upon Distribution

Fourth, before making any distribution, the Executor must insist on a receipt and refunding agreement and, if applicable, a bond from the devisees and legatees pledging to repay any distribution if these distributions are later found to be needed to pay taxes. A copy of a receipt and refunding agreement may be found in Appendix IV.

Consider Whether a Request for Prompt Assessment of Income Taxes Is Appropriate

Fifth, the Executor can request prompt assessment by the IRS of all income taxes for the estate. The Internal Revenue Code provides that any tax (other than the estate tax) for which a return is required for a Decedent or for the estate during the course of administration shall be assessed within 18 months after a written request has been made by the Executor.[10.37] By using this provision, the Executor can obtain a relatively fast determination of whether there is any income tax deficiency due and owing. Be forewarned, this request may trigger an audit or protective assessment but can aid the Executor in resolution of certain issues.

Determine Whether a Request for Discharge of Personal Liability Is Appropriate

Sixth, the Executor can request a discharge from personal liability. If a return has been filed, the Executor may apply in writing to the Secretary of the Treasury for a release from personal liability. Upon receipt of that application, the Secretary has nine months to notify the Executor of any additional amounts owing. After expiration of that period and payment of any additional amounts of tax claimed by the Secretary, the Executor is discharged from liability.[10.38] As is the case with the request for prompt assessment, the Executor should consider the possibility that a request for discharge from personal liability will trigger an audit or an arbitrary assessment. Unlike requesting prompt assessment of all taxes that releases the estate and the transferees—that is, the legatees and devisees—the discharge from personal liability releases only the Executor.

CHECKLIST: TAXES

It is essential that the Executor determine which of these returns and forms need to be filed.

Form		Necessary?
1. IRS Form 56 (open)	Yes	
2. IRS Form SS-4	Yes	

3. Income Tax (IRS Form 1040 and State) — Yes

4. Estate Income Tax (IRS Form 1041 and State) — Yes, if estate income exceeds minimum amount of income.

5. K-1s to devisees and legatees — Yes, if estate distributed income.

6. Gift Tax Returns (IRS Form 709 and State) — Yes, if gifts given are in excess of annual exclusion.

7. Federal Estate Tax Return (IRS Form 706) — Yes, if value of the estate exceeds amount sheltered by the unified estate and gift tax credit.

8. Large Transfers Report (Federal) — Yes, if fair market value of property transferred (other than cash) exceeds $1,300,000.

9. Generation-Skipping Tax (IRS Form 706 and State) — Yes, if gifts to skip person exceed exemption for Generation-Skipping Tax.

10. State Inheritance or Estate Tax — Yes, if state law requires.

11. Consent to Transfer (State) — Yes, if requested.

12. Personal Property Tax Return — Yes, if taxable personal property is owned.

13. Real Property Tax Return — Yes, if real estate is owned.

14. IRS Form 56 (close) — Yes

15. Disclaimer (Federal and State) — Case-by-case determination.

Special Considerations

There are a few special topics and concepts that may be important in the administration of the estate but that do not logically fit into any other chapter. These concepts include disclaimers, pre-marital agreements, survival and simultaneous death clauses, settlement agreements, *in Terrorem* clauses, and testamentary trusts.

DISCLAIMERS

Occasions arise where there is an advantage for a person to refuse a gift given in a Will. Gifts are sometimes refused to avoid adding income-producing assets to the estate of an already wealthy person, to avoid potential creditors, to assure that money does not go to a spouse but instead goes to children, or to avoid later payment of death taxes by using the unified credit for the estate of the first spouse to die. **Disclaimers** are a powerful tool when used by the survivors to accomplish significant estate planning and money-saving goals after the Decedent's death.

The named recipient may refuse any inheritance, devise, legacy, or gift. When a gift is refused, the gift is distributed according to the Will, by the beneficiary designation, or by intestate succession as if the named recipient had died before the Testator. The person who disclaims a gift does not direct where the gift will go. Instead, the person who disclaims can be aware to whom the gift will be given and, by the disclaimer, enable that distribution to go to that person or persons. (This process is also called renunciation.) The Executor and the person disclaiming a gift should take great care to consider the exact identity of the substitute beneficiary before any gift is disclaimed.

For a disclaimer to be valid, several requirements must be met. First, the named recipient may not take any benefit from or exercise control over the gift before disclaiming it. For example, if a check for insurance is received and cashed, the recipient cannot later disclaim the insurance proceeds even if the money is returned. Second, the gift must be formally refused by a signed, written document called a Disclaimer. A named recipient may refuse all or only a part of any gift. For instance, the named recipient may disclaim one-half or $100,000 of the spouse's IRA. Only the portion that is disclaimed will pass as if the recipient had died before the Decedent. The part not disclaimed will go to the named recipient.

Third, the disclaimer must be filed within the period of time allowed by state and federal statute.[11.1] The disclaimer must be filed with the transferor of the interest, the transferor's legal representative, the holder of the legal title, with the court in the probate proceeding to disclaim probate or joint assets or with the bank or insurance company to disclaim a gift given through a beneficiary designation.

PRE-MARITAL AND POST-MARITAL AGREEMENTS

A Pre-Marital (also called an Antenuptial or Prenuptial) Agreement can be written and signed before marriage to dictate the rights of each marriage partner at the death of the other.[11.2] A Pre-Marital Agreement varies the rights that the surviving spouse had under state law. The Pre-Marital Agreement may favor the surviving spouse or may favor the Decedent's other beneficiaries. Although the Pre-Marital Agreement is not a Will or a Trust, it is a contract that may be enforced in the Decedent's probate proceeding after the Decedent's death. In some states, a Post-Marital Agreement is also recognized as an enforceable contract. In certain states, the Post-Marital is recognized only if there was a valid Pre-Marital Agreement. The Executor must carefully consider the obligations of the estate under any Pre-Marital or Post-Marital Agreements. The beneficiaries of such a contract may be entitled to notice of all estate proceedings as creditors of the estate.

Those who have an interest in enforcing a Pre-Marital or Post-Marital Agreement must make their claim in the probate court within the time allowed creditors by state statute. The Executor and the estate attorney should be contacted to discuss how the Pre-Marital and Post-Marital Agreements affect the distribution of the estate. The Executor must consider the claims made under the Agreement and seek advice of the estate attorney and, perhaps, an order of the court. If the parties cannot reach an agreement, a claim based on the enforcement of a Pre-Marital Agreement will be a claim against the estate. Those seeking to enforce the Pre-Marital or Post-Marital Agreement against the estate should seek independent legal advice and representation.

SURVIVAL CLAUSES

Survival clauses help avoid the expense of double probates and double taxes. When a person who has been given a gift in a Will dies soon after the person who gave the gift, the gift must be administered in the estate of both the giver and the recipient. This process is, in essence, a double probate. In addition, it is possible that the same asset will be taxed in the estates of both the giver and the recipient. Some Wills have language that alleviates this problem to some extent with a survival clause that requires a devisee or legatee to live at least a certain number of days or months after the Decedent dies in order to receive the gift. If the named devisee or legatee fails to survive for that period of time, the Will provides for a successor. These clauses are used to avoid unnecessary taxes and administration costs. Some states have statutory provisions to alleviate this problem as well.[11.3]

SIMULTANEOUS DEATH CLAUSES

A cumbersome and expensive problem arises when two individuals die at the same time, leaving their estates to one another. These reciprocal gifts are common between husband and wife, parent and child, siblings, life partners, and friends. Without special provisions in a Will or under state law, the estate of each would be distributed into the other's estate to be administered and taxed unnecessarily. A Will can designate an alternative distribution in the event of a simultaneous death. The Uniform Simultaneous Death Act provides a formula of distribution in such cases,[1.4] but a direction in the Will takes precedence over the Uniform Act. In some instances, it is beneficial to presume that each person survived the other. This provision limits the administration of the assets to the bare minimum. However, in other instances, it is beneficial to presume that one person, the less wealthy, survived the wealthier person to take advantage of both persons' Unified Estate and Gift Tax Credit to shelter the maximum amount from estate tax.

SETTLEMENT AGREEMENTS

Many times the Decedent's estate planning was not completed before death or the Will was written under circumstances that no longer exist and the ultimate distribution called for in the Will is not fair. If all the devisees and legatees agree, the distributions directed by Will may be modified. This modification is accomplished by a Settlement Agreement. To be valid, a Settlement Agreement requires the agreement and signature of each and every devisee and legatee. If a single devisee or legatee does not sign, there is no agreement and the Will controls. The valid Settlement Agreement also must be filed and approved by the court in the probate proceeding. After approval, the Settlement Agreement controls the distribution of the probate assets instead of the Will.

Unless the written agreement of those who are affected is obtained, any distribution of assets that is not precisely as described by the Will or as required by statute creates a risk of liability for the Executor. In some instances, a Settlement Agreement is more effective than a waiver or consent to inform the interested persons of changes or deviations from the Will and limit the Executor's liability. The Executor should discuss with the estate attorney possible uses of this technique to solve problems of distribution of the estate.

IN TERROREM CLAUSES

The prospect of a family member contesting the Will is unacceptable to some Testators. To attempt to prevent such contests, some Wills are written with a clause that threatens anyone who contests the Will with the loss of their benefits under the Will. This is called an *in Terrorem* clause. These clauses are often effective as a persuasive psychological deterrent to a contest. However, the actual legal effectiveness of the *in Terrorem* clause varies from state to state. If the Will is contested on the grounds of the lack of proper witnesses or the incapacity of the Testator at the time of signing the Will and the Will is found to be invalid, the contest will be successful in spite of the clause. In such a case, the *in Terrorem* clause in the invalid Will cannot be enforced. The Executor should discuss any *in Terrorem* clause contained in the Will with the estate attorney before discussing any contest to the Will with heirs, devisees, or legatees. In the event a contest to the Will is brought, the Executor and the estate attorney must evaluate the potential outcome of the contest, the effect of the *in Terrorem* clause, and the course of action that is in the best interest of the estate. If settlement of the contest is determined to be in the best interest of the estate, the Executor should attempt to obtain the written agreement and consent to the settlement of all those whose interests are affected.

TESTAMENTARY TRUSTS

A **Testamentary Trust** is a Trust that is created in a Will. A Testamentary Trust is created at death and only through the probate proceeding. The Testamentary Trust is not the *Inter vivos* or Living Trust that is discussed so frequently in estate planning seminars and financial planning literature, although in some ways they serve the same purposes. The Testator can have a variety of reasons for creating a Testamentary Trust, including:

1. to provide for management and distribution of the assets of a minor child or other person who does not have legal capacity.
2. to protect the assets of an adult child from wasteful spending or to inhibit division of assets as marital property by a divorce court.
3. to provide for a surviving spouse during his or her lifetime but protect the assets from the survivor's new spouse and the children of that new spouse.
4. to assure that assets are managed and invested by an experienced money manager.
5. to allow support for certain persons during their lifetime but to direct that the remaining principal be paid to a charity or other beneficiaries at the death of those persons.
6. to avoid death taxes when the combined estates of a married couple are worth more than the Unified Estate and Gift Tax Credit will protect.

Generally, the Testator named a Trustee for the Testamentary Trust when the Will was written. The procedures for creating a Testamentary Trust and qualifying the Trustee are set out in the statutes of each state.[1.5] The Executor must petition the court to create the Trust and to qualify a Trustee so that the Trustee can receive the assets from the estate. In the event the Trustee named by the Testator is unable to serve, the successor Trustee named by the Testator in the Will shall serve. In the event the Trustee and the successor Trustee named by the Executor are unable to serve, the court, when asked to do so, will appoint a Trustee.

The Trustee is the person to whom the Executor must distribute the assets. The administration of a Testamentary Trust is then the responsibility of the Trustee. The Executor should obtain a Receipt and Refunding Agreement from the Trustee for all assets distributed to the Trustee.

Some Wills provide that if the Testamentary Trust is not created within a certain period of time, the assets of the estate must be distributed to an alternate legatee. The Executor must be aware that when the Will creates a duty for the Executor to create the Trust, the Executor does not have the option to choose not to have the Trust created unless that option or discretion is specifically stated in the Will.

LIVING TRUSTS

Revocable Living Trusts are the centerpiece for a many estate plans. The reasons for creating the **Revocable Living Trust** include all the six items listed previously for Testamentary Trusts. In addition, two other reasons are often cited:

7. to avoid ancillary probate to transfer real estate and tangible personal property located in a state other than the Decedent's domicile at death.
8. to avoid probate in the state where Decedent is domiciled at death.

The eighth reason is, by far, the most common reason given by those who have a Trust as the reason for using a Revocable Living Trust. With respect to this last concept, several facts must be noted.

1. *Duties of Executor and Trustee in administering the probate estate and the trust estate are nearly identical.* The duties of the fiduciary, whether Executor or Trustee, in administering the probate estate or the trust are nearly identical, with the exception of the requirement of the court's immediate involvement in the probate estate. Both the Executor and the Trustee must gather, inventory, value, and manage the assets of the decedent; file all required reports and returns; pay debts and taxes; and distribute the assets to the beneficiaries.
2. *Decedent's failure to fully fund the trust often results in administration of both a trust and probate estate.* A very low percentage of the Revocable Living Trusts are ever fully funded. The funding of the Trust is a cumbersome and detail-oriented task that the owner of the property must accomplish. When assets and property remain out of the trust, a probate proceeding is necessary to distribute those assets and property. As a matter of good estate planning a **Pour-Over** Will accompanies the Trust to transfer those assets left out of the Trust from the probate estate into the Trust. That Pour-Over Will must be admitted to probate and administered under the probate laws and procedures of the state before the assets are distributed to the Trust. When the Pour-Over Will is admitted to probate and the Executor of that Will appointed, the expenses of administering the Will are added to the expenses of administering the Trust. Obviously, the expense of conducting two administra-

tions, one probate and one trust, is greater than the expense of administering either one or the other.

4. *Probate administration offers quick determination and termination of the claims of creditors.* In some states, when a Will is offered for probate, the creditors who have been given legal notice have a limited time in which to make their claims against the probate estate. Once that time period has passed, the creditors can no longer enforce payment of their claims. However, when the Will is not administered under the probate laws, the creditors do not have legal notice and their claims against the property of the trust may remain enforceable beyond the period that is specially limited by the probate laws.

5. *The need for court intervention in Trust administration may add unexpected costs.* The costs of administration of the probate estate and the overall cost of creating, funding, and administering of the Trust from its beginning through the distribution after the Decedent's death are comparable. However, if the court must intervene to enforce the Trust, to force the production of assets, to force an accounting, or to replace a Trustee, or the like, the cost of involving the court in the administration of a Trust can be greater than the cost of the similar probate administration.

Revocable Living Trusts are a versatile, powerful tool for the reasons given here. However, the assurance that the estate will avoid probate administration is often an empty promise that was used to sell an expensive, and perhaps unnecessary, document.

CHECKLIST: SPECIAL CONSIDERATIONS

Consider the following carefully.

- Disclaimer: Would any devisee, legatee, or beneficiary have a reason to refuse to take a bequest, devise, or benefit? If yes, determine who would take the asset if that devisee or legatee had died before the Testator. File the Disclaimer with the transferor of the asset.
- Pre-Marital or Post-Marital Agreement: Was Decedent a party to a Pre- or Post-Marital Agreement? Does that agreement create an obligation on Decedent's estate? If yes, notify those who are protected by the Agreement as known creditors. Does that Agreement create a benefit to the Decedent's estate? If yes, make the claim for that benefit within the time period allowed.

- Survival Clause: Have all devisees or legatees survived the Decedent for the required length of time? If no, determine the alternate devisees or legatees and distribute to them.
- Simultaneous Death Clause: Did the Decedent die at or near the same time as a legatee or devisee under the Decedent's Will? If yes, read the Will and state statutes for instructions for distribution of the estate in the event of simultaneous death.
- Settlement Agreement: Are there reasons to change or modify the distribution made in the Will? If yes, obtain the written agreement of all devisees and legatees in a Settlement Agreement.
- *In Terrorem* Clause: Does the Will have an *in terrorem* clause? If yes, are there reasons the Will may be contested? Evaluate claims.
- Testamentary Trust: Does the Will require the Executor to create a Testamentary Trust? If yes, petition the court for creation of the Trust and qualification of the Trustee. Does the Will give the Executor discretion to create a Testamentary Trust? If yes, consider very carefully before choosing not to create the Testamentary Trust.
- Living Trust: Is the Trust fully funded or are there assets that require probate administration? Is there a Pour-Over Will that must be filed? Does a probate administration need to be filed to end creditor's claims? Is the court's authority necessary to resolve legal questions? Does the Trustee wish to seek court approval of actions taken and accountings to seek discharge?

Final Settlement, Distribution of Assets, and Discharge of the Executor

Final settlement and distribution of the estate are the steps that are most anticipated by all devisees and legatees. Final settlement is the process by which all the claims against the estate are settled and the assets of the estate are finally ordered to be distributed. Actual distribution of the assets comes only after the court hears the Petition for Final Settlement and orders distribution. The Petition for Final Settlement that begins this final phase may be filed as soon as the time limit for the creditors to make claims has passed and the debts, expenses, and taxes have been determined. Some states also require that a certain amount of time pass since the Decedent's death before the Petition for Final Settlement can be filed.[12.1] What follows is a brief summary of the steps necessary to obtain the court order for Final Settlement and distribution of the estate. The estate attorney will guide the Executor through details of the steps. The assistance of a CPA or accountant may also be necessary.

DETERMINATION OF THE ESTATE TO BE DISTRIBUTED

Before any asset is distributed to a devisee or legatee, the Executor must summarize the economic status of the estate, including all the adjustments, increases from appreciation and income, and losses to the probate inventory that may have occurred since the Decedent's death.

Then all the claims, demands, expenses of the administration, and taxes must be itemized. The total value of the assets available for distribution is calculated by subtracting the total claims, demands, expenses, and taxes from the total available assets. Only when all the claims, demands, expenses, and taxes are fully paid are the assets of the estate available to be distributed. The following sections discuss these calculations more specifically.

Original Inventory and Adjustments

The beginning point of calculating the settlement of the estate is the original inventory. This is the inventory filed with the probate court.

Corrections in Valuation

The original inventory must be amended for all corrections in the date of death value of the original assets. Sometimes an asset was not properly valued on the inventory or the tax returns. For example, if a house was reported at the value of $100,000 on the inventory and on the estate tax return, but sold at arm's length for $80,000, a correction must be made on the inventory and on any tax returns that were filed. If this difference is not taken into account, the devisees and legatees will expect more than the estate received for that asset.

Newly Discovered Assets

The original inventory must be corrected to include the value of all newly discovered assets. Often an asset is discovered after the inventory and tax returns are filed. For example, bonds are found in a box, a previously undisclosed loan is repaid, or a bank account is discovered that was not known at the time of the original inventory. These newly discovered assets are part of the Decedent's estate. These assets must be added to the inventory that was filed with the court and to any tax returns that were filed.

Changes in Market Value

Although the original inventory must be changed when the amount reported was incorrect at the time it was reported, the original inventory is not changed when the market value of an asset changes during administration. Stocks and bonds are particularly likely to have values that vary over time. The change in market value must be accounted for only in the final settlement.[12.2]

Amended Inventory and Tax Returns

When the Executor becomes aware of a newly discovered asset or a mistake in the original valuation of an asset, the Executor has a duty to file an amended inventory with the court and to correct any tax returns that contain that mistake. These mistakes or omissions must be disclosed to the court and to the state and federal taxing authority on any tax returns before the Petition for Final Settlement is filed. However, if the value of an asset merely increases or decreases during the period of administration because the market value changed, the original inventory and tax returns should not be changed.

Lost, Stolen, or Damaged Assets

If an asset is lost after the Decedent's death for any reason—for example, by theft or breakage—that loss needs to be accounted for at final settlement. If the loss is compensated for by insurance, the insurance proceeds must be included as well. Losses from the estate and insurance compensation for those losses must be reported to the probate court as soon as is reasonably possible. The losses and insurance compensation must also be reported in any tax return that included the lost asset.

Estate Income

The income that is earned on estate assets must be determined and the source of the income carefully identified and recorded. The income from the assets can be dividends, interest, rent, or realized gain or loss. "Realized gain" means the amount over the basis that is a profit that has been received by the estate in the sale of an asset. For example, if a mutual fund sells some of its stock holdings during the administration of the estate, the mutual fund will report gain or loss depending upon the basis of the stock or bond sold and the sale price. Statements of income during the period of administration should be requested for all income-producing assets. This income must be reported on the Estate Income Tax Return (Federal 1041 and State Estate Income Tax Return).

The ultimate distribution of this income and, therefore, the responsibility to report it as income on a legatee's personal income tax return is determined by the instructions given by the Testator in the Will. If the Will does not direct who is to receive the income from the assets, then the class of gift will determine who gets the income from that asset. The income from certain assets will be distributed to the legatee who receives that asset; income from other assets will not be distributed with the asset but will be distributed to those who take the Residue. The estate attorney or tax preparer will determine the distribution, calculate the deduction, and prepare the proper tax statements to be sent to the devisees and legatees.

Final Settlement Inventory and Income Accounting

In order to calculate the distribution, the Executor must make an accounting of the adjustments, corrections, and additions to the original inventory; the losses and reimbursement for lost assets; the value of the assets on the date of distribution; and the income from each asset. This updated final settlement inventory and income accounting is the total value of the estate available to pay claims, demands, expenses, and taxes, and finally to distribute and the basis of the final settlement of the estate.

CLAIMS AND DEMANDS ON THE ESTATE

Next the Executor must determine the exact amount of the claims and demands on the estate and the order of priority for payment as described in Chapter 9. These claims, demands, expenses, and taxes must be subtracted from the total estate to obtain the total value available for distribution.

If the claims, demands, expenses, and taxes are to be paid from the Residue and the estate has sufficient assets to pay all these from the Residue, the calculation of what is available for distribution is simple. Residue minus claims, demands, expenses, and taxes will leave a balance to be distributed as the Will instructs. However, if the estate does not have sufficient assets to pay all the claims from the Residue, then, in addition to determining the amount, the Executor must determine exactly which of the estate assets are to be used to pay these claims, demands, expenses, and taxes. To do this, the Executor must determine the exact nature and amount of the claims and allocate certain classes of assets to pay those claims.

As discussed in Chapter 9, the claims against the estate of the Decedent are separated into several types or classes. Each class of claims has a different priority for payment under the state statutes. The creditor's position in this hierarchy of claims controls whether that creditor gets paid from an estate that does not have enough to pay all the creditors. The Executor and the estate attorney must analyze each claim to determine its priority.

TYPES OF CLAIMS AND DEMANDS

Secured Creditors

The Will can direct the distribution of encumbered property, or the Will can require that the loans be paid from the other assets of the estate and the property be distributed unencumbered, or free of debt. If the Will does not give instructions regarding the secured creditors, the

Executor must consult the estate attorney for information about the state law with regard to secured debt.

Whenever an estate asset secures a debt, the court will order that debt paid at least to the extent of the value of the asset. If there are sufficient assets to pay all unsecured creditors, then any amount remaining on the debt over the value of the estate asset that secures the debt will be ordered paid from other assets along with the other unsecured creditors.

Frequently during the administration of the estate, assets are used to make payments on secured loans, especially mortgage and car payments, to prevent foreclosure or repossession of the asset. Specific instructions in the Will and state law must be consulted to determine who ultimately must bear the burden of those loan payments that are made during administration.

Homestead and Spousal and Minors' Allowance

State law guarantees a homestead right and spousal or minors' allowance from the Decedent's estate before payment of any other claim on the estate, except a security interest in a specific asset.[12.3] The only claims that can supersede these spousal and minors' rights are the mortgage and purchase money liens on assets. These rights and allowances must be formally requested, approved, and specifically ordered by the court. For final settlement, assets must be allocated to pay the spousal and minors' allowances from the designated classes of estate assets in the order set out in the state statutes. Usually, the court will have ordered the homestead and the spousal and minors' allowances early in the administration. To provide the court and the devisees and legatees with a complete record, the Executor should include these items and the allocation of assets to pay these allowances in the Petition for Final Settlement.

Funeral Expenses

Payment of funeral expenses is next in the hierarchy after the homestead right, the allowance for surviving spouse and minor children, and the security interest in specific assets.[12.4] However, the purchase of a headstone or other grave marker is not considered part of the essential funeral expense. Instead, the purchase of a headstone is considered a claim equal to that of an unsecured creditor. The request for approval and the allocation of assets to pay the funeral expenses should be included in the Petition for Final Settlement.

Medicaid Reimbursement

Money spent by the government for the long-term care of the Decedent may be recovered from the Decedent's estate or the estate of the

Decedent's spouse after that spouse's death. It is a matter of public policy that recovery is delayed when there is a surviving spouse. A home, car, and personal items are exempt so long as there is a surviving spouse.[12.5] The Executor should include the request for authority to pay the claim for Medicaid reimbursement and the allocation of assets to pay those expenses in the Petition for Final Settlement.

Expenses of Last Illness

State law makes the expenses of last illness a priority claim after security interests, homestead and support claims, reimbursement of medical assistance, and funeral expenses.[12.6] The claim for expenses of last illness and the allocation of assets to pay those expenses should be included in the Petition for Final Settlement.

Expenses of Administration of the Estate

The expenses of administration are paid after the homestead, spousal and minor support; funeral expenses; reimbursement of medical assistance; and expenses of last illness.[12.7] The expenses of administration must be reasonable and approved by the court. The expenses of administration of the estate include, but are not limited to, the costs of insurance, maintenance and repairs on estate property, utilities, postage, telephone, court filing fees, publications fees, attorney and accounting fees. The expense of packing, shipping, insuring, and storage of assets may be considered an expense of administration or an expense of the individual who is to receive an asset. The Will controls this issue. If the Will does not give instructions, the state law will control. The cost for shipping and insurance should be allocated before calculating the final distribution. The request for approval of these expenses can be included in the Petition for Final Settlement.

Taxes

Taxes are paid first from the assets according to the instructions of the Testator in the Will. A well-written Will customarily will have a special provision to assure that the payment of taxes is shared by the beneficiaries in proportion to the benefit each receives from the estate. Some Wills include a provision that those who take assets from the Decedent by joint tenancy with rights of survivorship or by pay-on-death beneficiary designations also share the tax proportionately. However, if the estate does not have sufficient funds to pay the other claims, demands, and the taxes, even these special tax provisions will not save a gift.

If the Will does not include instructions, the taxes are paid from the assets according to the order set out in the state statutes.[12.8] Debts owed to the state and federal government for taxes have priority over the other claims against the estate according to the law of the state in which the estate is being administered. In some states, the homestead, spousal, and minor support, funeral expenses, expenses of last illness, and the expenses of administration of the estate have priority and may be paid before taxes. In other states, taxes have priority. In all states, taxes have priority over the unsecured claims of creditors. The Petition for Final Settlement should request authority to pay these taxes and allocate the assets from which they are to be paid.

Judgments and Liens

Judgments that were ordered against the Decedent personally and judgments and liens against the Decedent's property are paid before the general unsecured creditors.[12.9] The request for authority to pay judgments and liens and the allocation of assets to pay those items should be included in the Petition for Final Settlement.

Debts of the Decedent

All unsecured creditors who are owed money by the Decedent at death are paid only after the homestead, spousal and minors' support, funeral expenses, expenses of last illness, expenses of administration, Medicaid reimbursement, taxes, judgments, and liens are paid.[12.10] These creditors may include any of those listed in Chapter 6. All creditors are required to be paid before any distribution is made to legatees or devisees. The request for authority to pay the demands and the allocation of assets to pay should be included in the Petition for Final Settlement.

Accounting for Claims and Demands

The careful explanation of the nature, classification, and amount of the claims and demands and the allocation of the assets from which those claims and demands are to be paid is essential information for the court and for the ultimate beneficiaries of the estate.

ABATEMENT OF GIFTS TO PAY DEBTS, TAXES, AND EXPENSES

As discussed earlier, when there are sufficient assets to pay all claims, demands, debts, taxes, and expenses of administration from the Residue and give the full amount set out in the Will to each devisee and legatee, there is no need to consider abatement. However, when there are not enough assets in the Decedent's estate to fully pay the claims, demands, debts, taxes, and expenses, some creditors will not receive the full payment they are owed and no devisee or legatee will receive the gifts the Testator intended. If there are sufficient assets to pay all the claims and demands, but not to give every gift the Will promises, the Executor must allocate the gifts of some to pay these claims and demands, while the gifts to others will remain untouched. The payment of claims, demands, debts, taxes, and expenses from certain assets of the estate and not from others and the payment of some gifts but not others are perhaps the least understood and potentially the most painful and disappointing aspect of estate administration. The Executor must use great care to avoid making mistakes in this area in order to avoid the liability that accompanies such mistakes. The primary rule is that claims, demands, debts, expenses, and taxes are paid before any legatee or devisee gets a penny, and certain classes of gifts are used first to pay claims, demands, debts, taxes, and expenses before the next class of gifts is touched.[12.11]

CLASSES OF GIFTS

Several of the important decisions that the Executor must make are dependent upon the class of the gift given, that is, whether the gift is a specific bequest, specific devise, a demonstrative bequest, a demonstrative devise, a general bequest, a general devise, or a residuary gift. Those decisions include: whether certain classes of gifts will be used to pay claims, demands, debts, taxes, and expenses; whether certain legatees and devisees will receive the gifts given in the Will and others will not; and whether the income that is generated from an asset accompanies the gift or remains to be distributed with the Residue. The Executor should carefully review the descriptions of the classes of gifts that may be given in a Will and the Schedule of Abatement in Chapter 9. (See the discussion in Chapter 9 regarding whether demonstrative devises and bequests are classified as specific or general gifts.)

The most common order of abatement is repeated here:

Residuary Devises are exhausted first.

Residuary Bequests are exhausted next.

General Devises are exhausted next.

General Bequests are exhausted next.

Specific Devises are exhausted next.

Specific Bequests are the last to be used.

If payment of the debt will require part of, but not exhaust, the last class of gift necessary to pay the claims, demands, debts, taxes, and expenses, then all those who receive that class of gift will pay a proportionate share of the remaining debt.[12.12]

A clear accounting of these payments and the explanation of the source of each payment is an important tool in explaining the final distribution of the estate to devisees and legatees. This is especially important when the assets given to one class of devisees and legatees is used to pay debts and expenses instead of sharing the payments *pro rata* among all the devisees and legatees.

LIMITS TO THE DISTRIBUTION OF THE ESTATE

Even when all these claims, demands, debts, expenses, and taxes are paid, the distribution of the balance of the estate is further limited by state law, by certain provisions of the Will, by Settlement Agreements, and by the Executor's discretion. The most important of those limitations include the surviving spouse's right to elect against the Will, class gifts (gifts to a group of people), ademption by satisfaction and by extinction (the asset is no longer in the estate because it has been given to the person who was to receive it under the Will or has been given or sold to someone else), and **lapse** (the person who was to receive the gift is no longer living). These and several other possible limitations are discussed briefly here.

Witness to Will

Some states do not allow a person who wrote or is a necessary witness to the Will to benefit as a primary beneficiary under that Will. If this provision of state law is violated, that person may not take under the Will.[12.13]

Murder

Many states do not allow a person to benefit from the Will of a person he or she has been convicted of murdering.[12.14]

Divorce

In most states, a divorce invalidates any gifts given in a Will to a person who was the spouse of the Testator at the time the Will was written.[12.15] Gifts to an ex-spouse must be reaffirmed in a new Will or a codicil after a divorce to allow the gift to remain in effect.

Lapse

When the person who was to receive a gift dies before the Testator, the gift in a Will to that person lapses or terminates. If the Will makes a provision for that possibility, the instructions in the Will control the distribution. For example, if a bequest is worded thus, "I give $1,000 to my brother Sam, if he survives, or if he fails to survive to his wife, Sarah." The instructions in the Will control the distribution. If Sam dies before the Testator, Sam's wife, Sarah, gets the $1,000. However, if the Will does not address the possibility, the gift lapses or is ineffective. However, some states have anti-lapse statutes that provide in certain circumstances that the gift does not lapse but goes to the descendants of the intended recipient.[12.16] If the Will did not give instructions about what to do if Sam dies, but says only "I give $1,000 to my brother Sam," the $1,000 would go to Sam's children instead. Those anti-lapse statutes require that specific requirements be met—for example, the original gift must be to a spouse or a relative of the Testator and that spouse or relative must have died leaving descendants.

Settlement Agreement

A Settlement Agreement can vary the provisions of a Will if all interested persons—that is, all those who would take under the Will—agree to the deviation from the Will.[12.17] The Settlement Agreement must be attached to the Petition for Final Settlement for approval by the court.

Election by Surviving Spouse

In many states a surviving spouse can choose to take what he or she is given under the Decedent's Will or the share of the Decedent's estate that is guaranteed by state statute, but not both.[12.18] Most commonly, the share guaranteed by state statute is the amount the surviving spouse would have received if the Decedent had died without a Will. This choice or election must be made within a certain period of time in the probate court proceedings. If the surviving spouse consented to the Will before the Decedent's death, then the option to elect against that Will is not available.

Some states have adopted statutes that give a percentage of the Decedent's estate to the surviving spouse depending upon the number of years the Decedent and the surviving spouse were married.[12.19] The percentage increases over the years of marriage up to the full intestate share—the amount the surviving spouse would have received if the Decedent had died without a will—when the couple has been married long enough. Some states have adopted provisions that permit a surviving spouse to take a share of not only the probate estate but also the Decedent's entire estate, including property held in joint tenancy, insurance proceeds, brokerage and bank accounts with pay-on-death beneficiaries, land transferred by pay-on-death deeds, and other assets that pass outside of probate to others.

Ademption (Asset no longer in the estate)

The Will may instruct the Executor to give an individual a specific asset that is not part of the Decedent's estate at death. That asset may have been given to the named recipient before the Decedent's death. In that event, the gift is said to be **adeemed by satisfaction** or advancement. Or the asset may have been sold or given to another person. Such a gift has been **adeemed by extinction**. A specific bequest or devise is extinguished if the asset is not in the estate. No replacement or compensation for the specific gift is given from the Decedent's estate.

Class Gifts

A class gift is a gift of a specified sum of money to a group of persons whose number is unknown at the time of the gift—for example, "I give $50,000 to be divided equally among my grandchildren living at my death." The gift is to be divided equally among those who qualify as legatees at the time of the Testator's death. The amount of the gift to each person is dependent upon the number of grandchildren who are born and who survive the Testator's death. For example, if there is only one grandchild, that grandchild will receive $50,000. But if there are ten grandchildren, each will receive $5,000.

Executor's Discretion

If the Will or the state law permits, the Executor will have some degree of discretion in the distribution of assets. For example, the Executor may be excused from equalizing the tax impact of distribution of certain assets or may be empowered to make distributions of personal property without obtaining approval of all the legatees. Granting these powers of discretion to the Executor simplifies difficult questions in the administration of an estate and thus reduces the potential for conflict and expense. The Executor must follow the Will if specific instructions are given, but may exercise discretion if that power is granted.

PROCESS FOR DETERMINING DISTRIBUTION

The estate attorney should prepare a statement of the proposed distribution based on the application of the state laws and the instructions in the Will. This proposed distribution must be filed with the court with the Petition for Final Settlement of the Estate. What follows is a step-by-step process for determining the distribution of the estate. This is a simplified guide to the process commonly followed by the estate attorney. It is provided here as a guide to the process.

1. Calculate the value of estate.
2. Allocate estate assets to pay the following pursuant to the Will's instructions or, if there are no instructions in the Will, according to the abatement schedule in the state's statutes.
   ____ Homestead
   ____ Spousal and minors' allowance
   ____ Spousal elective share
   ____ Funeral expenses
   ____ Expenses of last illness
   ____ Medicaid reimbursement
   ____ Expenses for administration of the estate
   ____ Taxes
   ____ Judgments and liens
   ____ Debts
3. After payment of all claims, demands, debts, expenses, and taxes, determine the value and identity of the assets that are available to be distributed.
4. Determine the class of each gift given in the Will.
5. Consider the following limitations to the distribution of the balance of the estate.
   ____ Is there a valid Settlement Agreement?
       ____ If yes, follow the Settlement Agreement.
       ____ If there is no Settlement Agreement, and there is a surviving spouse
           ____ has the surviving spouse consented to the Will?
               ____ If the surviving spouse has not consented to the Will, does the surviving spouse wish to elect against the Will?
                   ____ If the surviving spouse does not wish to elect against the Will, obtain the surviving spouse's consent to the Will.
                   ____ If the surviving spouse wishes to elect against the Will, calculate the consequences of the surviving spouse's election against the Will and/or the spousal share.
               ____ If the surviving spouse has consented to the Will, allocate the estate assets accord-

ing to the instructions in the Will as follows next.

6. Sprecific Gifts—Consider each of the Specific Devises and Bequests given in the Will.

_____ Is the asset given as a Specific Devise or Bequest available
to be distributed?

_____ If the asset is not available to be distributed, was the
asset in the estate at the time of death?

_____ If the asset was not in the estate at the time of
death, then a Specific Devise or Bequest fails.
(Adeemed by extinction or satisfaction)

_____ If the asset was in the estate at the time of death,
was the asset lost or destroyed?

_____ If the asset was lost or destroyed, any
insurance, damage, or restitution related
to the loss is paid to the named devisee or
legatee, otherwise a specific gift fails. A
Legatee entitled to a specific gift could
expect to recover the loss from the Executor personally if the Executor intention-
ally or negligently caused the loss.

_____ If the asset was in the estate at the time of death,
was the asset allocated for payment of a claim,
demand, debt, expense, or tax?

_____ If the asset was allocated for payment of
a claim, demand, debt, expense, or tax,
then the other assets of the estate have
been exhausted to pay claims and demands and the specific gift fails.

_____ If the Specific Devise or Bequest is available to be
distributed

_____ Is the Devisee or Legatee living?

_____ If the Devisee or Legatee is not living,
was a successor Devisee or Legatee
named in the Will?

_____ If yes, allocate that asset to the successor.

_____ If no, does an anti-lapse statute direct the gift to some other person?

_____ If yes, allocate that asset to
the person indicated.

_____ If no, the gift fails, and the
asset falls back into the Residue.

_____ Is the Devisee or Legatee disqualified from taking the gift given in the Will?
    _____ If not disqualified, distribute the gift to
the named Devisee or Legatee.
    _____ If disqualified, is there an alternate Devi-
see or Legatee?
        _____ If yes, distribute the asset to the
alternate.
        _____ If there is no alternate, the asset
falls back into the Residue.

7. General Gifts—Consider each of the General Devises and General Bequests given in the Will.

_____ Is the asset given as a General gift available to be distributed?
    _____ If the asset is not available to be distributed
        _____ Was the asset in the estate of the Decedent at the time of death?
            _____ If the asset was not in the estate (adeemed), then a General gift is paid from the Residue of the estate.
            _____ If the asset was in the estate at the Decedent's death, has the asset been destroyed or lost? If the asset has been lost or destroyed, the General gift is paid from any insurance or restitution for the loss, then from the Residue of the estate.
        _____ If the asset was in the estate at Decedent's death, was the asset allocated for payment of some claim, demand, debt, expense, or tax?
            _____ If the General Devise or Bequest has been allocated for payment of a claim, demand, debt, expense, or tax, the other assets of the estate have been exhausted to pay claims and demands and the general gift fails.
    _____ If the asset is available to be distributed
        _____ Is the Devisee or Legatee living?
            _____ If not living, was a successor Devisee or Legatee named?
                _____ If yes, check whether state law disqualifies the successor.
                _____ If no successor was named, does an anti-lapse statute direct the gift to some other person?

_____ If yes, allocate that General
gift to the person indicated.
_____ If no successor is designated
by statute, the gift fails, and
the asset falls back into the
Residue.

_____ Is the Devisee or Legatee disqualified under some provision
of state law from taking the gift given in the Will?
_____ If not disqualified, distribute the General gift to the
named Devisee or Legatee.
_____ If there is a disqualification, is there an alternate or
successor Devisee or Legatee?
_____ If yes, distribute the General gift to the successor
or alternate.
_____ If there is no alternate, the General gift falls to
the Residue.

8. Residuary gifts—Consider the Residuary gifts given in the Will.
_____ Are the Residuary assets available to be distributed?
_____ If the Residuary assets are not available to be distributed
_____ Were the assets in the estate of the Decedent at the
time of death?
_____ If yes, have assets been lost or destroyed? If the
assets have been lost or destroyed, any insurance or restitution for the loss is paid to the
Residue of the estate and distributed to the
Residuary Legatees, unless the insurance proceeds or restitution are necessary to pay claims
or demands.
_____ If the assets were in the Decedent's estate at the
time of death and have not been lost or destroyed, then the Residuary assets have been
exhausted to pay claims, demands, debts, expenses, taxes, general devises, and bequests,
and the gift fails because of lack of funds.
_____ If there are Residuary assets available to be distributed
_____ Are the Residuary Legatees living?
_____ If a Residuary Legatee is not living, was a successor or alternate Legatee named?
_____ If a successor or alternate was named, determine whether that person is qualified
to take the Residuary share.
_____ If no successor or alternate was named,
does an anti-lapse statute direct the gift
to some other person or persons?

_____ If yes, allocate that asset to the person or persons indicated.

_____ If no, the Residuary gift fails, and the assets are distributed to other Residuary legatees.

_____ Is any Residuary Legatee, alternate, or successor Legatee disqualified by some provision of state law from taking under the Will?

_____ If there is no disqualification, distribute to the Legatee.

_____ If disqualified, is there an alternate Legatee?

_____ If yes, is that alternate Legatee disqualified under some provision of state law? If disqualified, determine qualified subsequent Legatee. If there is no qualified subsequent Legatee, the gift falls back to the Residue to be distributed to the others who are entitled to the Residue.

PETITION AND ORDER FOR FINAL SETTLEMENT

Once the Executor and the estate attorney have determined the proper distribution of the assets of the estate, the estate attorney must prepare the Petition for Final Settlement and a Final Accounting to file with the court. The Executor will approve and sign the final draft of the Petition for Final Settlement. The estate attorney will give the required legal notices of the hearing for final settlement to all interested parties. A copy of the Petition for Final Settlement with the proposed distribution and the Final Accounting must accompany the notice of the hearing. Any questions or corrections that interested persons may have concerning the proposed distribution or the accounting must be dealt with at this time. Any questions or disagreements about the proposed distribution should be addressed first to the Executor. If the question remains, the interested persons should ask for an explanation from the estate attorney. Most questions can be answered and most problems solved with adequate information. If the question is not adequately answered, or the interested person does not agree with the analysis or explanation, the interested person should seek independent legal counsel in advance of the hearing on the Petition for Final Settlement. Any dispute may be resolved finally by the court at the hearing. The Order of Final Settlement signed by the court is the document that gives the Executor authority to distribute the estate assets.

TRANSFER ASSETS TO NEW OWNERS

Only after the court has ordered distribution of assets may the Executor and the estate attorney begin to distribute assets of the estate. A plan for the transfer of each and every asset must be made. The plan should include whether the asset is to be distributed in cash or in-kind and who will be responsible for liquidation or transfer. Highly **liquid assets** that will be used to pay expenses and debts or distributed in a check, including accounts in banks, savings and loans, and credit unions, are often deposited in the estate account; income statements are requested a week or two before the hearing on the final settlement so that the final accounting can be prepared. As a practical matter, much of the transfer work for the assets will need to be done by the estate attorney. Deeds for transfer of real property, assignments of mineral interests, assignments of installment contracts, and notice of these assignments to payors will need to be prepared by the estate attorney to assure that they are properly written and filed. Stocks, bonds, and mutual funds will require letters of instruction for transfer.

INSTRUCTIONS FOR TRANSFER OF SPECIFIC TYPES OF ASSETS

Instructions and suggestions for transfer of the most common types of property are listed for each asset in the last section of the Summary of Assets in Appendix V of this *Executor's Guide*. The Summary of Assets is not meant as a do-it-yourself guide for transfers. It is only an aid for the Executor to monitor and participate in the process. The help of an experienced estate attorney will be necessary to correctly accomplish the tasks of distribution.

RECEIPT AND REFUNDING AGREEMENTS

When making distributions, the Executor should protect himself or herself from unnecessary personal liability. Each recipient of an asset of the estate should sign and return a Receipt and Refunding Agreement before any asset is distributed to that person. Asking for the receipt after the assets have been distributed is a lot like closing the barn door once the cows are out—that is, not of much real use. In signing the Receipt and Refunding Agreement, the recipient acknowledges that the asset is being received and that in the event the Executor or the estate is asked to pay additional sums for claims, demands, debts, expenses, or taxes, the recipient will return his or her share of the assets or pay the amount in cash back to the estate. A sample Receipt and Refunding Agreement is included in Appendix IV. Although the Receipt and Refunding Agreement provides some protection, a wise Executor should be aware that if it becomes necessary to recover an asset, that asset may have already been sold or spent and the Executor may be personally liable for any amounts that have been paid out that the recipients cannot return.

DISTRIBUTION OF HOUSEHOLD AND PERSONAL PROPERTY

The household and personal property of the Decedent is often difficult to distribute. These items have great sentimental value to those receiving them, and the economic value is often not easy to determine. In order to distribute these items, certain difficulties must be overcome, including the valuation of the items, the identification of sets of items that are to stay together—such as dining sets, silverware, jewelry, and the like—and the method of choosing who gets which items. One proposal for distribution that addresses these difficult issues is included in this *Executor's Guide* at Appendix III.

It is useful for the Executor to correspond in writing early in the administration with all those persons who are entitled to take a share of the personal and household items to inform them of the gift, to involve them in the necessary decision-making regarding the distribution of these items, and to inform them of the time at which these items can be distributed.

The cost of shipping and insuring the personal property can be considerable. The determination of whether the estate or the recipient will pay these costs should be part of the court's order for distribution.

DISTRIBUTION TO MINORS AND DISABLED PERSONS

The Executor may not distribute assets directly to a minor or disabled person. If the Will does not provide for distribution to a Trustee or Custodian for the benefit of a minor, or if the state does not provide for the informal distribution of a small estate (e.g., less than $5,000), a legal Conservatorship will be necessary. A well-written Will takes into account the possibility that assets may be distributed to individuals who are not of legal age or who are disabled, impaired, or incompetent. A brief clause in the Will can avoid the need to create a Conservatorship (in some jurisdictions called a Guardianship of the Estate). The Will should be reviewed carefully for express authority to distribute to a Trustee or Custodian for the minor or disabled person. The estate attorney will be knowledgeable about special state law provisions for distribution of small estates to minors. If distribution to a Conservator for the benefit of a minor or disabled person is necessary, the estate attorney will prepare the documents and instruct the Executor in the other procedures necessary to appoint a Conservator. Chapter 5 discusses creation of a legal Conservatorship.

DISTRIBUTION TO TRUSTEE

Where the Will requires distribution of assets to a Trustee of a Testamentary Trust—that is, a Trust created in a Will—the Trustee must be qualified and be approved by the court. The Executor may not distribute assets to the named Trustee until the court has granted Letters of Trusteeship.

A Will can direct distribution of assets to a Trustee of a Trust that already exists. The Trustee of this existing Trust is treated as any other Devisee or Legatee. Court approval of the Trust or Trustee of the *Inter vivos*, or Living Trust, is not necessary. A Receipt and Refunding Agreement should be obtained for all assets transferred to a Trustee.

CLOSING THE ESTATE AND DISCHARGING THE EXECUTOR

From the date the court orders final settlement until actual distribution, some amount of time will pass—perhaps only a week, perhaps several months. The amount of time depends upon the difficulty of completing the distribution of the assets and the promptness with which the Executor and estate attorney act. In the time before distribution the assets may earn additional income. A supplemental accounting must be filed to account for this additional income and to verify the distribution.

After a full and complete distribution of all the estate assets, the technical closing of the estate is often delayed for several months or longer in order to ensure that all the assets have been discovered and distributed and all matters relating to the estate are resolved. The authority of the Executor ends when the estate is closed, which means that the Executor no longer has the legal ability to act for the estate. If after the estate is closed some matter arises that needs the Executor's signature, such as a tax return, the transfer of another asset, or collection of a debt, a closed estate must be reopened to give the Executor the authority to act. Reopening an estate entails added expense and time. In determining when the estate should be formally closed, the Executor should remember two things: 1) There is a statute of limitations for tax matters regarding the Decedent's personal and estate taxes; and 2) there is a time limit during which an interested party can contest or appeal the court's final order of distribution. The estate attorney will know when these time limits have passed and will advise the Executor when the estate can be closed.

AFTER DISCHARGE

After being discharged, the Executor should retain all the supporting documents, receipts, and worksheets that show the Executor's work. The Executor should also retain original documents that relate to the Decedent's estate. The Executor should obtain a copy of the state law, if any, from the estate attorney giving instructions for preservation of documents. The case file at the courthouse is a permanent file of the legal documents filed with the court and is available for viewing upon request. The estate attorney may retain pertinent supporting documents and a complete court file in the office.

REOPENING THE ESTATE

In the event an asset is discovered after the estate is closed or there is some act that requires the authority of the Executor, such as signing a tax return or transferring an asset, the Executor must petition the court to reopen the probate proceeding to deal with that asset. The Executor should discuss reopening an estate with the estate attorney.

CHECKLIST: FINAL SETTLEMENT, DISTRIBUTION OF ASSETS, CLOSING OF THE ESTATE, AND DISCHARGE OF THE EXECUTOR

_____ Read the Will again to be sure that all instructions have been followed.

_____ Review the Checklists from each previous Chapter to assure that all tasks are completed.

_____ Review the probate inventory, make all corrections, and prepare and file an Amended Inventory with the court, if necessary.

_____ Prepare and file amended estate, succession, and inheritance tax returns, if necessary.

_____ Calculate the current value of all assets as of date proposed for distribution. (Inventory plus changes in market value)

_____ Calculate all income. Prepare statement of estate income by asset.

_____ Calculate the value of estate available for distribution. (Current total assets plus income)

_____ Calculate claims, demands, debts, expenses, and taxes.

_____ Determine whether the estate has sufficient value to pay all claims, demands, debts, expenses, and taxes. If not, create a detailed abatement plan.

_____ Determine whether the estate has sufficient value to distribute all specific and general bequests and devises. If not, determine the amount to be distributed. Prepare a written statement of all calculations.

_____ Prepare Proposed Distribution.

_____ Determine whether gifts are valid and whether Devisees and Legatees are qualified.

_____ Prepare plan for distribution of each asset with special attention to who receives income and who is to complete each transfer.

_____ Check to be sure tax authorities have sent tax-closing letters to be filed with the court.

_____ Prepare estate income tax return.

_____ Send the required reports of income to Devisees and Legatees.

_____ Prepare final accounting for the court.

_____ Review and sign Petition for Final Settlement.

_____ If necessary, attend hearing on Petition for Final Settlement.

_____ Assure that estate attorney has filed a certified Order of Final Settlement with the Register of Deeds in every county where real estate is located.

_____ Upon the court's order, pay all claims, demands, debts, expenses, and taxes.

_____ Upon the court's order, make distribution of all assets following the plan for distribution. Obtain Receipt and Refunding Agreements.

_____ Prepare supplemental accounting showing distributions.

_____ Petition for ancillary proceedings if real estate or tangible personal property is located out of state.

_____ Wait to close estate until statutes of limitations and time for appeal have passed.

_____ Close estate; sort and store all necessary papers. Calendar follow-up dates for disposing of papers.

Appendix I

Probate Timetable: Court Proceedings

Primary Court Proceedings(All Estates)	Additional Court Proceedings Possible
File Petition to Admit Will and Appoint Executor	Determination of heirs, Appointment of *Guardian ad Litem*
Mail and Publish Notice of Hearing to Admit Will and Appoint Executor	Contest of Will for validity, Testator's capacity, etc., and objections to the fitness of the Executor
Hearing to Admit Will and Appoint Executor	Homestead, spousal and minors' allowances, and elective share must be claimed.
	Appointment of Guardian or Conservator
Probate Inventory due, with Date of Death Values	Motion for Authority to Sell Estate Assets
	Contest on Sales Price
Period runs for creditors to make claims	Hearing on Allowance and Classification of Demands
Payment of debts and taxes	
	Appointment of Successor Executor
Determination of Distribution	Motion for Instruction or Approval of Contested Matter
File Petition for Final Settlement	
Mail and Publish Notice Hearing for Final Settlement	
Hearing for Final Settlement and Approval of Accounting	Contest of Actions and Accounting of Executor
	Establish Testamentary Trust and Qualification of Trustee
	Ancillary Probate in another state where real estate is located
Distribution of Estate	
Petition to Close Estate and Approve Final Accounting	
Hearing on Final Accounting and Discharge of Executor	Final Order of Distribution filed in County where real estate is located.

Appendix II

Timetable Necessary for All Estates

All Estates	Income, Estate, and Inheritance Tax Concerns
Date of Death (DOD)	
Obtain death certificates	
	File IRS Form SS-4 and IRS Form 56
File Death Certificates against Real Estate held in Joint Tenancy, TOD, and Pay On Death with Register of Deeds	
	706 Inventory at Date of Death Value
Distribute Non-Probate Property to Beneficiaries	Determine Income Potential of Estate Assets
	Review Elections
	File for 1040 & 1041 Extension, File for 706 Extension
	706 Alternative Valuation Date 6 months from Date of Death.
	State Estate/Inheritance Tax Returns must be filed within 9 months of date of death.
	Federal Estate Tax Return must be filed within 9 months of date of death.
	Federal tax closing letters received
	Statute of Limitation runs for IRS Claims
	File Decedent's Final 1040
	File Decedent's Estate 1041
	File Form 56

Appendix III

Proposed Method for Distribution of Personal and Household Items

The following plan for distribution can be used in situations where the Executor or Legatees wish the process to be as objective and equitable as possible.

1. An appraiser shall be chosen by the Executor. These instructions shall be given to that appraiser.
2. Executor shall correspond with each Legatee to explain the procedure and timetable for distribution.
3. The appraiser shall make a complete list of the items available for distribution with sufficient description to enable the Legatees to make reasonable choices without actually seeing the items.
4. The appraiser shall assign groups of items to sets that are by their nature parts of sets, such as silverware, glassware, and china of the same pattern, furniture that matches other pieces of furniture, and jewelry that is part of a matched set. The appraiser shall identify such a group of items as a set and give the number of pieces included in such a set. In some instances, sets that have a large number of pieces may be divided into smaller sets—for example, a twelve place setting of silver or china may be divided into two sets of six place settings each.
5. The appraiser shall assign groups of items to lots that are by their nature similar and that would be best organized for distribution in lots—for example, bed linens, table linens, household utensils, tools, and so on. The appraiser shall identify such a group as a lot and give the number of pieces included in such lot.

6. The appraiser shall assign a value to each piece, set, and lot.
7. The appraiser shall calculate the total value of the inventory and the value of the share to which each Legatee is entitled, that is, the Legatee's portion of the total value.
8. The appraiser shall provide each Legatee a copy of the inventory and valuation, the calculation of the total value of the property, and the calculation of the legatee's share.
9. If a Legatee believes that the description or valuation made by the appraiser is significantly incorrect, that Legatee may send to the appraiser a written statement of the description of the error believed to have been made. A copy of the statement of an error must also be sent to each of the Legatees at the same time. The responsibility for sending this statement of an alleged error or request for correction rests solely on the individual making the statement of error. The appraiser, in his or her sole discretion, may amend the inventory or leave the inventory as written. If the appraiser makes an amendment, the appraiser shall send a copy of the amended inventory to all the Legatees. If the appraiser chooses not to amend the inventory, the Legatee's notice of the error to all parties will serve to make all the interested parties aware of any alleged errors in the inventory.
10. The items to be distributed shall be made available for each Legatee to view not only for the purpose of choosing items but also for the purpose of allowing all the Legatees to have a sentimental last look at the items of the Decedent before the distribution.
11. The choosing of the items shall be accomplished by each Legatee choosing one item, one set of items, or one lot of items in turn.
12. The order of choosing shall be determined by a method of choosing a number and having the person whose number is closest to a randomly drawn number be the first to choose, the person whose number is second closest to the randomly drawn number be the next to choose, and so on.

   Each distributee will choose a number from 1 to ___ and inform the others of that number in writing. If any of the Legatees pick numbers that are identical, then all the legatees will pick new numbers and none of the new numbers can be the same as any of the numbers that were chosen before by any of the Legatees. For example, if Bill chooses 48, Sarah chooses 48, and John chooses 2, then all the parties must pick a new number and no one may choose the numbers 48 or 2 again. In this example, for the second number selection, Bill chooses 52, Sarah chooses 50 and John chooses 49. When the random number is known, the person with the number nearest the random chosen number will be the first to choose. If there are two numbers that are equally close to the random number, for example, Sarah chose 50 and Bill chose 52 and the random number is 51, the person with the number closest without going over the random number is the winner. In this example, Sarah would go first. Then between Bill's 52 and John's 49, Bill is closer and would choose second. This is true even though Bill went over, because Bill's 52 is closer to 51 than John's 49 and the "closest without going over" rule is activated only when the numbers are equally close.

13. As each Legatee chooses an item, set, or lot, the value of the item, set, or lot chosen will be added to each Legatee's account. When each Legatee has chosen items whose total value equals that to which that Legatee is entitled, that legatee shall not be entitled to participate in making further choices. The choosing will continue until each Legatee has chosen items equal in value to the amount to which that Legatee is entitled from the total inventory.

14. The form of the inventory shall provide space for each Legatee to make his or her choices and a space to number each consecutive choice.

15. The form of the tally sheet shall include a column for each Legatee's choices and the value of each choice. The columns shall be subtotaled frequently to assure that each Legatee has not exceeded his or her allotted distribution.

16. The first person to choose shall make his or her choice on the working copy of the inventory and on the tally sheet, make a copy of those documents, and send the documents to the next to

Example of a Working Copy of Inventory and Valuation

Number Chosen	Inventory Number	Item with description	Value	Person who chose this item
4	A	Maple Dresser, bed frame, nightstand (lot with 3 pieces)	400.00	Sarah
1	B	Floor Lamps with Tiffany shades (set of two)	260.00	Sarah
6	C	Silverware (Gorham, 8 place setting)	900.00	Bill
2	D	Britannica Encyclopedia (1999 ed.) (Set of 45 volumes)	200.00	John
5	E	Computer (Gateway 2000)	400.00	John
3	F	Grandfather clock	750.00	Bill
8	G	Signed baseball	50.00	John
7	H	Oil Painting ( )	1,000.00	Sarah
10	I	Dining set (table and 6 chairs)	1,000.00	John
11	J	Linens (lot of 30 pieces)	11.00	John
9	K	Household utensils	9.00	Bill

Distribution Tally Sheet

Sarah Item chosen	Sarah amount	John Item chosen	John amount	Bill Item chosen	Bill amount
Floor Lamps with Tiffany shades (set of two) Inv. # B	260.00	Britannica Encyclopedia (1999 ed.) (Set of 45 volumes) Inv. # H	200.00	Grandfather clock Inv. # F	750.00
Maple Dresser, bed frame, nightstand (lot with 3 pieces) Inv. # A	400.00	Computer (Gateway 2000) Inv. # E	400.00	Silverware Inv. # C	900.00
Subtotal	660.00		600.00		1650.00
Oil Painting Inv. # H	1000.00	Signed baseball Inv. # G	50.00		9.00 Inv. # L
Subtotal	1660.00		650.00		1659.00
		Dining set (table and 6 chairs) Inv. # J	1000.00		
Subtotal	1660.00		1650.00		1659.00
		Linens (lot) Inv. # K	11.00		
Total	1660.00		1661.00		1659.00
Total of three columns	4980.00				

choose. If the parties are all present for the distribution, the original inventory and tally sheet can be passed around. The number in the left column of the working inventory is the order in which the items were chosen.

17. If someone has already chosen an item, that item cannot be chosen by another.

18. The working copy of the inventory shall be sent from person to person until one person has chosen the total value to which he or she is entitled. Then the working copy of the inventory shall be sent to only those persons who are entitled to continue to make choices.

19. Once all the items have been chosen, each person shall be sent a final copy of the completed working inventory showing who took each item and the accounting for each item.

20. The appraiser, or other person designated by the Executor, shall separate and pack the items chosen by each person into boxes clearly labeled with the name of the recipient and shall supervise the distribution of those items to the persons entitled. Each

recipient shall sign a Receipt and Refunding Agreement before or upon delivery of the items.

21. If any part of the above described process is disrupted, the legatees agree that the resolution of the problem shall be submitted to the Executor, or if the Executor is a participating legatee, to an independent person for an absolute decision.

SAMPLE LETTER
TO
LEGATEES OF TANGIBLE PERSONAL PROPERTY
(A letter to a legatee may be worded this way.)

Dear (Legatee):

You have been given a portion of personal and household property under the Will of (<u>Decedent's name</u>). Your share of that property will be _____% of the value of the items. The value of the personal property to be divided is approximately $_____. So the value of your share will be approximately $ _____. The property cannot be distributed until the court first has made an order of distribution. I expect that will be on (<u>date</u>). Until that order of distribution, I must store the personal and household property.

It may be advisable to give the items to a charity or to sell them and distribute the sales proceeds among all the legatees. (I would recommend _____ for these reasons _____. However, you are entitled to take your portion regardless of what other legatees choose to do. The final decision is yours.) I would like to make the distribution as easy as possible. Please read the choices available. Choose only one and return promptly. I cannot guarantee that I will be able to fulfill your wishes if other legatees have different wishes, but I will make all reasonable attempts to comply. Please indicate your preference below.

Choice 1. _____DONATE ALL TO CHARITY. Give all personal and household items to charity. *Name of charity* _____. (_____ Charity is recommended by _____ for these reasons_____.) Take the charitable deduction for estate.

Choice 2. _____SELL AND DISTRIBUTE CASH. Sell all personal and household items at an estate sale and divide the proceeds among the legatees.

Choice 3. _____DISTRIBUTE PERSONAL PROPERTY BY A CHOOSING METHOD. Distribute all property to named legatees by the method of allowing each person to choose an item or set of items in turn until the value of his or her share is achieved.

Choice 4. _____DISTRIBUTE SOME ITEMS, SELL BALANCE, AND DISTRIBUTE CASH. Distribute some items to the named legatees, sell the balance at an estate sale, and divide the proceeds of that sale among the legatees. If this is your choice, list the items you believe should be distributed on a separate page.

Choice 5. _____DISTRIBUTE SOME ITEMS, DONATE BALANCE TO CHARITY. Distribute some of the items to the legatees; give the balance to charity, *name of charity* _____. If this is your choice, list items you wish to have distributed to legatees on a separate page.

Choice 6. _____ALL TO ANOTHER PERSON. Distribute all the personal and household items to a person. Name of person

_____.

_____ Count the value of personal and household items as part of that person's legacy.

_____ Do not count as part of that person's legacy.

Choice 7. _____ OTHER_____

_____

Appendix IV

Worksheets and Forms

Information about Decedent Worksheet
Obituary Information
Cemetery and Funeral Worksheet
Will Evaluation Worksheet
Heirs Contact Worksheet
Legatees and Devisees Worksheet
Agents and Representatives Worksheet
Asset Evaluation Form
Estate Accounting Voucher
Receipt and Refunding Agreement

INFORMATION ABOUT DECEDENT WORKSHEET

Decedent's Name as shown on birth certificate: _____

Decedent's Married Name(s): _____

Variations on name used by Decedent: _____

Nicknames or aliases: _____

Date of birth: _____ Place of birth: _____

Date of death: _____ Place of death: _____

Domicile at death (Consult Estate Attorney): _____

Length of Decedent's residence in state: _____ in United States: _____

_____

MILITARY SERVICE

If Decedent was a veteran, rank: _____ Branch of Service: _____
    Serial number: _____

Date and place entered service: _____
    Date discharged from service: _____

_____

LEGAL HEIRS

SPOUSE

Was the Decedent married at time of death? If yes,

Spouse's name: _____

Spouse's date of birth: _____ Place of birth: _____

Spouse's address: _____

Social Security Number _____ Is there a Premarital Agreement? _____

LEGAL HEIRS (continued)

DECEDENT'S CHILDREN

Did the Decedent have children? If yes, list below.

Child's Name	Address	Social Security Number	Date of Birth	Date of Death

Did any child die before the Decedent? If yes, did that deceased child have any children?

Name of deceased child _____
    Names, addresses,   _____
    and social security   _____
    numbers of deceased   _____
    child's children   _____

Name of deceased child _____
    Names, addresses,   _____
    and social security   _____
    numbers of deceased   _____
    child's children   _____

Name of deceased child _____
    Names, addresses,   _____
    and social security   _____
    numbers of deceased   _____
    child's children   _____

If Decedent is survived by a spouse, children, or grandchild, STOP HERE!

LEGAL HEIRS (continued)

If Decedent did not leave a surviving spouse, children, or grandchildren, complete the following for the Decedent's parents:

Parent's Name	Date of Birth	Date of Death	Social Security Number	Street Address, City, State, and Zip

If both parents are deceased, list Decedent's brothers and sisters.

Sibling's Name	Address	Social Security Number	Date of Birth	Date of Death

Did any sibling die before the Decedent? If yes, did that deceased sibling have any children?

Name of deceased sibling
   Names, addresses,
   and social security
   numbers of deceased
   sibling's children _____

Name of deceased sibling
   Names, addresses,
   and social security
   numbers of deceased
   sibling's children _____

Name of deceased sibling
   Names, addresses,
   and social security
   numbers of deceased
   siblings's children _____

Name of deceased sibling
   Names, addresses,
   and social security
   numbers of deceased
   sibling's children _____

Consult the estate attorney for interpretation of the state law concerning heirs.

OBITUARY INFORMATION

Name and address of newspaper: _____

Name and address of newspaper: _____

The following information should be provided to the newspapers listed above for the Decedent's obituary:

Decedent's full name: _____ **Nickname or alias?** _____

Occupation: _____

Date of birth: _____ **Place of birth:** _____

Date of death: _____ **Place of death:** _____

Residence: _____

Previous city and state of residence: _____ **Photo:** _____

Special achievements, interesting facts, important accomplishments, volunteer associations:

_____

_____

_____

Memorial established: _____

Preceded in death by: _____

_____

Survived by (List only those whose names are to appear in the obituary):

Spouse: _____

Children: _____

_____

_____

_____

Parents: _____

Grandchildren: _____

_____

_____

_____

Brothers and Sisters: _____

_____

_____

Others: _____

CEMETERY AND FUNERAL WORKSHEET

THIS WORKSHEET SHOULD BE BROUGHT TO THE FUNERAL HOME WHEN MAKING FUNERAL ARRANGEMENTS

Facts for Funeral Director

Decedent's full name (including maiden name): _____

Date of birth: _____ Birthplace: _____

Residence: _____ Race or national origin: _____

Social Security Number: _____ Business or occupation: _____

Marital status: _____ Spouse's name: _____

Father's name, date of birth, and birthplace _____
_____

Mother's maiden name, date of birth, and birthplace: _____
_____

If veteran, rank: _____ Branch of service_____
    Serial number: _____

Date and place entered service: _____
    Date discharged from service: _____

Name of next of kin (if there is no surviving spouse): _____

Cemetery Plot or Mausoleum Space

Location: _____

Deed number: _____ Location of deed: _____

Date purchased: _____

Other informaiton (e.g., perpetual care): _____

Funeral

Pre-arranged funeral plans located at: _____
Funeral should be paid for by:
_____

Life Insurance

Bring policy if proceeds will be used for funeral expenses.
          Insurer   Policy Number
_____
_____   _____
_____   _____

WILL EVALUATION WORKSHEET

DECEDENT INFORMATION

Testator's name: _____   Any alias? _____

Testator's county of residence   State of residence
at death: _____   at death: _____

Testator's date of birth: _____ Place of birth: _____

Testator's date of death: _____ Place of death: _____

Spouse's name: _____

Spouse's date of birth: _____

WILL INFORMATION: Location of original Will: _____Codicils: _____

Type of Will: _____   Is Will contractual? _____

State of Execution: _____   Date Will was signed: _____

Who wrote the Will? _____   Address: _____

Is Will self-proved? _____   Name and address of notary: _____

Names and addresses of Witnesses: _____

Is there a Letter Directing Distribution of Personal Property? _____

Is there a Testamentary Trust? _____ Trustee's name and address: _____

Executor's name: _____   Address: _____
Executor's county: _____   Executor's state: _____
Is bond excused for Executor? _____

Co-Executor's name and address: _____
Co-Executor's county: _____ Co-Executor's state: _____
Powers of Executor:
  Power to sell personal property without court approval? _____
  Power to sell real property without court approval? _____
  Other specific powers? _____

Guardian's name and address: _____

Conservator's name and address: _____

HEIRS CONTACT WORKSHEET
(Refer to the Legal Heirs in the Information about Decedent Worksheet)

Names, Addresses, and Telephone Numbers

Name: _____ Relationship to Decedent: _____
Address: _____
_____
Telephone no. _____

Name: _____ Relationship to Decedent: _____
Address: _____
_____
Telephone no. _____

Name: _____ Relationship to Decedent: _____
Address: _____
_____
Telephone no. _____

Name: _____ Relationship to Decedent: _____
Address: _____
_____
Telephone no. _____

Name: _____ Relationship to Decedent: _____
Address: _____
_____
Telephone no. _____

Name: _____ Relationship to Decedent: _____
Address: _____
_____
Telephone no. _____

Name: _____ Relationship to Decedent: _____
Address: _____
_____
Telephone no. _____

Name: _____ Relationship to Decedent: _____
Address: _____
_____
Telephone no. _____

LEGATEES AND DEVISEES WORKSHEET
(Only Those Who Are Named in the Will)

Names, Addresses, Telephone Numbers, and Social Security Numbers

Name: _____   Relationship to Decedent: _____
Address: _____   Soc. Sec. # _____
_____   Gift given in Will: _____
Telephone no. _____   _____

Name: _____   Relationship to Decedent: _____
Address: _____   Soc. Sec. # _____
_____   Gift given in Will: _____
Telephone no. _____   _____

Name: _____   Relationship to Decedent: _____
Address: _____   Soc. Sec. # _____
_____   Gift given in Will: _____
Telephone no. _____   _____

Name: _____   Relationship to Decedent: _____
Address: _____   Soc. Sec. # _____
_____   Gift given in Will: _____
Telephone no. _____   _____

Name: _____   Relationship to Decedent: _____
Address: _____   Soc. Sec. # _____
_____   Gift given in Will: _____
Telephone no. _____   _____

Name: _____   Relationship to Decedent: _____
Address: _____   Soc. Sec. # _____
_____   Gift given in Will: _____
Telephone no. _____   _____

Name: _____   Relationship to Decedent: _____
Address: _____   Soc. Sec. # _____
_____   Gift given in Will: _____
Telephone no. _____   _____

Name: _____   Relationship to Decedent: _____
Address: _____   Soc. Sec. # _____
_____   Gift given in Will: _____
Telephone no. _____   _____

AGENTS AND REPRESENTATIVES WORKSHEET

Names, Addresses, and Telephone Numbers

Name: _____   Company represented: _____
Address: _____   Position:_____

Telephone no. _____

Name: _____   Company represented: _____
Address: _____   Position:_____

Telephone no. _____

Name: _____   Company represented: _____
Address: _____   Position:_____

Telephone no. _____

Name: _____   Company represented: _____
Address: _____   Position:_____

Telephone no. _____

Name: _____   Company represented: _____
Address: _____   Position:_____

Telephone no. _____

Name: _____   Company represented: _____
Address: _____   Position:_____

Telephone no. _____

ASSET EVALUATION FORM
(Use a separate sheet for each asset)

_____
Name of Decedent

_____
❑ Real Estate ❑ Tangible ❑ Intangible

_____
Specific Type of Asset
Page _____ Summary of Assets

Legal description: _____
_____
_____

Asset location: _____

Ownership: (Choose one)

_____ Individual without Beneficiary: (Probate Inventory)

_____ Individual with Beneficiary(s) _____

_____ Joint Tenancy with Right of Survivorship:

Joint Owner(s) names _____

_____ Tenancy in Common: (Probate Inventory)

Joint Owner(s) names _____

_____ Trust, Name of Trust _____

_____ Other _____

Method of valuation: (Choose one)

_____ Statement of Account for intangible personal property (Attach copy)

_____ Formal Appraisal by _____ (Attach copy)

_____ Informal Statement of Value by _____ (Attach copy)

_____ Published Value Reference Source_____ (Attach copy)

_____ Other: _____

Value on date of death: _____ Value at 6 months: _____
Confirmed by: _____ Confirmed by: _____

Management instructions:

_____
_____
_____

Income on this asset: (Attach Statement) _____

Transfer instructions:

_____
_____
_____

ESTATE ACCOUNTING VOUCHER

_____		_____
Account Name		Account Number

Amount of payment: _____ Date paid: _____ Check number: _____
Reason for payment: _____
Payment made to: _____
Address of payee: _____

Is this payment for
_____ spousal or minor's allowance? If yes, has the court ordered payment? ___
_____ funeral expense? If yes, is the amount reasonable? _____
_____ expense of last illness? If yes, has the court ordered payment? _____
_____ expense of administration? If yes, is the amount reasonable? _____
_____ taxes? Specify: _____ Has a court ordered payment? _____
_____ debt of Decedent? If yes, has the court ordered payment? _____
_____ a distribution? If yes, has the court ordered distribution?_____
_____ other? Specify _____

DOCUMENTATION
Attach a copy of the billing statement.
Attach a copy of the receipt.
Attach a copy of the check.

(Use a separate voucher for each check.)

RECEIPT AND REFUNDING AGREEMENT

Received of _____, Executor, $_____

in (partial/full) payment of my (legacy/devise/residuary be-

quest/pecuniary bequest/distributive share) of the Estate of

_____.

In consideration of this distribution at this time I agree to refund

any portion of the distribution made to me that may be required be-

cause of any additional assessment of estate, inheritance, succession,

gift, or income taxes by the federal or state government, or other ex-

pense that is properly payable out of my share of the estate. This

agreement is expressly made for the benefit of the Executor and the

Decedent's estate.

Dated this _____ day of _____, _____.

_____

SUBSCRIBED AND SWORN TO before me this _____ day of

_____, 20___.

_____

NOTARY PUBLIC

My Commission Expires _____

Appendix V

Summary of Assets

TYPES OF ASSETS

Asset names in **bold type** are titles to sections in the Summary of Assets. All other listed assets are included under the asset name indicated.

Annuities

Antiques

Art

Audiotapes, see **Family Memorabilia**

Automobiles and Other Motor Vehicles

Bank, Savings and Loan, and Credit Union Accounts, see **Deposit Accounts**

Bonds

Burial Lots, see **Cemetery Lots**

Cash and Uncashed Checks

Cemetery Lots

Certificates of Deposit, see **Deposit Accounts**

Checks, see **Cash and Uncashed Checks**

Corporate Bonds, see **Bonds**

Credit Union Accounts, see **Deposit Accounts**

Death Benefits (Social Security, Veteran's Benefits, etc.)

Real Property

Refunds

Rental Property, see **Real Property**

Residence, see **Real Property**

Retirement Plans

Savings Accounts, see **Deposit Accounts**

Savings and Loan Accounts, see **Deposit Accounts**

Stocks

Stock Bonus Plan, see **Retirement Plans**

Tangible Personal Property

Trusts

U.S. Government Bonds, see **Bonds**

Videos, see **Family Memorabilia**

401(k), see **Retirement Plans**

403(b), see **Retirement Plans**

A SURVEY OF SPECIFIC TYPES OF ASSETS

This survey describes many of the types of property that an individual may have owned before death. Though few estates have all types of assets, it is useful for the Executor to know what types are possible. The most frequently owned types of assets are listed in this Summary of Assets in alphabetical order.

Each asset is discussed with respect to the following 11 questions.

1. "What is this asset?" identifies and describes the specific type of asset.
2. "What type of asset is this?" places each asset in one of three main categories: real estate, tangible personal property, or intangible personal property. These three main categories determine which state law applies to the distribution of this particular probate asset. For example, as described in Chapter 6, **real property**/real estate is land and whatever is attached to it. At death, the law of the state where the real estate is located governs sale and distribution of real estate by the probate court. **Personal property** is, simply stated, anything that is not real estate. There are two types of personal property, intangible personal property and tangible personal property. **Intangible personal property** is personal property that represents value but is not valuable in and of itself. For instance, an insurance policy is merely paper and ink that

represents value. Other examples of intangible personal property are cash, stocks, bonds, mutual funds, bank accounts, annuities, mortgages, and notes. No matter where the intangible personal property is located, the laws of the Decedent's state of domicile at death govern sale and distribution of intangible personal property by the probate court. **Tangible personal property** is property that has intrinsic value, that is, its usefulness is not merely representative. Tangible personal property includes jewelry, clothes, guns, furniture, clothing, books, china, crystal, silverware, and art. The laws of the state where tangible personal property is located govern the sale and distribution of tangible personal property by the probate court.

3. "How is this asset described?" sets out the information necessary to make a complete legal description of the asset on the probate inventory and on any tax returns that must be filed. The probate inventory and the estate tax return require the description of each asset to include the precise name of the owner or owners (see Chapter 3 for a discussion on importance of using the precise name), the mode of ownership (see Chapter 6 for a discussion of ownership modes), a complete legal description, and the name of any beneficiary.

4. "How is the property valued?" discusses how the Executor may obtain a value to report on the probate inventory and on the estate tax return. The discussion does not include the specific method by which an appraiser will arrive at a value and does not attempt to train the Executor as an appraiser. Instead, the section describes the sources the Executor can contact to obtain a value that is of sufficient authority for the IRS and the court. (See Chapter 6, Inventory and Valuation of Assets, for a discussion on valuation of assets.) The various methods of valuation that are recommended include a statement of account for intangible personal property such as bank, investment, and retirement accounts; an appraisal by a qualified appraiser for real estate, tangible personal property, and some types of intangible personal property; an informal statement of value from an individual who regularly deals with that type of property (for example, a realtor, a coin dealer, an auctioneer, or a reference book on asset value); a stock quotation in the *Wall Street Journal* or local newspaper for certain stocks, bonds, and mutual funds; and in some circumstances, the Executor may determine the value of an asset using his or her best judgment.

5. "How is information about the asset confirmed?" emphasizes the need for the Executor to obtain and preserve a written record of

all the information about ownership, legal description, and value that is used to report the asset on the inventory and tax returns.

6. "What are the management concerns regarding this asset?" The answer to this question highlights the most common concerns for managing this type of asset. (See Chapter 7, Management of Assets, for a general discussion of asset management issues.) The Executor has the responsibility and authority to manage only those assets that are part of the probate estate. All assets that are jointly owned with rights of survivorship and all assets that have a beneficiary designation are managed by the new owner.

7. "May this asset be liquidated during the administration of the estate?" deals with one particular aspect of estate management, that is, the sale of an asset during the administration of the estate. For each asset, the answer to this question focuses on the special concerns for sale or liquidation of that particular asset.

8. The Executor is responsible for filing the state and federal income tax returns of the estate on the Federal 1041 and the state income tax return. "What income does this asset generate?" alerts the Executor to the potential of income from an asset and, where applicable, identifies the report that shows the amount of the income that must be reported on the tax returns. (See Chapter 10, Taxes.)

9. "On what federal estate tax schedule is this asset reported?" The answer to this question helps the Executor complete the basic inventory information that the estate attorney and the tax preparer need to file the estate tax return.

10. "Is this asset reported on the probate inventory?" The short answer to this question is that if the Decedent owned the asset solely and there were no beneficiaries named to take the asset after death, then the asset is reported on the probate inventory. The comments under this question give the Executor guidance on what to look for with each type of asset to determine whether the asset was solely owned.

11. "How is this asset transferred out of the estate?" The answer to this question sketches the method of transferring each asset from the estate to the new owner and emphasizes the need for continued caution and care in handling the assets and the necessity of receipts and refunding agreements to protect the Executor. (See Transfer of Assets to New Owners in Chapter 12.)

Taken together, the summary for each asset gives the answers that the Executor must know to adequately deal with each asset in the probate estate.

ANNUITIES

What is an annuity? Originally, an annuity was simply a regular payment made to an individual called the annuitant for life or for a specific period of time, usually by an insurance company. The premium for an annuity could be paid over time or in a lump sum. Under federal tax laws that allow the deferral of payment of income tax on the income, a qualified annuity is an investment that permits tax-deferred accrual of income. An annuity that had not been annuitized before annuitant's death may have a death benefit payable to the estate of the Decedent or to named beneficiaries. If the annuity had been annuitized during annuitant's lifetime, the benefit of a regular payment may continue for another individual or all benefits may end at the death of the annuitant.

What type of asset is an annuity? An annuity is intangible personal property. No matter where the annuity contract or the annuity company is located, the laws of the Decedent's state of domicile govern the administration and distribution of the annuity in the probate estate.

How are annuities described? The description of the annuity includes the name of the company issuing the annuity contract, the contract number, the name of the owner, the name of the annuitant (that is, the person entitled to receive payments), and the names of beneficiaries, if any.

How are annuities valued? The insurance company will provide upon request a statement of the value of the annuity on the Decedent's date of death. An annuity for which all payments ceased at the Decedent's death has no value and the annuity is not reported on the probate inventory or on the federal estate tax return. The annuity may still be required to be reported under some other provision of tax law—for example, as a power of appointment.

How is information about annuities confirmed? The statement issued by the insurance company is the confirmation of ownership of the annuity, the full description, the beneficiaries, the value of the annuity, and any basis and tax deferral information.

What are the management concerns for annuities? The Executor must notify the annuity company of the death of the Decedent. The Executor must determine whether there is a lump sum payment or continuing benefits for a survivor by requesting that information from the annuity company. The Executor may file or assist in filing claims for annuities for which the Decedent was the annuitant.

May an annuity be liquidated during the administration of the estate?
The Executor must review the Will for instructions concerning the intangible personal property generally and the annuity specifically. An annuity for which the Decedent's estate is the beneficiary may be liquidated to raise cash to pay debts, expenses, or taxes; or to divide the proceeds among legatees. There are circumstances in which an annuity must be liquidated even when prohibited by the Will. See Chapter 9 for a discussion of these circumstances.

The liquidation of an annuity can be accomplished as soon as the Executor has been appointed by the court. The value of the annuity will be controlled by the annuity contract signed by the Decedent at the time the annuity was purchased. To liquidate the annuity, claim forms must be requested from the annuity company. The forms must be completed, signed by the Executor, and returned to the company. The proceeds will be disbursed by check from the annuity company. Money payable to the estate from an annuity must be deposited into the estate account. The court will order payment of the proceeds of the annuity and the Executor will write a check to distribute those funds. The Executor must keep a copy of all documents relating to the transaction and a copy of the payment check to support the accounting.

What income is generated by an annuity? An annuity generates income that is reported by the insurance company on a IRS Form 1099-R as the income is earned or as the income is withdrawn from a qualified annuity.

Because the income from the qualified annuity was not previously taxed as income, the full amount of the accrued income will be included as income of the estate or to the beneficiary of the plan. The proceeds from a qualified annuity that are in excess of the principal invested are not subject to the basis step-up rule.

On what federal estate tax schedule are annuities reported? Schedule I. Annuities.

Are annuities reported on the probate inventory? Generally, no. Usually the Decedent has named a beneficiary of the annuity. That beneficiary will receive payments directly from the company. However, if the Decedent named the estate as the beneficiary, if the named beneficiary has died before the Decedent and no contingent beneficiary was named, or if the named beneficiary chooses to disclaim the annuity, then the estate will be the beneficiary of the annuity and the annuity will be reported on the probate inventory.

The Decedent may have placed intangible personal property such as an annuity into a trust that transfers the asset to a beneficiary at the

Decedent's death. The annuity is not reported on the probate inventory if it is held in such a trust.

How are annuities transferred out of the estate? If the annuity will remain as an investment, transfer of ownership forms and instructions for transfer must be requested from the annuity company. Those forms must be completed, signed as instructed, and returned to the annuity company. The annuity company will confirm the transfer of ownership by a statement sent to the new owner.

ANTIQUES

What are antiques? Antiques are items that were made in a bygone era such as furnishings, clothing, toys, decorations, machines, and utensils.

What type of assets are antiques? Antiques are tangible personal property. The laws of the state where antiques are located govern administration, sale, and distribution of antiques in the probate estate.

How are antiques described? The description of antiques must include a complete description of each piece; the name of the manufacturer; the date of manufacture, if known; the type of material from which the item is made; and any distinguishing features or marks.

How are antiques valued? The value on the date of death and, if necessary, the alternate valuation date must be determined by the Executor. The alternate valuation date is the date exactly six months after the date of death. Valuation of antiques requires that a market for the piece be identified and a comparable market price be established. For an estate that is not required to file a federal estate tax return and where appraisal by a licensed appraiser is not required by state statute, valuation by an antiques dealer may be sufficient. An independent appraisal is recommended for all antiques of significant value. If an estate tax return will be filed, an appraisal by a licensed appraiser is required for any antique that is worth more than $3,000. If antiques are sold in an arm's length sale before the estate is distributed, the sale price of the antiques is the fair market value. If a value different than the sale price was reported to the court on an inventory or to the state and federal governments on any tax return, the inventory and any tax returns need to be amended to reflect the fair market value.

How is information about antiques confirmed? The written statement of the appraiser or dealer will confirm the description and the value of the antique.

What are the management concerns for antiques? The Executor must assure that all tangible personal property is safely stored and adequately insured. Some antiques are affected by heat, light, cold, and humidity. Consult with an antiques dealer for special instructions for care of antiques. Early distribution or sale of these assets will minimize the risk of loss and the costs of storage, maintenance, and insurance. Personal and household items, including antiques, are the subject of state spousal and minors' allowances. The Executor should consult with the estate attorney to determine whether the antiques will be considered part of the spousal and minors' allowance.

May antiques be sold during the administration of the estate? The Executor must review the Will and any personal property memorandum for instructions concerning the distribution or sale of tangible personal property. Antiques may be sold to pay debts, expenses, or taxes; to avoid the costs of storage, insurance, and maintenance; to prevent losses in value because of a declining market; or to divide the proceeds of a sale among legatees. There are circumstances in which assets must be sold even when their sale is prohibited by the Will. See Chapter 9 for a discussion of these circumstances.

Antiques that are located in a state other than the state in which the primary probate proceeding is being conducted will be subject to an ancillary, which is an additional and supplementary probate proceeding for administration, sale, and distribution of the antiques. The Executor must consult with the estate attorney to determine how, when, and where to begin the ancillary probate proceedings.

The sale of antiques can be accomplished as soon as the Executor has been appointed by the court and has proper authority for the sale. The Executor must review the Will to be sure that it expressly permits the Executor to sell tangible personal property. If the Will does not give express authority to sell personal property, the estate attorney must obtain a court order specifically authorizing the Executor to sell personal property.

In seeking the court order, the petition must state that the sale is necessary to pay debts, expenses, taxes, or legacies; that the value of the asset may decline during the administration of the estate; or that the sale of the antique is in the best interest of the estate for some other reason. When none of these conditions is met, all interested persons can agree in writing that the sale is in the best interest of the estate and the court will give permission for the sale.

For obvious reasons, the sale of estate property to a family member or associate of the Executor is prohibited by state statute even where the Executor has authority to sell property without court supervision. Such a sale is known as self-dealing. See Chapter 8 for a discussion concerning the requirement to avoid self-dealing. This requirement may be overcome if the duty not to self-deal is waived in the Will, or if the court, with full knowledge of the relationship between the buyer and the Executor, approves of the buyer and the sale price before the sale.

Within the limits of the state requirement for a minimum price, setting the sale price is the responsibility of the Executor. The advice of the estate attorney or an antiques dealer will be a helpful guide, but the Executor has the final decision. Although the Executor should attempt to get the best possible price, it is also important to complete the sale within a reasonable time. Storage costs and insurance are expenses that cannot be recovered. A prompt sale removes these expenses from the estate.

State statutes control the minimum sale price for personal property. This required price is usually a percentage, for example, 80 percent, of the value reported in the probate inventory. The estate attorney must be consulted before any asset is sold to ensure that the sale price complies with the required minimum price. If there are no buyers at the required minimum price after the antique has been offered for sale for a reasonable time, the estate attorney must seek court authority to amend the probate inventory to reflect the lower market value and to reduce the minimum sale price.

Antiques should be sold "as is," and the buyers must be required to inspect the pieces for themselves or to hire professionals to inspect for them. Whether the sale is accomplished by private sale, at an estate sale, or by auction, the Executor should make no statements concerning the condition of the property to the buyers. The statements of the Executor may be considered by the buyer as a warranty or guarantee of the condition of the property. This is an area of potentially serious personal liability for the Executor and for the estate. If the Executor's statements prove to be incorrect, the buyers may make a claim for their losses against the estate and against the Executor personally.

Antiques may be sold at an estate sale or by auction. Sale of tangible personal property by a local professional is highly recommended for the reasons set out in detail in Chapter 8. The Executor should contact several reputable estate sale, at an estate sale, or auction companies to discuss the timing of the sale, sale costs and commissions, reserved bids, and advertising. These professionals will charge a percentage of the total sale proceeds as their sales commission. The Executor or estate attorney should negotiate and confirm in writing a reasonable commission before the sale. This cost is a reasonable expense of the estate and will be paid from estate assets. The professional must provide a detailed receipt for items sold and the amount of the proceeds.

In all cases, an accounting of the sale must be filed and approved by the court before the estate can be closed and the Executor discharged, even when the court ordered the sale or the Will waived the court's supervision. The Executor must keep a copy of all documents relating to the sale and a copy of the payment check to support the accounting of the sale. All proceeds of a sale must be deposited into the estate account for administration and await the court's order of distribution.

What income is generated by antiques? Generally, antiques do not generate ordinary income. The proceeds of a sale are taxable gain if they exceed the basis in the assets and deductible as a loss if the basis exceeds the proceeds. However, because the basis is stepped up at death to the market value on the date of death, the sale price and the basis are usually the same and there is no gain or loss. A gain arises only when the value of the asset increases between the date of death and the sale date. A loss arises when the value of the asset decreases between date of death and the sale date. See Chapter 10 for a discussion of basis in the sale of estate assets.

On what federal estate tax schedule are antiques reported? Schedule F. Other Miscellaneous Property.

Are antiques reported on the inventory? Generally, yes. Antiques usually do not have a title or other document of ownership that can transfer the assets at death by a beneficiary designation or show ownership by joint tenants with right of survivorship. The Decedent may have placed tangible personal property such as antiques into a trust that transfers the property to a beneficiary at Decedent's death. The antiques are not reported on the probate inventory if they are held in such a trust.

How are antiques transferred out of the estate? The transfer of ownership of the antiques from the estate to the Legatee is made by court order either as an early distribution during the time the estate is being probated or in the final distribution of the estate. The transfer is made by actual delivery of possession into the hands or the control of the Legatee. The Executor should obtain a receipt from the Legatee before or at the time the asset is delivered. If the asset cannot be delivered directly but must be shipped, then the determination of whether the estate or the recipient will pay the cost of shipping must be part of the court's order for distribution. The Executor must also ensure that the asset is adequately insured until delivery to the Legatee. Insurance for the risk of loss or damage to the asset during shipping must be purchased as part of the shipping cost. An ancillary, that is, an additional and supplementary, probate proceeding may be necessary to obtain a court order of distribution if tangible personal property is located in a state other that the state in which the primary probate proceedings' are being conducted.

ART

What is art? Art can be paintings, pencil drawings, watercolors, glass, vases, stained glass, sculpture, and a myriad other items. Art is, as they say, in the eye of the beholder.

What type of asset is art? Art is tangible personal property. The laws of the state where the art is located govern the administration, sale, and distribution of art in the probate estate.

How is art described? The description of art should include the type and size of the art object, the materials used, a description of the subject matter, the artist's signature, and any distinguishing marks or inscriptions.

How is art valued? The value on the date of death and, if necessary, the alternate valuation date must be determined. The alternate valuation date is the date exactly six months after the date of death. Valuation of art requires that a market for the piece be identified and a comparable market price be established. Appraisal by someone with knowledge and experience with this type of art will be required. An independent appraisal is recommended for all art pieces of significant value. For an estate that is not required to file an estate tax return, valuation by an art dealer may be sufficient. If an estate tax return will be filed, an appraisal by a licensed appraiser is required for any art that is worth more than $3,000. All single works of art with a claimed value of $20,000 or more must be referred to the IRS Art Advisory Panel for Review. If art is sold in an arm's length sale before the estate is ordered to be distributed, the price for which the art sold is the fair market value. If a value different than the sale price was reported to the court on an inventory or to the state and federal governments on any tax return, the inventory and any tax returns may need to be amended to reflect the fair market value.

How is information about art confirmed? The written statement of the appraiser or the art dealer will confirm the description and the value of the art piece. The purchase receipt and a catalog listing are also evidence of the value and may provide a description of the piece.

What are the management concerns for art? The Executor must assure safe storage and adequate insurance of all art works. Consult with an art dealer for special instructions for storage, handling, and care of the piece. Early distribution or sale of art works will minimize the risk of loss and the costs of storage, maintenance, and insurance. Personal and household items, including art, are the subject of state spousal and minors' allowances. The Executor should consult with the estate attorney to determine whether the art will be considered part of the spousal and minors' allowance.

May art be sold during the administration of the estate? The Executor must review the Will and any personal property memorandum for instructions concerning the distribution or sale of tangible personal property generally and art specifically. Art may be sold to pay debts, expenses, or taxes; to avoid the costs of storage, insurance, and maintenance; to prevent losses in value because of a declining market; or to divide the proceeds of the sale among legatees. There are circumstances in which art must be sold even when its sale is prohibited by the Will. See Chapter 9 for a discussion of these circumstances.

Art that is located in a state other than the state in which the primary probate proceeding is being conducted will be subject to an ancillary, that is, an additional and supplementary, probate proceeding for administration, sale, and distribution of the art. The Executor must consult with the estate attorney to determine how, when and where to begin the ancillary probate proceedings.

The sale of art can be accomplished as soon as the Executor has been appointed by the court and has proper authority for the sale. The Executor must review the Will to be sure that it expressly permits the Executor to sell tangible personal property. If the Will does not give express authority to sell personal property, the estate attorney must obtain a court order specifically authorizing the Executor to do so.

In seeking the court order, the petition must state that the sale is necessary to pay debts, expenses, taxes, or legacies; that the value of the art may decline during the administration of the estate; or that the sale of the art is in the best interest of the estate for some other reason. When none of these conditions is met, all interested persons can agree in writing that the sale is in the best interest of the estate and the court will give permission for the sale.

For obvious reasons, the sale of estate property to a family member or associate of the Executor is prohibited by state statute even where the Executor has authority to sell property without court supervision. Such a sale is known as self-dealing. See Chapter 8 for a discussion concerning the requirement to avoid self-dealing. This requirement may be overcome if the duty not to self-deal is waived in the Will, or if the court, with full knowledge of the relationship, approves of the buyer and the sale price before the sale.

Within the limits of the state requirement for a minimum price, setting the sale price is the responsibility of the Executor. The advice of the estate attorney or an art dealer will be a helpful guide, but the Executor has the final decision. Although the Executor should attempt to get the best possible price, it is also important to complete the sale within a reasonable time. Storage costs and insurance are expenses that cannot be recovered. A prompt sale removes these expenses from the estate.

State statutes control the minimum sale price for personal property. This required price is usually a percentage, for example, 80 percent, of the value reported in the probate inventory. The estate attorney must be consulted before any asset is sold to ensure that the sale price is at least the required minimum price. If there are no buyers at the required minimum price after the art has been offered for sale for a reasonable length of time, the estate attorney must seek court authority to amend the probate inventory to reflect the lower market value and to reduce the minimum sale price.

Art should be sold "as is," and the buyers must be required to inspect the pieces for themselves or to hire professionals to inspect for them. Whether the sale is accomplished by private sale or by auction, the Executor should make no statements concerning the condition of the property to the buyers. The statements of the Executor may be considered by the buyer as a warranty or guarantee of the condition of the property. This is an area of potentially serious liability for the Executor personally and for the estate. If the Executor's statements prove to be incorrect, the buyers may make a claim for their losses against the estate and against the Executor personally.

Art may be sold at an estate sale, on consignment by an art dealer, by private sale, or by auction. Sale of tangible personal property by a professional is highly recommended for the reasons set out in detail in Chapter 8. The Executor should contact several reputable art dealers or auction companies to discuss the timing of the sale, sale costs and commissions, insurance, reserved bids, and advertising. These professionals will charge a percentage of the total sale proceeds as their sales commission. The Executor or estate attorney should negotiate and confirm in writing a reasonable commission before the sale. This cost is an expense of the estate and will be paid from estate assets. The professional must provide a detailed receipt for items sold and the amount of the proceeds.

In all cases, an accounting of the sale must be filed and approved by the court before the estate can be closed and the Executor discharged, even when the court ordered the sale or the Will waived the court's supervision. The Executor must keep a copy of all documents relating to the sale and a copy of the payment check to support the accounting.

All proceeds must be deposited into the estate account for administration and to await the court's order of distribution.

What income is generated by art? Generally, art does not generate ordinary income. In the instance where art has been leased, the lease payment is income. The proceeds of a sale of art is taxable gain if those proceeds exceed the basis in the assets and is deductible as a loss if the basis exceeds the proceeds. However, because the basis is stepped up at death to the market value on the date of death, the sale price and the basis are usually the same and there is no gain or loss. A gain arises when the value of the asset increases between the date of death and the sale date. A loss occurs when the value of the asset decreases between date of death and the sale date. See Chapter 10 for a discussion of basis in the sale of estate assets.

On what federal estate tax schedule is art reported? Schedule F. Other Miscellaneous Property.

Is art reported on the probate inventory? Generally, yes. Art works do not have a legal title or other document of ownership that can be transferred at death by a beneficiary designation. However, the Decedent may have placed tangible personal property such as art into a trust that transfers the property to a beneficiary at Decedent's death. The art is not reported on the probate inventory if it is held in such a trust.

How is art transferred out of the estate? The transfer of ownership of art from the estate to the Legatee is made by court order either as an early distribution during the time the estate is being probated or in the final distribution of the estate. After obtaining the order of the court, the Executor should obtain a receipt from the Legatee and deliver the asset directly to the Legatee. If the asset must be shipped, then the determination of whether the estate or the recipient will pay the cost of shipping must be part of the court's order for distribution. Insurance for the risk of loss or damage to the asset during shipping must be purchased as part of the shipping cost. An ancillary, that is, an additional and supplementary, probate proceeding may be necessary to transfer tangible personal property located in a state other than the state in which the primary probate proceedings are being conducted.

AUTOMOBILES AND OTHER MOTOR VEHICLES

What are motor vehicles? Motor vehicles are machines used to transport persons, animals, and materials for business, personal, or recreational purposes. Automobiles, trucks, vans, recreational vehicles, farm machinery, boats, trailers, snowmobiles, motorcycles, and airplanes are examples of motor vehicles.

What type of assets are motor vehicles? Motor vehicles are tangible personal property. The laws of the state where each motor vehicle is located govern the administration, sale, and distribution of motor vehicles in the probate estate.

How are motor vehicles described? Motor vehicles are described by the year of manufacture, the model name, the name of the manufacturer, the vehicle identification number, and any other information that distinguishes this vehicle (for example, the engine size, custom work, or extra features). Unlike most other items of tangible personal property, motor vehicles often have a title. The title to a motor vehicle shows the name of the owner, the make and model of the vehicle, the vehicle identification number, and any pay-on-death beneficiary on the face of the title. (See Tangible Personal Property in this Summary of Assets.)

How is a motor vehicle valued? The date-of-death value and, if necessary, the value on the alternate valuation date, for automobiles, trucks, motorcycles, boats, recreational vehicles, planes, and manufactured houses can be obtained by reference to the National Automobile Dealer Association (NADA) published values that are available at car dealerships, local banks, the public library, and on the Internet at www.NADA.com. The value of used farm machinery by region may be obtained by reference to the North American Equipment Dealers Association (NAEDA) publication *Official Guide* or on the Internet at www.NAEDA.com. For more unusual or older equipment it may be necessary to refer to the *Ad Price Survey*. Consider any circumstances such as condition and mileage that may cause the value of the motor vehicle to vary from the published value. When the motor vehicle has no published value and the state does not require appraisal by a licensed appraiser, an appraisal of the value by a dealer may be sufficient. Keep in mind that a dealer may value the vehicle below the retail market value if the dealer also intends to offer to purchase the vehicle for resale. If a federal estate tax return must be filed or the state law requires appraisal by a licensed appraiser, then when there is no published value, the value of motor vehicles must be determined by a licensed appraiser.

If a motor vehicle is sold in an arm's length sale before the estate is distributed, the price for which the motor vehicle sold is the fair market value. If a value different than the sale price was reported to the court on an inventory or to the state and federal governments on any tax return, the inventory and any tax returns need to be amended to reflect the fair market value.

How is information about motor vehicles confirmed? The title will confirm the ownership, the vehicle description, the vehicle identification number, and any beneficiary designation. For motor vehicles without a title, the statement of the dealer or appraiser will confirm the description and condition. A copy of the published NADA or NAEDA value, a copy of a dealer's statement of value, or a copy of the appraisal will confirm the value of the vehicle.

What are the management concerns for motor vehicles? The Executor is responsible for assuring that motor vehicles are not operated by anyone without proper liability and collision insurance. The Executor must secure the keys to any car or other motor vehicle owned solely by the Decedent. The Executor is responsible for storing and maintaining motor vehicles. Careful maintenance of vehicles is necessary to avoid deterioration. Consult with a mechanic or the maintenance department of a car dealership for special instructions. The storage and maintenance of a motor vehicle is an expense of the estate until the vehicle is sold or distributed. Sale or early distribution of motor vehicles by court order will minimize the costs of storage, maintenance, and insurance. Automobiles and other motor vehicles are the subject of state spousal and minors' allowances. The Executor should consult with the estate attorney to determine whether the motor vehicles will be considered part of the spousal and minors' allowances.

Can motor vehicles be sold during the administration of the estate? The Executor must review the Will and any personal property memorandum for instructions concerning distribution or sale of tangible personal property generally and any motor vehicles specifically. Motor vehicles may be sold to pay debts, expenses, or taxes; to avoid the costs of storage, insurance, and maintenance; to prevent losses in value because of a declining market; or to divide the proceeds of sale among Legatees. There are circumstances in which motor vehicles must be sold even when their sale is prohibited by the Will. See Chapter 9 for a discussion of these circumstances.

Motor vehicles that are located in a state other than the state in which the primary probate proceeding is being conducted will be subject to an ancillary, that is, an additional and supplementary, probate proceeding for administration, sale, and distribution of the vehicle. The Executor must consult with the estate attorney to determine how, when, and where to begin the ancillary probate proceedings.

The sale of motor vehicles can be accomplished as soon as the Executor has been appointed by the court and has proper authority for the sale. The Executor must review the Will to be sure that it expressly permits the Executor to sell tangible personal property and that the motor vehicle is not specifically given to someone. If the Will does not give express authority to sell personal property, the estate attorney must obtain a court order specifically authorizing the Executor to sell personal property.

In seeking the court order, the petition must state that the sale is necessary to pay debts, expenses, taxes, or legacies; that the value of the asset may decline during the administration of the estate; or that the sale of the vehicle is in the best interest of the estate for some other reason. When none of these conditions is met, all interested persons can agree in writing that the sale is in the best interest of the estate and the court will give permission for the sale.

For obvious reasons, the sale of estate property to a family member or associate of the Executor is prohibited by state statute even where the Executor has authority to sell property without court supervision. Such a sale is known as self-dealing. See Chapter 8 for a discussion concerning the requirement to avoid self-dealing. This requirement may be overcome if the duty not to self-deal is waived in the Will, or if the court, with full knowledge of the relationship, approves of the buyer and the sale price before the sale.

Within the limits of the state requirement for a minimum price, setting the sale price is the responsibility of the Executor. The advice of the estate attorney or a dealer in motor vehicles property will be helpful, but the Executor has the final decision. Although the Executor should attempt to get the best possible price, it is also important to complete the sale within a reasonable length of time. Storage and maintenance costs, personal property taxes, and insurance are expenses that cannot be recovered. A prompt sale removes these expenses from the estate.

State statutes control the minimum sale price for personal property. This required price is usually a percentage, for example, 80 percent, of the value reported in the probate inventory. The estate attorney must be consulted before any asset is sold to ensure that the sale price is at least the required minimum price. If there are no buyers at the required minimum price after the vehicle has been offered for sale for a reasonable length of time, the estate attorney must seek court approval to amend the probate inventory to reflect the lower market value and to reduce the minimum sale price.

Any motor vehicle should be sold "as is," and the buyers must be required to inspect the vehicle or hire a professional mechanic to inspect for them. Whether the sale is accomplished by private sale or by auction, the Executor should make no statements concerning the condition of the vehicle to the buyers. The statements of the Executor may be considered by the buyer as a warranty or guarantee of the condition of the property. This is an area of potentially serious liability for the Executor personally and for the estate. If the Executor's statements prove to be incorrect, the buyers may make a claim for their losses against the estate and against the Executor personally.

Motor vehicles may be sold at an estate sale, privately to an individual or a dealer, on consignment, or by auction. Sale of vehicles by a professional is highly recommended for anyone not familiar with vehicle sales. The Executor should contact reputable estate sale, car dealer, or auction companies to discuss the timing of the sale, sale costs and commissions, reserved bids, insurance, and advertising. These professionals will charge a percentage of the total sale proceeds as their commission. The Executor or estate attorney should negotiate and confirm in writing a reasonable commission before the sale. This cost is a reasonable expense of the estate and will be paid from estate assets. The professional must provide a receipt for the vehicle sold and the amount of the proceeds.

Even when the court ordered the sale or the Will waived the court's supervision, an accounting of the sale must be filed and approved by the court before the estate can be closed and the Executor discharged. The Executor must keep a copy of all documents relating to the sale and a copy of the payment check to support the accounting. All proceeds of a sale must be deposited into the estate account for administration and to await the court's order of distribution.

What income is generated by motor vehicles? Generally, motor vehicles do not generate ordinary income. However, if the vehicle was leased to a third party prior to Decedent's death, then the ongoing lease payment is ordinary income to the estate of the Decedent. For income tax purposes, the proceeds of the sale of a motor vehicle are taxable gain if those proceeds exceed the basis in the vehicle and deductible as a loss if the basis exceeds the proceeds. However, because the basis is stepped up at death to the market value on the date of death, the sale price and the basis are usually the same and there is no gain or loss. A gain arises when the value of the vehicle increases between the date of death and the sale date. A loss arises when the value of the vehicle decreases between date of death and the sale date. See Chapter 10 for a discussion of basis in the sale of estate assets.

On what federal estate tax schedule are motor vehicles reported? Schedule F. Other Miscellaneous Property.

Are motor vehicles reported on the probate inventory? Motor vehicles are often owned solely by the Decedent without a co-owner or a beneficiary and must be reported on the probate inventory. However, the title to a motor vehicle provides the opportunity to name a co-owner and, in some states, a Transfer-On-Death beneficiary. If there is a co-owner or a Transfer-On-Death beneficiary who survives the Decedent, the motor vehicle will not be reported on the probate inventory.

The Decedent may have placed tangible personal property such as a motor vehicle into a trust that transfers the asset to a beneficiary at Decedent's death. The motor vehicle is not reported on the probate inventory if it is held in such a trust.

How are motor vehicles transferred out of the estate? The transfer of ownership of a motor vehicle from the estate to the Legatee is made by court order, either as an early distribution during the time the estate is being probated or in the final distribution of the estate. The transfer is made by actual delivery of possession of the motor vehicle into the hands or control of the Legatee. The Executor should obtain a Receipt and Refunding Agreement from the Legatee before or at the time the asset is delivered. If the vehicle must be shipped, then the determination of whether the estate or the recipient will pay the cost of shipping must be part of the court's order for distribution. The Executor must also ensure that the asset is adequately insured until delivery to the Legatee. Insurance for the risk of loss or damage to the asset must be purchased as part of the shipping cost. An ancillary, that is, an additional and supplementary, probate proceeding may be necessary to transfer tangible personal property located in a state other than the state in which the primary probate proceedings are being conducted.

The Executor will transfer the title to a motor vehicle owned by the Decedent's estate by completing the form usually found on the back of the title and the other forms required by the state department of motor vehicles. The Executor should discuss with the attorney and the state department of motor vehicles the local law for transfer of the ownership of a motor vehicle.

BONDS (Corporate Bonds, Municipal Bonds, U.S. Government and Agency Bonds)

What are bonds? Bonds are evidence of debts owed by a government or corporation. Bonds are purchased for par value (face value), for a premium (more than the face value), or for a discount (less than the face value). Almost all bonds pay interest to maturity; some bonds have coupons for interest attached that must be clipped and redeemed. All bonds can be redeemed for face value at maturity. The types of bonds most commonly held in estates are mentioned here. U.S. Government Bonds include E, EE, H, HH, I Savings Bonds and Treasury bills, notes, and bonds and are guaranteed by the federal government. Agency Bonds are bonds backed, but not guaranteed, by the federal government, and include Student Loan Marketing Association Bonds (Sallie Mae Bonds), Federal National Mortgage Association Bonds (Fannie Mae Bonds), Federal Home Loan Mortgage Corporation Bonds (Freddie Mac Bonds), and Government National Mortgage Association Bonds (Ginnie Mae Bonds). Municipal Bonds include general obligation bonds, special tax bonds, revenue bonds, and industrial revenue bonds (IRBs). **Corporate Bonds** include bonds of private corporations, including mortgage bonds, equipment trust certificates, debentures, convertible bonds, variable interest rate bonds, and zero-coupon bonds. Bond funds are mentioned briefly in the section Mutual Funds in this Summary of Assets.

What type of assets are bonds? Bonds are intangible personal property. No matter where the government or corporation that issued the bond is located and no matter where the bonds are stored, the laws of the Decedent's state of domicile govern the administration sale and distribution of bonds in the probate estate.

How are bonds described? Generally, bonds are described by the type of bond, name of the issuer, the face value of the bond, the interest rate, date of issue, maturity date, a CUSIP number, the name of the owner or owners, the mode of ownership (whether owned solely, with another as tenants in common, or as joint tenants with right of survivorship), the name of any beneficiary, and restrictions on the bond. If the bond is held in book-entry form, the description also includes the account number and name of the investment company that holds the bond.

How are bonds valued? The value of marketable bonds is determined by the sale price on the day of valuation. The Executor must request the date of death value, and if necessary on marketable bonds, the value on the alternate valuation date, which is six months after Decedent's date of death. Marketable bonds include corporate bonds, municipal bonds, and U.S. Government Treasury Bills, Notes, and Bonds and Agency Bonds. The value of the marketable bonds will vary with the quality of the bond. The quality of a bond is rated on the risk that the issuer of the bond will not be able to repay the interest or the principal on the bond, the interest rate that the bond pays, and consumer confidence.

If the bond is held in book-entry form, the value of the bond can be obtained by requesting a written statement of the value on the

Decedent's date of death from the investment company that holds the bond or from the U.S. Treasury for U.S. Government Bonds held in Treasury Direct. If the bond is held in certificate form, the value of some bonds can be determined from the quotes in a financial newspaper such as the *Wall Street Journal* or from the Internet at a site such as www.askresearch.com. Ask the estate attorney for assistance. A registered representative of an investment company can also provide a statement of value for a bond that is not held in book-entry form. There may be a fee for this service.

The value of nonmarketable governmental bonds, such as Series E, EE, I, H, and HH Bonds, are determined by referring to tables published by the U.S. government.

How is information about bonds confirmed? When bonds are held in book-entry form, the statement from the company or *Bond Direct* that holds the bonds will confirm the owner, description, beneficiaries, and value. The face of the bond certificate confirms the description, issue date, interest rate, maturity date, and ownership of a bond held in certificate form. The date-of-death values for bonds that are held in certificate form can be obtained from a copy of the *Wall Street Journal* or other financial newspaper, from the public library reference section, or on an Internet site, such as www.askresearch.com. Keep a copy of the newspaper or print a copy of the Internet screen you use to determine the values. The written statement of the financial institution or investment company can also confirm the value of a bond held in certificate form. A fee may be charged for this service.

What are the management concerns for bonds? The Executor must assure that bonds held in certificate form are safely stored either by depositing them with an investment brokerage company to be placed in a book-entry account or by placing them in a safe deposit box held in the name of the estate. The Executor must review the bond holdings for sale before maturity. The risk of default for each bond should be determined by reference to a standard rating system to help judge whether the bonds should be held or sold. Consult *Moody's Bond Record* and *Moody's Manuals* or *Standard and Poor's Bond Guide* and *Standard and Poor's Corporation Records* for bond ratings. The Executor must examine the bonds to determine whether there is income to collect. Some bonds have coupons that must be clipped and redeemed to obtain payment of interest. If the bonds have stopped earning interest, the Executor must consider redeeming the bonds and placing the proceeds in an investment that bears interest. Unless the Will authorizes sale of personal property, the Executor may not sell bonds without a court order. Bonds may not be distributed to any Legatee until the court orders distribution.

May bonds be sold during the administration of the estate? The Executor must review the Will for instructions concerning the sale of intangible personal property generally and bonds specifically. Bonds may be sold to pay debts, expenses, or taxes; to prevent losses in value because of a declining market; or to divide the proceeds of an asset among Legatees. The Executor may need to consider sale of bonds for other reasons as well. There are circumstances in which bonds must be sold even when their sale is prohibited by the Will. See Chapter 9 for a discussion of these circumstances.

The sale of bonds can be accomplished as soon as the Executor has been appointed by the court and has proper authority for the sale. The Executor must review the Will to be sure that it expressly permits the Executor to sell personal property. If the Will does not give express authority to sell personal property, the estate attorney must obtain a court order expressly authorizing the Executor to sell personal property.

In seeking the court order, the petition must state that the sale is necessary to pay debts, expenses, taxes, or legacies; that there is a risk of loss of value in the bond; or that the sale of the bond is in the best interest of the estate for some other reason. When none of these conditions is met, all interested persons can agree in writing that the sale is in the best interest of the estate and the court will give permission for the sale.

The sale price or redemption value of nonmarketable bonds is the value published by the U. S. government. For sale of nonmarketable bonds issued by the U.S. Treasury including Series E, EE, H, HH, and I Bonds contact a Federal Reserve Bank or a local financial institution that handles treasury bonds.

The sale price of marketable bonds is controlled by the market price at the time of the sale. For sale of marketable bonds held in book-entry form in a brokerage investment account, including Treasury Bills, Notes, and Bonds, agency bonds, municipal and corporate bonds, the Executor or estate attorney should request instructions for sale from the account representative of the company that holds the bonds. For marketable bonds held in book-entry form with *TreasuryDirect*, contact www.publicdebt.treas.gov. For marketable bonds held in certificate form, the Executor can contact an investment company. The account representative will provide instructions for sale of these bonds. The Executor should inquire about transaction fees before the sale. These transactions can take several communications before all the requirements are fulfilled. Be persistent and patient!

For obvious reasons, the sale of estate property to a family member or associate of the Executor is prohibited by state statute even where the Executor has authority to sell property without court supervision.

Such a sale is known as self-dealing. See Chapter 8 for a discussion concerning the requirement to avoid self-dealing. This requirement may be overcome if the duty not to self-deal is waived in the Will, or if the court, with full knowledge of the relationship, approves of the buyer and the sale price before the sale.

Whether the court ordered the sale or the Will waived the court's supervision, an accounting of the sale must be filed and approved by the court before the estate can be closed and the Executor discharged. The Executor must keep a copy of all documents relating to the sale and a copy of the payment check to support the accounting. All proceeds must be deposited into the estate account until the court orders distribution.

What income is generated by bonds? Interest is paid on bonds. The bond issuer will send IRS Form 1099-INT to the registered owner of the bond to report that interest. The sale of marketable bonds before maturity can generate a loss or gain that is also reportable as income. The proceeds of the sale of bonds is taxable as a capital gain if those proceeds exceed the basis in the asset, and a loss is deductible if the basis exceeds the proceeds. However, because the basis is stepped up to the market value on the Decedent's date of death, the sale price and the basis are usually the same and there is no gain or loss. A gain arises when the value of the asset increases between the date of death and the sale date. A loss arises when the value of the asset decreases between date of death and the sale date. See Chapter 10 for a discussion of basis and gain in the sale of estate assets.

The increase in the value of Series E, EE, and I Savings Bonds do not have the benefit of the basis step-up rule. Federal income tax must be paid on the income accrued before the Decedent's death in U.S. Savings Bonds. The tax on the interest in E or EE bonds may have been paid on an annual basis. When a Series E or EE Savings Bond is redeemed, the bank or financial institution will issue a 1099-INT showing the interest earned and the social security or tax identification number to which that income will be reported. If the Decedent had elected to report the interest income each year on his or her 1040 income tax return, rather than when the bond is redeemed, the amount of interest shown on the 1099-INT will not be reduced by the total amount of income the Decedent had already reported in the prior years. A copy of the Decedent's 1040 federal income tax returns with Schedule B will be necessary to show that the interest was already reported and taxed in prior years.

Before redeeming a bond, the Executor must determine the next date upon which interest will be posted to the bond. Any interest that has not yet been posted to the bond will be lost. It is possible to unwittingly forfeit up to six months of interest by redeeming the bond before this interest is posted.

On what federal estate tax schedule are bonds reported? Schedule B. Stocks and Bonds.

Are bonds reported on the probate inventory? Bonds may be owned by the Decedent solely and have no pay-on-death beneficiary named. These bonds plus the interest accrued on the bonds are part of the Decedent's probate estate, reported on the probate inventory, and subject to probate administration. However, bonds often have a co-owner or a pay-on-death beneficiary named. If there is a joint tenant with right of survivorship on the bond, that co-owner will own the bond after the death of the Decedent. If there is a named beneficiary who survives, that beneficiary will own the bond after the Decedent's death. If there is no beneficiary named, the beneficiary does not survive, or the beneficiary disclaims the account, the estate will be the owner of the bond and the bond must be included in the probate inventory. However, the Decedent may have placed bonds into a trust that transfers those bonds to a beneficiary at the Decedent's death. The bonds are not reported on the probate inventory if they are held in such a trust.

How are bonds transferred out of the estate? Upon the court's order, the Executor will distribute the bonds to the new owners. Bonds are transferred in-kind. An in-kind distribution means that the bond is transferred directly into the name of the new owner.

When bonds are held in book-entry form, the bonds in the account can be distributed directly into an account owned by the new owner. To receive this in-kind distribution of bonds held in book-entry form, each Legatee either must already have or must open a brokerage account in his or her own name before the distribution. The Legatee's investment account number and the investment company's Depository Transfer Clearing (DTC) number must be provided to the Executor by each Legatee. The account number and the DTC number for each legatee will be included in the Letter of Instruction that is sent to the holder or transfer agent of the bonds. When bonds are transferred "in-kind" to a new account, there is no reinvestment fee for the new owner. There may be, however, a transaction fee. The Legatees and the Executor should inquire about fees prior to requesting the transfer. If bonds are liquidated before distribution and the Legatees are paid in cash, a sales commission or fee will be charged for reinvestment by the new owner.

When the bonds are held in certificate form, the bonds can be place into book-entry form to ease transfer. If the bonds are to be reissued in certificate form, the transaction must be conducted through the bond's transfer agent. Seek the assistance of the estate attorney or an investment advisor to find the name and address of the transfer agent for the bond.

The estate attorney or the Executor must request instructions for transfer from each transfer agent or from the registered representative of the investment account. Usually the transfer agent or the registered representative will require a certified death certificate, a Letter of Instruction giving precise instructions for distribution signed by the Executor with the signature Medallion Guaranteed, a copy of the Letters Testamentary certified by the clerk of the court in the last 30 to 60 days, and a copy of the court's order of distribution certified by the clerk of the court in the last 30 to 60 days. A tax waiver for state death taxes and an Affidavit of Domicile may also be required. The instructions of the transfer agent or the registered representative should be followed carefully. These transactions can take several communications with the transfer agent or registered representative before all the requirements are fulfilled to the transfer agent's or brokerage company's satisfaction. Be persistent and patient.

CASH AND UNCASHED CHECKS

What are cash and uncashed checks? The currency and coin from any country that is in current use in that country is cash. A check is a signed, written document that orders payment to the Decedent or the Decedent's estate from an account.

What type of assets are cash and uncashed checks? Cash and checks are intangible personal property. No matter where the intangible personal property is located, the laws of the Decedent's state of domicile govern distribution of cash and uncashed checks in the administration of the probate estate.

How are cash and uncashed checks described? Cash is simply described as "cash" and the amount is stated. Checks are described by stating the source of the check, the signer, the payee, the purpose for the payment, and the amount of the check.

How are cash and checks valued? Domestic currency is valued at its face value on the Decedent's date of death. Foreign currency is valued at its foreign exchange rate for the Decedent's date of death. A check, if collectible, is valued as if it were cash. Collections of coins and currency require special valuation techniques. Consult the estate attorney or a reputable coin and currency dealer for estates that do not require appraisal by a licensed appraiser, or consult a licensed appraiser for estates that require a qualified appraisal.

How is information about cash and uncashed checks confirmed? The Executor may count the cash and make a photocopy of checks before deposit as confirmation.

What are the management concerns for cash and uncashed checks? Money from any country except when that money is part of a bona fide collection and all uncashed checks should be deposited in the estate account as soon as possible to avoid the risk of loss and to assure that the checks do not become void and require reissue. The Executor should be careful to wait for collection of any checks that are deposited before drawing on that money. Those checks may be refused for any number of reasons—for example, too much time may have passed since the check was issued, the check may have been replaced and cashed previously, or the payor may have stopped the check.

May cash and uncashed checks be used during the administration of the estate? The Executor must review the Will for instructions concerning the distribution of cash. Cash, after it has been deposited into the estate account, may be used to pay expenses, taxes, and debts as ordered by the court.

What income is generated by cash and uncashed checks? Cash and uncashed checks, as such, do not earn income. However, once placed in the estate account, the interest income from that account is reported to the estate on a 1099-INT and must be reported by the estate on the estate's federal and state income tax returns.

On what federal estate tax schedule are cash and uncashed checks reported? Schedule C. Mortgages, Notes, and Cash.

Are cash and uncashed checks reported on the probate inventory? Generally, yes. There is no opportunity to name a beneficiary for cash and uncashed checks. These items are the property of the Decedent at death.

How are cash and uncashed checks transferred out of the estate? All cash and checks payable to the estate must be deposited into the estate account. The court will order payment of the account, and the Executor will write a check to distribute those funds.

CEMETERY LOTS

What are cemetery lots? Cemetery, funeral, or burial lots are the spaces platted in real estate for the sole purpose of the burial of human remains. Local governments—including cities, townships, and counties, corporations, and associations—can organize, maintain, and sell lots in those cemeteries. Traditionally, burial lots are real estate. In some states, the owners of the lots are shareholders in the corporation that own the lots. In other jurisdictions, funeral lots have been declared by statute to be personal property. Mausoleum spaces are also set aside for entombment of human remains, but are not parcels of real estate.

What type of assets are cemetery lots? Depending upon state and local law, cemetery lots may be real estate or intangible personal property. The law of the state where the real estate is located governs the administration, sale, and distribution of real estate in the probate estate. Sale and distribution of intangible personal property by the probate court is governed by the laws of the Decedent's state of domicile, no matter where the intangible personal property is located. However, the statutes that control the sale and disposition of funeral lots and mausoleum spaces may require application of the law of the state where the cemetery is located. The manager or the administrator of the cemetery or the estate attorney will be able to provide information about the sale or transfer of cemetery property.

How are cemetery lots described? A cemetery lot is described by the name and location of the cemetery including city, county, and state; the lot location on the cemetery plat map, usually designated by lot numbers; the name of the owner; and the mode of ownership.

How are cemetery lots valued? Once a body is buried in the space, the cemetery or burial lot has no value and, generally, cannot be disturbed. The value of an empty lot is the fair market value on Decedent's date of death if that lot were sold. The cost of a lot from the cemetery if it were purchased on Decedent's date of death is evidence of the value. If an unoccupied lot is sold in an arm's length sale before the estate is distributed, the price for which the lot sold is its fair market value. If a value different than the sale price was reported to the court on an inventory or to the state and federal governments on any tax return, the inventory and any tax returns may need to be amended to reflect the fair market value. The discussion in the section on Real Estate in this Summary of Assets should be read for additional information about valuation.

How is information about cemetery lots confirmed? The title or other ownership papers of the cemetery lot or a letter from the manager or administrator of the cemetery will confirm the lot location and ownership. The value of a cemetery lot is shown by a statement from the cemetery manager or administrator of the current sale price of similar lots from that cemetery or the written statement of appraisal by a licensed appraiser.

What are the management concerns for cemetery lots? The on-site maintenance of a cemetery lot is usually handled by the cemetery manager. The Executor must assure that the title to a cemetery lot is kept in a secure place.

May cemetery lots be sold during the administration of the estate? The Executor must review the Will for instructions concerning the sale of cemetery lots. Unused cemetery lots may need to be sold to pay debts, expenses, or taxes or to divide the proceeds among Legatees or Devisees. There are circumstances in which cemetery lots must be sold even when sale is prohibited by the Will. See Chapter 9 for a discussion of these circumstances.

The sale of cemetery lots can be accomplished as soon as the Executor has been appointed by the court and has proper authority for the sale. The Executor must review the Will to be sure that it expressly permits the Executor to sell real estate if the lots are classified as real estate under the state law, or that it expressly permits the Executor to sell personal property if the lots are deemed personal property under the state law. If the Will does not give express authority to sell the type of property that the cemetery lots are considered to be under the state law, the estate attorney must obtain a court order specifically authorizing the Executor to sell the lots.

In seeking court order, the petition must state that the sale is necessary to pay debts, expenses, or taxes due from the estate; that the value of the asset may decline during the administration of the estate; or that the sale of the real estate is in the best interest of the estate for some other reason. Even if none of these conditions is met, the court will give permission for the sale if all interested persons agree in writing that the sale is in the best interest of the estate.

For obvious reasons, the sale of any property to a family member or associate of the Executor is prohibited by state statute even where the Executor has authority to sell property without court supervision. Such a sale is known as self-dealing. See Chapter 8 for a discussion concerning the requirement to avoid self-dealing. This requirement may be overcome if the duty not to self-deal is waived in the Will, or if the court, with full knowledge of the relationship, approves of the buyer and the sale price before the sale.

Even when the court ordered the sale or the Will waived the court's supervision, a complete accounting of the sale must be filed and approved by the court before the estate can be closed and the Executor discharged. The Executor must keep a copy of all documents relating to the sale and a copy of the payment check to support the accounting of the sale. All proceeds of a sale must be deposited into the estate account to await the court's order of distribution.

Within the limits of the state's requirement for a minimum price, setting the sale price is the responsibility of the Executor. The advice of the estate attorney and the sale prices of similar lots in the same cemetery or in the area will be a helpful guide to a sale price, but the Executor has the final decision. Although the Executor should attempt to get the best possible price, it is also important to complete the sale within a reasonable time.

State statutes control the minimum sale price for estate assets. This required minimum price is usually a percentage, for example, 80 percent, of the value reported in the probate inventory. The estate attorney must be consulted before any asset is sold to ensure that the sale price complies with the minimum price requirement. If there are no buyers at the required minimum price after the property has been offered for sale for a reasonable time, the estate attorney must seek court approval to amend the probate inventory to reflect the lower market value and to reduce the minimum sale price.

The Executor may sell the real estate by offering the property for sale in the newspaper or other media that offer items for sale. The Executor must notify the cemetery of the sale and complete transfer papers provided by the cemetery administrator.

What income is generated by cemetery lots? Cemetery lots generate no income. For income tax purposes, the proceeds of the sale are taxable gain if the proceeds exceed the basis in the asset and deductible as a loss if the basis exceeds the proceeds. However, because the basis is stepped up at death to the market value on the date of death, the sale price and the basis are usually the same and there is neither a gain nor a loss. A gain arises when the value of the asset increases between the date of death and the sale date. A loss arises when the value of the asset decreases between date of death and the sale date. See Chapter 10 for a discussion of basis.

On what federal estate tax schedule are cemetery lots reported? If the state law classifies cemetery lots as real estate, report on Schedule A. Real Estate. If the state law classifies ownership of a share of the company that owns the cemetery (and entitles the owner to a cemetery lot) as corporate stock, report on Schedule B. Stock and Bonds. If the state law classifies cemetery lots as miscellaneous intangible property report on Schedule F. Other Miscellaneous Property.

Are cemetery lots reported on the probate inventory? The space that the Decedent is to occupy purchased prior to death will be reported at no value on the probate inventory and the federal tax return. If the Decedent owns a cemetery lot in which there is no body buried, the fair market value of the lot must be reported on the probate inventory.

Some cemeteries are operated under contracts that allow the decedent to name a beneficiary or joint owner of a lot. Such lots are not part of the probate estate if they are transferred according to contract provisions. The Executor can contact the manager or administrator of the cemetery for instructions. Property such as cemetery lots can be placed into a trust that transfers the property to a beneficiary at Decedent's death. The cemetery lots are not reported on the probate inventory if they are held in such a trust.

How are cemetery lots transferred out of the estate? A transfer of the cemetery lot by deed or assignment pursuant to the court's order of distribution will transfer the lot to a new owner prior to final distribution of the estate. The estate attorney will prepare the assignment or deed, or the cemetery may have transfer documents that may be requested. The court's final order will transfer the cemetery lot at the final distribution of the estate. The Executor should notify the cemetery of the transfer.

DEATH BENEFITS

What are miscellaneous death benefits? The Decedent's estate, the Decedent's surviving spouse and minor children, or named beneficiaries may be entitled to certain benefits from numerous sources. The Social Security Administration and the Civil Service Retirement System may provide a monthly benefit for a surviving spouse and minor children and a lump sum benefit for Decedent's burial. There may be additional benefits for survivors of government workers whose deaths are work related. The Armed Services may provide benefits for survivors for personnel who die in service-related deaths while on active duty. The federal Veteran's Administration may provide insurance and a burial allowance for a qualified Decedent and pension benefits for a qualified surviving spouse. The state Veteran's Administration may provide benefits as well. The Federal Government Railroad Retirement Board provides a monthly annuity for a surviving spouse and minor children who qualify, a lump-sum benefit to survivors of certain employees, and a residual one-time payment in certain circumstances. Employers, whether Decedent was employed at the time of death or was employed many years before, may provide benefits such as severance pay, vacation time, retirement benefits, group insurance, deferred compensation, and credit union or thrift plans to the estate, a surviving spouse, or dependent minors. Trade unions, fraternal organizations, credit unions, and federal, state, or local government employee benefit programs may provide benefits to a surviving spouse, children, or named beneficiaries. Life or casualty insurance, including no-fault vehicle insurance provisions, may provide death benefits to the estate, survivors, or to named beneficiaries for deaths that result from motor vehicle accidents.

What type of assets are death benefits? Death benefits are intangible personal property. No matter where the death benefit originates, the benefits paid to the Decedent's estate are administered and distributed according to the laws of the Decedent's state of domicile.

How are miscellaneous death benefits described? The death benefit is described by the source of the benefit, the payee, the amount, and the reason for the payment.

How are the miscellaneous death benefits valued? The amount of the check received in payment of the death benefit is the value.

How are the miscellaneous death benefits confirmed? A copy of the check, the check stub, or the accompanying letter will confirm the source, the recipient, and the value of the benefit.

What are the management concerns for miscellaneous death benefits? The Executor must inquire of all past employers for retirement programs, thrift plans, deferred compensation, and group insurance. The Executor may be required to apply for these benefits. The Executor must check with the Social Security Administration, the Railroad Retirement Board, the federal and state Veteran's Administrations, any employers, trade unions, fraternal organizations, and credit unions to which the Decedent belonged, and life and casualty insurance companies, including no-fault insurance programs, for potential benefits and make application for benefits where appropriate.

May death benefits be liquidated during the administration of the estate? The Executor may apply for death benefits due to the estate as soon as the Executor has been appointed by the court.

What income is generated by miscellaneous death benefits? Money received as an employee death benefit is income to the recipient, even when the recipient is the surviving spouse. There is no longer a $5,000 exemption for death benefits. An exemption is available for survivors of the 9-11 disaster in New York City in September 2001. Death benefits that are required to be paid because of a contract with the employer are "Income-in-Respect of Decedent."[SA1] Where an estate tax has been paid by the estate on the death benefit, the recipient is entitled to an income tax deduction for those payments. See IRS Publication 559 for additional information.

On what federal estate tax schedule are miscellaneous death benefits reported? When the benefit is payable to or for the benefit of the estate, the death benefit is reported on Schedule F. Other Miscellaneous Property. However, neither the social security lump-sum death benefit nor the values of monthly benefits to a surviving spouse are includable in the gross estate for estate tax purposes (Rev. Rul. 55-87, 1955-1 CB 112). Check with a CPA or the estate attorney to determine whether other benefits are subject to estate, inheritance, or succession tax.

Are miscellaneous death benefits reported on the probate inventory? Benefits that are payable to the estate of the Decedent are probate property and reported on the probate inventory. If the death benefit is payable to the surviving spouse, Decedent's children, or to a beneficiary, the benefit is not reported on the probate inventory.

How are these benefits transferred out of the estate? Money payable to the estate for death benefits must be deposited into the estate account. The court will order distribution, and the Executor will write a check to distribute those funds.

DEBTS OWED TO THE DECEDENT

What is a debt? A debt is money owed to the Decedent. The debt may be shown by a mortgage or a promissory note, by a written admission of the debtor, or by other evidence. (See also Promissory Notes in this Summary of Assets.)

What type of assets is a debt? A debt is intangible personal property. No matter where the debt originates, the administration, sale, and distribution of a debt owed to the Decedent are governed by the laws of the Decedent's state of domicile in the probate estate.

How is a debt owed to the Decedent described? A debt is described by the name of the debtor, the mode of ownership, the name of all those who are owed money, and the terms of the debt, including the principal amount, the date of note, the interest rate, any demand right, the schedule of repayment, any security for the debt, and the amount of principal and accrued interest due at the date of death.

How is a debt owed to the Decedent valued? The value of a debt is calculated from the face of the note and from the records of payments. The mortgage agreement or the promissory note will show the owner- ship and contain the terms of the debt. It may be necessary to consult the estate attorney or accountant for assistance in calculating the date- of-death value for the debt. If a debt is sold in an arm's length sale before the estate is ordered to be distributed, the price for which the debt sold is the fair market value. If a value different than the sale price was reported to the court on an inventory or to the state and federal govern- ments on any tax return, the inventory and any tax returns may need to be amended to reflect the fair market value.

How is information about a debt owed to the Decedent confirmed? The evidence of the debt, the record of payments received, and the written calculation, are necessary to confirm the value of the debt.

What are the management concerns for a debt owed to the Decedent? The Executor or the estate attorney must write to all persons indebted to the Decedent informing them of the Decedent's death and demand- ing payment. Instructions for payment to the estate should be included in the letter to the debtors. (See Promissory Notes in this Summary of Assets.) If payments are not made timely, the Executor has a duty to make all reasonable efforts to collect the debt. This includes seeking enforcement of the debt in court, if necessary. If the Executor fails to make all reasonable efforts to collect the debt, the Executor may be personally liable for failure to collect the debt. Collection of the debt may be accomplished as soon the Executor is appointed by the court. The Executor has the authority to collect the debt whether or not the Executor has the authority to sell assets.

May debts owed to the Decedent be sold during the administration of the estate? The Executor must review the Will for instructions con- cerning any debt. If the debt is not fully collectible before the estate will be distributed, the debt may be sold to prevent loss in value or to divide the proceeds of an asset among legatees. The sale of the debt can be accomplished as soon as the Executor has been appointed by the court and has proper authority. In order to have proper authority to sell the debt, the Executor must review the Will to be sure that it expressly permits the Executor to sell personal property. If the Will does not give express authority to sell personal property, the estate attorney must obtain a court order expressly authorizing the Executor to sell the debt. In seeking the court order, the petition must state that the sale is necessary to pay debts, expenses, taxes, or legacies; that there is a risk of loss of value in the asset; or that the sale of the debt is in the best interest of the estate for some other reason. When none of these conditions is met, all interested persons can agree in writing that the sale is in the best interest of the estate and the court will give permission for the sale.

The sale price of the debt is controlled by the interest rates at the time of the sale, the likelihood that the debt is collectible (debtor's credit record), the value of the collateral, and other factors.

For obvious reasons, the sale of estate property to a family member or associate of the Executor is prohibited by state statute even where the Executor has authority to sell property without court supervision. Such a sale is known as self-dealing. See Chapter 8 for a discussion concerning the requirement to avoid self-dealing. This requirement may be overcome if the duty not to self-deal is waived in the Will, or if the court, with full knowledge of the relationship, approves of the buyer and the sale price before the sale.

Whether the court ordered the sale or the Will waived the court's supervision, a complete accounting of the sale must be filed and approved by the court before the estate can be closed and the Executor discharged. The Executor must keep a copy of all documents relating to the sale and a copy of the payment check to support the accounting for the sale. All proceeds must be deposited into the estate account until the court orders distribution.

What income is generated by a debt owed to the Decedent? The payment on a debt generally includes interest as well as principal. If there is no interest stated in the evidence of debt, the federal tax laws impute a rate of interest. That imputed interest is income and is reportable on the federal and state estate income tax returns. The debtor may or may not produce a report of interest paid. The obligation to report the interest income is not excused by the debtor's failure to send a report.

The Executor should alert a Legatee of the income tax consequences of a provision in a Will that forgives a debt. The federal tax code requires that the amount of the forgiven debt be included as taxable income to the debtor, unless a state statute saves the gift—that is, transforms the forgiveness of the debt into a gift that is not taxable. The Executor should consult with the estate attorney, a CPA, or the tax preparer concerning "imputed interest" and "forgiveness of indebtedness income."

On what federal estate tax schedule are debts owed to the Decedent reported? Schedule C. Mortgages, Notes, and Cash.

Are debts owed to the Decedent reported on the probate inventory? Generally, yes. Commonly, the right to repayment was owned solely by the Decedent, and there is no opportunity to assign a beneficiary for the note. Some notes are owned by the Decedent with another co-owner as tenants in common. This mode of ownership requires that the portion owned by the Decedent be treated as probate property. The portion owned by the surviving co-owner is not affected by the Decedent's death. Although it is somewhat rare, a note can be owned by joint tenants with right of survivorship. At the death of one joint owner, the right to repayment belongs to the surviving joint tenant and the asset is not part of the probate estate. Intangible personal property such as debts can be placed into a trust that transfers the debt to a beneficiary at Decedent's death. The debts are not reported on the probate inventory if they are held in such a trust.

How is a debt owed to the Decedent transferred out of the estate? If the debt cannot be fully collected or sold, the right to collect the payment is transferred to the new owners by court order. The Executor should notify the debtor of the transfer of the debt and instruct the debtor to pay the new owners directly.

DEPOSIT ACCOUNTS

What are deposit accounts? Deposit accounts are accounts held at a bank, savings and loan, or credit union or other institution and include savings, checking, money market, and certificate of deposit (CD) accounts. Deposit accounts also include demand deposits at farm co-operatives and brokerage firms.

What type of assets are deposit accounts? Deposit accounts are intangible personal property. No matter where the deposit accounts are located, the laws of the Decedent's state of domicile govern administration and distribution of deposit accounts in the probate estate.

How are deposit accounts described? The account is described by the name and address of the bank, savings and loan, credit union, or other institution holding the account; the nature of the account, that is, savings, checking, money market, time deposit, certificate of deposit, and the like; the names of all owners; the mode of ownership; the account number; and any beneficiary designations.

How are demand deposits valued? The balance in the account on the Decedent's date of death less any outstanding checks on the Decedent's date of death is the value of the account. The Executor must request a written statement of the balance of the account on Decedent's date of death. The Executor must also determine what checks were outstanding on the date of death, usually from a bank statement issued after the date of death or from the checkbook register.

How is information about demand deposit accounts confirmed? A written statement from the bank or other institution requested by the Executor will confirm the owner's name, account number, the type of account, any beneficiaries, and the account balance on the date of death. The records of the Decedent showing outstanding checks or a statement from the bank, savings and loan, or credit union showing checks that cleared after the date of death will confirm the checks that were outstanding but that had not cleared on the date of death.

What are the management concerns for deposit accounts? The Executor must keep a record of all transactions, balance each account within a day or two of receiving the monthly statement, and report any discrepancies to the bank immediately. Enough cash should be maintained in an estate account to assure timely payment of debts (upon the court's order) and expenses. If a low-interest or no-interest checking account has funds that are not necessary for payment of debts and expenses, it may be necessary to transfer some funds to an interest-bearing account. Often Certificates of Deposit (CDs) were purchased by the Decedent at a higher interest rate than paid on savings or money market accounts. It is wise to allow that money to remain at higher interest as long as possible. CDs can be cashed for a period of time after the death of the owner without penalty. The Executor must not let that time pass without making provisions for withdrawing the funds from the CD. The Executor must consider carefully the needs of the estate before putting cash into any account that is time restricted with a penalty provision.

May deposit accounts be liquidated during the administration of the estate? The Executor must review the Will for instructions concerning the disposition of intangible personal property. If an account is not specifically given to someone in the Will, a deposit account may be used to pay debts, expenses, or taxes or to divide the proceeds of an asset among legatees. There are circumstances in which money in accounts must be used even when those accounts are specifically bequeathed in the Will. See Chapter 9 for a discussion of abatement.

The money in a deposit account can be used as soon as the Executor has been appointed by the court. Remember, however, that the Executor must seek court approval for payment of debts. An accounting of deposits and payments from the account must be filed and approved by the court before the estate can be closed and the Executor discharged. The Executor must keep a copy of all documents relating to any deposit and withdrawal and a copy of the payment check to support the accounting. The money from deposit accounts cannot be distributed to those named in the Will until the court orders distribution.

What income is generated by deposit accounts? The interest paid on all deposit accounts is income. The bank or other institution will report the income to the taxpayer on an IRS Form 1099-INT. Income earned after the Decedent's death is income to the estate. Income earned before the death of the Decedent but not paid before death is Income in Respect of Decedent. See the Income-in-Respect of Decedent in this Summary of Assets.

On what federal estate tax schedule are deposit accounts reported? Schedule C. Mortgages, Notes, and Cash.

Are deposit accounts reported on the probate inventory? Deposit accounts often have a co-owner or a pay-on-death beneficiary named. If there is a co-owner or beneficiary who survives, that co-owner or beneficiary will receive the balance in the account directly and the deposit account is not reported in the probate inventory. If there is no co-owner, no beneficiary is named, the beneficiary does not survive, or the beneficiary disclaims the account, the estate will be the owner of the account and the account must be included in the probate inventory. Intangible personal property such as deposit accounts can be placed into a trust that transfers the deposit accounts to a beneficiary at Decedent's death. The deposit accounts are not reported on the probate inventory if they are held in such a trust.

How are deposit accounts transferred out of the estate? The court will order distribution of the money, and the Executor will write a check to distribute those funds. The Executor should obtain a Receipt and Refunding Agreement before or at the distribution of any funds.

DEVISES, LEGACIES, AND INHERITANCES FROM THE ESTATE OF ANOTHER

What are devises, legacies, and inheritances? Often before death a Decedent was entitled to assets from the estate of another but had not yet received those assets. In most instances, when the estate of another was in the process of administration when a Decedent dies, the estate of the Decedent is entitled to the assets the Decedent would have received.

What types of assets are devises, legacies, or inheritances? Devises, legacies, and inheritances from the estate of another can be tangible or intangible personal property or real estate. The administration, sale, and distribution of real estate received by the Decedent's estate after the Decedent's death are governed by the law of the state where the real estate is located. Also administration, sale, and distribution of any tangible personal property that is received by the Decedent's estate after the Decedent's death are governed by the laws of the state where that tangible personal property is located. However, wherever intangible personal property is located, administration, sale, and distribution of intangible personal property received by the Decedent's estate after the Decedent's death is governed by the laws of the Decedent's state of domicile.

How is a devise, legacy, or inheritance described? The description of the devise, legacy, or inheritance includes the name of the estate from which the gift is to be received; the city, county, and state where the estate is being administered; the case number of the court proceedings; and the description of any assets that will be received from the estate. Consult the specific type of asset in this Summary of Assets for more detailed instructions for describing property that is included in the devise, legacy, or inheritance.

How is a devise, legacy, or inheritance valued? The value of the devise, legacy, or inheritance will be stated in the court order from the estate of another that distributes the asset, in the inventory and accounting from the Executor or Administrator of the estate of the gift giver, in the inventory or accounting of the Trustee of the trust from which the assets come, or in a receipt for the assets received. If the value of the gift is not available from these sources, the asset may be valued in the same manner as that type of asset is valued as if originally a part of the Decedent's estate. See the individual asset in this Summary of Assets for specific instructions.

How is information about a devise, legacy, or inheritance confirmed? The information can be confirmed by the court's order of distribution from the estate of another, the statement of distribution, or a receipt for the devise, legacy, or inheritance.

What are the management concerns for devises, legacies, or inheritances? The Executor must notify the Executor, Administrator, or other personal representative of the estate of another of the Decedent's death; of the appointment of the Executor; and of instructions that all legal notices, correspondence, and distributions should be made to the estate of the Decedent. The Executor may be asked to sign waivers of notice, settlement agreements, or receipts in regard to these bequests, devises, or inheritances. The Executor should consult with the estate attorney for Decedent's estate before signing any legal document pertaining to the estate of another. The Executor should explore the use of disclaimers to avoid unnecessary taxes and probate costs. Secure storage, insurance, and maintenance must be provided for these assets when they are received by the Executor. See the individual asset in this Summary of Assets for specific instructions.

May devises, legacies and inheritances be liquidated during the administration of the estate? Once the assets from the estate of another are received by the estate of the Decedent, the Executor may sell or liquidate those assets in the same manner as that type of asset is sold or liquidated in Decedent's estate. See the individual asset in this Summary of Assets for specific instructions.

What income is generated by devises, legacies, or inheritances? Generally, inheritances, devises, legacies, and other assets that are received because of the death of another are not income. However, when the asset is a tax qualified plan—for example, an IRA, 401(k) retirement plan, or Series EE bonds that allowed the deferral of income tax —all or a portion of proceeds of the sale or liquidation of that asset will be income. If a specific bequest or devise is made in the Will, income that accrues on the legacy or devise in that estate will be distributed to and will be taxable in the Decedent's estate. Any income earned on the Residue of the estate of another that is distributed out of that estate to the Decedent's estate also will be taxable in the Decedent's estate if the income tax is not paid before it is distributed. The type of asset that is received will control whether there is income that must be reported on the estate income tax return. A report of income should be sent to the Executor by the Administrator or Executor of the other estate; however, the income must be reported even if that report is not received.

On what federal estate tax schedule are devises, legacies, and inheritances reported? Assets received from the estate of another are reported on the federal estate tax return according to the type of asset received. See the individual asset in this Summary of Assets for specific instructions. However, if the assets have not yet been received by Decedent's estate, the value of the devise, legacy, or inheritance is reported on Schedule F. Other Miscellaneous Property.

Are devises, legacies, or inheritances reported on the probate inventory? Generally, yes. If the asset has not yet been transferred to the Decedent at the time of the Decedent's death, the right to receive that property is owned solely by the Decedent. As such, the asset is part of the Decedent's probate estate. If the Decedent had received that asset before death, then the Decedent may have placed the inheritance into an account with a joint owner with right of survivorship or with a beneficiary. In that case, the joint owner or beneficiary will be the owner at the Decedent's death, and the asset will no longer be part of the Decedent's probate estate. All gifts from the estate of another may have been placed by the Decedent into a trust that transfers the devises, legacies, or inheritances to a beneficiary at Decedent's death. The devises, legacies, or inheritances are not reported on the probate inventory if they are held in such a trust.

How are devises, legacies, or inheritances transferred out of the estate? Each asset received from the estate of another will be transferred out of the Decedent's estate in the manner that each specific type of asset is transferred as if the asset had been part of the Decedent's estate from the Decedent's date of death. See the individual asset in this Summary of Assets for specific instructions.

FAMILY MEMORABILIA, PHOTOGRAPHS, AND VIDEOS

What is family memorabilia? Memorabilia are items that evoke memories of important events or special times. Personal or family memorabilia include photographs, albums, videos, and newspapers. Keepsakes such as tickets, ribbons, wedding dresses, and medals are also family memorabilia.

What type of assets are photographs, videos, and family memorabilia? These items of family memorabilia are tangible personal property. The laws of the state where the items are located govern the administration, sale, and distribution of photographs, videos, and other family memorabilia in the estate.

How is family memorabilia described? These assets are usually grouped together in the inventory as "family memorabilia." If a more detailed description is necessary to allow the Executor to divide the assets, the description of the memorabilia must include a full description of the type of item—baseball, service medal, photograph, video, audio, compact disc, memory stick, and so on—and the subject recorded including sufficient description that would serve to distinguish each item.

How is family memorabilia valued? Family memorabilia is generally without significant monetary value. The exception to this rule occurs when the memorabilia has some connection with a famous or noteworthy person or the item has a special significance to a larger public, such as a baseball signed by Willie Mays or a moon rock. If no estate tax return is required and the state statutes do not require appraisal by a licensed appraiser, the value of such items may be estimated by a dealer for that type of asset. However, keep in mind that a dealer may value pieces below the retail market value if the dealer also intends to offer to purchase those items for resale. If a federal estate tax return is required to be filed or state law requires, the Executor must obtain an appraisal of those items by a licensed appraiser to assure that the full value of the items is reported and to avoid personal liability for distribution or sale for less than full market value. If the personal mementos of a famous person or valuable items are to be distributed according to their value, the Executor must take great care to establish a value that interested parties agree upon before distribution. If an agreement on value cannot be reached, as a final resort, an appraisal of those items by a licensed appraiser will be necessary.

How is information about family memorabilia confirmed? Generally, the value of family memorabilia is negligible, and the inventory and valuation by the Executor is all that is necessary. The statement from a licensed appraiser or a dealer will confirm the description and value of the family memorabilia of a famous person or of valuable articles. Ownership of family memorabilia is most commonly determined by possession. Purchase receipts, insurance coverage for specific assets, presentation certificates, and other written documents also may give evidence of ownership.

What are the management concerns for family memorabilia? The Executor must assure that all family memorabilia are safely stored and maintained. Early distribution or sale of memorabilia will minimize the risk of loss and the costs of storage, maintenance, and insurance (if insurance is necessary). However, the Executor may not distribute the assets without a court order and may not sell without a court order unless sale of personal property is specifically authorized by the Will. Personal and household effects, including family memorabilia, is the subject of state spousal and minors' allowances. The Executor should consult with the estate attorney to determine whether the family memorabilia will be considered part of those allowances.

May family memorabilia be sold during administration of the estate? The Executor must review the Will and any personal property memorandum for instructions concerning the distribution and sale of family memorabilia. Generally, family memorabilia are of great sentimental value but not of significant monetary value. This lack of significant value usually makes the sale of these items more cumbersome that the value warrants. However, if the items have sufficient value to warrant a sale, family memorabilia may be sold to pay debts, expenses, or taxes, to avoid the costs of storage, insurance, and maintenance; or to divide the proceeds among legatees. There are circumstances in which assets must be sold even when their sale is prohibited by the Will. See Chapter 9 for a discussion of these circumstances.

Items of family memorabilia that are located in a state other than the state in which the primary probate proceeding is being conducted will be subject to an ancillary, that is an additional and supplementary, probate proceeding for administration, sale, and distribution of those items. The Executor must consult with the estate attorney to determine how, when, and where to begin the ancillary probate proceedings.

The sale of the family memorabilia can be accomplished as soon as the Executor has been appointed by the court and has proper authority for the sale. The Executor must review the Will to be sure that it expressly permits the Executor to sell personal property. If the Will does not give express authority to sell personal property, the estate attorney must obtain a court order specifically authorizing the Executor to sell personal property.

In seeking the court order, the petition must state that the sale is necessary to pay debts, expenses, taxes, or legacies or that the sale of the items is in the best interest of the estate for some other reason. When none of these conditions is met, all interested persons can agree in writing that the sale is in the best interest of the estate and the court will give permission for the sale.

For obvious reasons, the sale of estate property to a family member or associate of the Executor is prohibited by state statute even where the Executor has authority to sell property without court supervision. Such a sale is known as self-dealing. See Chapter 8 for a discussion concerning the requirement to avoid self-dealing. This requirement may be overcome if the duty not to self-deal is waived in the Will, or if the court, with full knowledge of the relationship, approves of the buyer and the sale price before the sale. In the case of family memorabilia, the court is likely to approve a sale to family members so long as the price is reasonable.

Within the limits of the state requirement for a minimum price, setting the sale price is the responsibility of the Executor. The advice of the estate attorney or a dealer in personal property will be a helpful guide, but the Executor has the final decision. Although the Executor should attempt to get the best possible price, it is also important to complete the sale within a reasonable time. Storage costs and insurance are expenses that cannot be recovered. A prompt sale removes these expenses from the estate.

State statutes control the minimum sale price for personal property. This required price is usually a percentage, for example, 80 percent, of the value reported in the probate inventory. The estate attorney must be consulted before any asset is sold to ensure that the sale price is at least as much as the required minimum price. If there are no buyers at the required minimum price after the assets have been offered for sale for a reasonable length of time, the estate attorney must seek court approval to amend the probate inventory to reflect the lower market value and to reduce the minimum sale price.

Family memorabilia should be sold "as is," and the buyers must be required to inspect the items for themselves or to hire a professional to inspect for them. Whether the sale is accomplished by private sale, at an estate sale, or by auction, the Executor should make no statements concerning the condition of the items to the buyers. The statements of the Executor may be considered by the buyer as a warranty or guarantee of the condition of the property. If the Executor's statements prove to be incorrect, the buyers may make a claim for their losses against the estate and against the Executor personally. This is an area of potentially serious liability for the Executor personally and for the estate.

Family memorabilia may be sold by private sale, at an estate sale, or by auction. Sale of tangible personal property by a professional is highly recommended for the reasons set out in detail in Chapter 8. The Executor should contact several reputable estate sale or auction companies to discuss the timing of the sale, sale costs and commissions, reserved bids, and advertising. These professionals will charge a percentage of the total sale proceeds as their sales commission. The Executor or estate attorney should negotiate and confirm in writing a reasonable commission before the sale. This cost is an expense of the estate and will be paid from estate assets. The estate sale or auction professional must provide a detailed receipt for items sold and the amount of the proceeds.

In all cases, an accounting of the sale must be filed and approved by the court before the estate may be closed and the Executor discharged. This is true even when the court ordered the sale or the Will waived the court's supervision. The Executor must keep a copy of all documents relating to the sale, including a copy of the payment check, to support the accounting. All proceeds of a sale must be deposited into the estate account for administration and to await the court's order of distribution.

What income is generated by family memorabilia? Generally, family memorabilia does not generate ordinary income. However, the proceeds of a sale are taxable gain if those proceeds exceed the basis in the assets and are deductible as a loss if the basis exceeds the proceeds. However, because the basis is stepped up to the market value on the date of death, the sale price and the basis are usually the same and there is no gain or loss. A gain occurs when the value of the family memorabilia increases between the date of death and the sale date. A loss arises when the value of the family memorabilia decreases between date of death and the sale date. See Chapter 10 for a discussion of basis and gain in the sale of estate assets.

On what federal estate tax schedule are family memorabilia reported? Schedule F. Other Miscellaneous Property.

Are family memorabilia reported on the probate inventory? Generally, yes. Memorabilia are usually in the possession of the owner and do not have a title or other document of ownership that can transfer ownership of the asset at death by a beneficiary designation. Tangible personal property such as family memorabilia can be placed into a trust that transfers the property to a beneficiary at Decedent's death. The family memorabilia are not reported on the probate inventory if they are held in such a trust.

How are family memorabilia transferred out of the estate? The transfer of ownership of family memorabilia from the estate to the legatee is made upon the court's order, either as a partial distribution during the time the estate is being administered or in the final distribution of the estate. The transfer is made by actual delivery of possession of the items into the hands or control of the Legatee. The Executor should obtain a receipt from the Legatee and deliver the items directly to the Legatee. If the items cannot be delivered but must be shipped, the determination of whether the estate or the recipient will pay the cost of shipping must be part of the court's order for distribution. The Executor must also ensure that the asset is adequately insured until delivery to the Legatee. Insurance for the risk of loss or damage to the asset must be purchased as part of the shipping cost. An ancillary, that is, an additional and supplementary, probate proceeding may be necessary to transfer ownership of family memorabilia located in a state other than the state in which the primary probate proceeding is conducted.

GIFTS MADE BEFORE DEATH (WITHIN THREE YEARS OF DATE OF DEATH)

What are gifts made within three years prior to date of death?
Certain gifts made in the three years prior to death are deemed to be assets for estate tax purposes. These gifts were already given away and are no longer in the Decedent's probate estate. However, the gift is deemed or considered to be part of the estate for estate tax purposes. The gift of a life insurance policy (IRC § 2042), the right to use property until death (which is called a retained life estate [IRC § 2036]), the right to have property returned to the giver after a certain period of time (which is called a reversionary interest [IRC § 2037]), and the right to cancel or take back a gift that has already been given away (which is called a power to revoke a gift [IRC § 2038]) are all gifts that must be included in the taxable estate if they were given away in the three years prior to Decedent's death. All other gifts given within the three years prior to Decedent's date of death are not deemed to be part of the Decedent's taxable estate and are not part of the Decedent's probate estate.

What type of assets are gifts made within three years prior to date of death? Gifts of the specific classes noted above can be real estate or tangible or intangible personal property. Because these gifts have already been transferred prior to death, there is no need to concern ourselves with which state law applies to govern sale and distribution of the gifts. For estate tax purposes, these gifts are deemed an asset. However, state gift tax considerations may also require attention. Consult with the estate attorney or CPA for questions concerning federal and state gift and estate tax.

How are gifts made within three years prior to date of death described? Gifts in the classes specified that were given before death are described in the same manner as that type of asset would be described if it were in the Decedent's estate. The description of the asset on the federal gift tax return (IRS Form 709) should be used if that return was filed. Consult the appropriate section in this Summary of Assets for specific instructions for the description of each type of asset.

How are gifts made within three years prior to date of death valued? The gifts are valued as of the time of the gift, not the Decedent's date of death. The valuation of each type of item is described in this Summary of Assets under the type of asset. The value reported on the federal gift tax return must be used unless there is some compelling evidence that the value used was incorrect.

How is information about gifts made within three years prior to date of death confirmed? The information about gifts made three years prior to death is confirmed on the gift tax return (IRS Form 709) filed or as each type of asset is confirmed as described in this Summary of Assets.

What are the management concerns for gifts made within three years prior to date of death? Because the assets are no longer in the Decedent's estate, no management of the assets is required. However, the Executor must ensure that the asset is correctly reported on the gift tax return and estate, inheritance, or other death tax returns.

May gifts made within three years prior to date of death be liquidated during the administration of the estate? No. These gifts have already been transferred out of the estate and are not part of the probate estate.

What income is generated by gifts made within three years prior to date of death? There will be no income to the estate generated by these gifts made prior to death.

On what federal estate tax schedule are gifts made within three years prior to date of death reported? Schedule G. Transfers During Decedent's Life.

Are gifts made within three years prior to death included in the probate inventory? No. The property has already been removed from the estate.

How are gifts made within three years prior to date of death transferred out of the estate? It is not necessary to transfer these gifts because they have already been transferred prior to death.

GIFT TAX PAID THREE YEARS PRIOR TO DATE OF DEATH

What is gift tax paid within three years prior to date of death? When the Decedent gave taxable gifts and paid gift tax on those gifts within three year of Decedent's date of death, the amount of the gift tax paid is included in the Decedent's estate for purposes of the federal estate tax return. Gift tax paid within three years prior to death is deemed an asset for federal estate tax purposes although the money that was paid as tax is no longer owned by the Decedent at death.

What type of asset is gift tax paid within three years prior to death? Gift tax paid within three years prior to death is deemed an asset for federal estate tax purposes although the money was paid from the Decedent's estate as tax and is no longer owned by the Decedent at death.

How is gift tax paid within three years prior to date of death described? The gift tax paid is described by reference to the federal gift tax return, IRS Form 709, and that includes the description of the gift, its recipient, and its value.

How is gift tax paid within three years prior to date of death valued? The amount of gift tax paid is the value. The gift tax is calculated on the federal gift tax return, IRS Form 709.

How is information about gift tax paid within three years prior to date of death confirmed? The information about the gift tax paid is confirmed by the federal gift tax return (IRS Form 709) filed to report the gift. The information reported on the gift tax return can be confirmed as described in this Summary of Assets for each type of asset.

What are the management concerns for gift tax paid within three years prior to date of death? Because the tax has already been removed from the estate of the Decedent, there are no management concerns for this deemed asset.

May gift tax paid within three years prior to date of death be liquidated during the administration of the estate? No. These taxes have already been paid and are not part of the probate estate.

What income is generated by a gift tax paid within three years prior to date of death? No income is generated for the estate when a gift tax was paid before death.

On what federal estate tax schedule is gift tax paid within three years prior to date of death reported? Schedule G. Transfers During Decedent's Life; and credit for gift tax paid. Also, see Part 1, line 17 of IRS Form 706.

Are gift taxes paid within three years prior to death reported on the probate inventory? No. The money to pay the gift tax has already been removed from the probate estate.

How is gift tax paid within three years prior to date of death transferred out of the estate? The money used to pay the gift taxes has already been transferred prior to death and requires no additional transfer.

GOODS IN STORAGE

What are goods in storage? Goods in storage are the tangible personal property that is stored apart from the Decedent's home or business including household furnishings placed in a self-storage unit when the Decedent moved from his or her home, wheat or other crops that are stored at the co-operative grain elevator waiting for a favorable sale price, furs held in a vault and antiques, art pieces, collections or family memorabilia that are stored by a storage company for safe-keeping.

What types of assets are goods in storage? Goods in storage are tangible personal property. In the probate estate, administration, sale, and distribution of goods in storage are governed by the laws of the state where the goods are located.

How are goods in storage described? A description of each piece in storage is necessary. See the individual assets in this Summary of Assets for specific instructions for describing each type of asset.

How are goods in storage valued? See the individual assets in this Summary of Asset for specific instructions for valuation of each type of asset.

How is information about goods in storage confirmed? The specific section for the different assets in this Summary of Assets discusses the requirements for confirmation of the information for each type of asset.

What are the management concerns for goods in storage? The Executor must assure that all tangible personal property is safely stored. The Executor must notify the caretaker of goods in storage of the Decedent's death and the appointment of the Executor and give instructions for continuing storage or removal of the property. As soon as possible the Executor should prepare an inventory of all goods in storage for inventory, management, tax reports, insurance, and distribution purposes. The Executor must obtain adequate insurance on goods in storage. Early distribution or sale of these assets will minimize the risk of loss and the costs of storage, maintenance, and insurance. However, the Executor may not distribute tangible personal property without a court order. In addition, unless the Will authorizes the sale of personal property, the Executor must obtain a court order to sell these assets.

May goods in storage be sold during the administration of the estate?
The Executor must review the Will and any personal property memorandum for instructions concerning the tangible personal property.
Unless items are specifically bequeathed or sale is prohibited by the
Will, goods in storage may be sold to pay debts, expenses, or taxes; to
avoid the costs of storage, insurance, and maintenance; to prevent
losses in value because of a declining market; or to divide the proceeds
of the sale among Legatees. There are circumstances in which assets
must be sold even when their sale is prohibited by the Will. See Chapter
9 for a discussion of these circumstances.

Goods in storage that are located in a state other than the state in
which the primary probate proceeding is being conducted will be
subject to an ancillary, that is an additional and supplementary, probate
proceeding for administration, sale, and distribution of those goods.
The Executor must consult with the estate attorney to determine how,
when, and where to begin the ancillary probate proceedings.

The sale of goods in storage can be accomplished as soon as the
Executor has been appointed by the court and has proper authority for
the sale. The Executor must review the Will to be sure that it expressly
permits the Executor to sell tangible personal property. If the Will does
not give express authority to sell personal property, the estate attorney
must obtain a court order specifically authorizing the Executor to sell
the goods in storage.

In seeking the court order, the petition must state that the sale is
necessary to pay debts, expenses, taxes, or legacies; that the value of the
asset will decline as time goes by; or that the sale of the items is in the
best interest of the estate for some other reason. When none of these
conditions is met, all interested persons can agree in writing that the
sale is in the best interest of the estate and the court will give permission
for the sale.

For obvious reasons, the sale of estate property to a family member
or associate of the Executor is prohibited by state statute even where
the Executor has authority to sell property without court supervision.
Such a sale is known as self-dealing. See Chapter 8 for a discussion
concerning the requirement to avoid self-dealing. This requirement
may be overcome if the duty not to self-deal is waived in the Will, or if
the court, with full knowledge of the relationship, approves of the buyer
and the sale price before the sale.

Within the limits of the state requirement for a minimum price,
setting the sale price is the responsibility of the Executor. The advice of
the estate attorney, a dealer in personal property, or an auctioneer will
be a helpful guide, but the Executor has the final decision. Although the
Executor should attempt to get the best possible price, it is also important to complete the sale within a reasonable time. Storage costs and

insurance are expenses that cannot be recovered. A prompt sale removes these expenses from the estate.

State statutes control the minimum sale price for personal property. This required price is usually a percentage, for example, 80 percent, of the value reported in the probate inventory. The Executor must consult the estate attorney before any asset is sold to ensure that the sale price complies with the required minimum price. If there are no buyers at the required minimum price after the goods have been offered for sale for a reasonable time, the estate attorney must seek court approval to amend the probate inventory to reflect the lower market value and to reduce the minimum sale price.

Goods in storage should be sold "as is," and buyers must be required to inspect the property for themselves or to hire a professional to inspect for them. Whether the sale is accomplished by private sale or by auction, the Executor should make no statements concerning the condition of the property to the buyers. This is an area of potentially serious liability for the Executor personally and for the estate. The statements of the Executor may be considered by the buyer as a warranty or guarantee of the condition of the property. If the Executor's statements prove to be incorrect, the buyers may make a claim for their losses against the estate and against the Executor personally.

Goods in storage may be sold at an estate sale or by auction. Sale of tangible personal property by a professional is highly recommended for the reasons set out in detail in Chapter 8. The Executor should contact several reputable estate sale or auction companies to discuss the timing of the sale, sale costs, commissions, reserved bids, and advertising. These professionals will charge a percentage of the total sale proceeds as their sales commission. The Executor or estate attorney should negotiate and confirm in writing a reasonable commission before the sale. This cost is a reasonable expense of the estate and will be paid from estate assets. The estate sale professional or auctioneer must provide a detailed receipt for items sold and the amount of the proceeds.

In all cases, an accounting of the sale must be filed and approved by the court before the estate can be closed and the Executor discharged, even when the court ordered the sale or the Will waived the court's supervision. The Executor must keep a copy of all documents relating to the sale and a copy of the payment check to support the accounting. All proceeds of a sale must be deposited into the estate account to await the court's order of distribution.

What income is generated by goods in storage? Goods in storage generally do not generate ordinary income. However, the proceeds of the sale are taxable gain if those proceeds exceed the basis in the assets, and a loss is deductible if the basis exceeds the proceeds. However, because the basis is stepped up at death to the market value on the date of death, the sale price and the basis are usually the same and there is no gain or loss. A gain arises when the value of the asset increases between the date of death and the sale date. A loss occurs when the value of the asset decreases between date of death and the sale date. See Chapter 10 for a discussion of basis in the sale of estate assets.

On what federal estate tax schedule are goods in storage reported? Schedule F. Other Miscellaneous Property.

Are goods in storage reported on the probate inventory? Generally, yes. Goods in storage usually do not have a title or other document of ownership that can be transferred at death by a beneficiary designation or create joint ownership with rights of survivorship. Intangible personal property such as goods in storage can be placed into a trust that transfers the goods in storage to a beneficiary at Decedent's death. The goods in storage are not reported on the probate inventory if they are held in such a trust.

How are goods in storage transferred out of the estate? The transfer of ownership of the goods in storage from the estate to the Legatee is made by court order, either as an early distribution during the time the estate is being administered or in the final distribution of the estate. The Executor should obtain a receipt from the Legatee and deliver the asset directly to the Legatee. If the asset must be shipped, the determination of whether the estate or the recipient will pay the cost of shipping must be part of the court's order for distribution. The Executor must ensure that the asset is adequately insured until delivery to the Legatee. Insurance for the risk of loss or damage to the asset during shipping must be purchased as part of the shipping cost. An ancillary, that is, an additional and supplemental, probate proceeding may be necessary to transfer ownership of goods in storage located in a state other than the state in which the primary probate proceeding is conducted.

INCOME-IN-RESPECT OF DECEDENT

What is Income-in-Respect of Decedent? Income-in-Respect of Decedent (IRD) is income that the Decedent earned but had not yet received before death.[1] IRD includes commissions, wages, salary, and fees due the Decedent. IRD is an asset as well as income.

What type of asset is Income-in-Respect of Decedent? Income-in-Respect of Decedent is intangible personal property. No matter what the

---

1 IRC § 691(a) Income-in-Respect of Decedent

source of the Income-in-Respect of Decedent or where that source is located, the laws of the Decedent's state of domicile govern administration and distribution of the Income-In-Respect of Decedent.

How is Income-in-Respect of Decedent described? Income-in-Respect of Decedent is described by the source and amount of the income, the reason for payment, and the time period to which it applies.

How is Income-in-Respect of Decedent valued? The amount of the check received in payment is the value of Income-in-Respect of Decedent.

How is information about Income-in-Respect of Decedent confirmed? A copy of the check is sufficient to confirm the source, ownership, and the value for the probate inventory and estate tax purposes. The Executor should contact the payor to ask that the income report be sent to the Executor for income tax reporting.

What are the management concerns for Income-in-Respect of Decedent? The Executor must collect salary, wages, unused sick pay, unused vacation pay, commissions, and fees due the Decedent. The Executor should make provisions to collect ongoing commissions, trails, royalties, interest, dividends and other income. A letter should be sent as soon as possible to all sources of Income-in-Respect of Decedent with instructions for payment to the Decedent's estate in care of the Executor. All income must be deposited in the estate account.

May Income-in-Respect of Decedent be liquidated during the administration of the estate? The Executor must collect all income owed to the Decedent as soon as is reasonably possible after the Executor has been appointed by the court.

What income is generated by Income-in-Respect of Decedent? Income-in-Respect of Decedent is both an asset of the estate and taxable as income to the estate. An income tax deduction for estate tax paid may be available.

On what federal estate tax schedule is Income-in-Respect of Decedent reported? Schedule F. Other Miscellaneous Property.

Is Income-in-Respect of Decedent reported on the probate inventory? Generally, the right to income was owned solely by the Decedent, and there is no opportunity to name a co-owner or beneficiary for the income. Income that is solely owned by the Decedent is included as probate property on the probate inventory. Some employers pay the uncollected salary or wages to a surviving spouse under an employment agreement. Income paid to the surviving spouse or other beneficiary under an employment contract is not probate property.

How is Income-in-Respect of Decedent transferred out of the estate? Commissions, wages, salary, fees, and all other income due the Decedent are collected and deposited in the estate bank account. Any right to receive income that cannot be collected before the estate is terminated must be assigned pursuant to the court's order of distribution. The Executor must notify those who owe the money to the Decedent of the court's order and their obligation to pay the new owner.

INTANGIBLE PERSONAL PROPERTY

What is intangible personal property? Intangible personal property is property that has no intrinsic value but is merely representative or evidence of value. Intangible personal property is any property that is not real estate and not tangible personal property. Examples of intangible person property include annuities; accounts at banks, savings and loans, and credit unions; bonds; cash and uncashed checks; club memberships; contracts; insurance; intellectual property such as patents, trademarks, and copyrights; investments; lawsuits; leases; limited liability company shares; limited partnership units; mortgages; mutual fund stock; partnership interests; promissory notes; refunds; stock; and stock options.

What type of property is intangible personal property? Intangible personal property is personal property that represents value but is not valuable in and of itself. No matter where intangible personal property is located at the Decedent's death, administration, sale, and distribution of intangible personal property by the probate court are governed by the laws of the Decedent's state of domicile.

How is intangible personal property described? The description of intangible personal property varies with the type of asset. Consult the specific type of asset in this Summary of Assets for instructions for the description of each type of intangible personal property.

How is intangible personal property valued? A written statement of the value of the asset on the Decedent's date of death and, if necessary, the alternate valuation date must be requested by the Executor. The alternate valuation date is the date exactly six months after the date of death. See the individual assets in this Summary of Assets for specific instructions for valuation of each type of intangible asset.

How is information about intangible personal property confirmed? The statement issued for the account is the confirmation of the description, ownership, the value, the beneficiaries, and sometimes, any tax basis and tax deferral information. The face of a security is the confirmation of the ownership and any beneficiaries of assets that are not held in an account. The market quotation in a financial newspaper or on the Internet is the confirmation of the value of some assets that are not held in accounts. The face of the promissory note or mortgage is the confirmation of the information about those assets. The statement of an appraiser is the confirmation for those assets that do not have another source of that information. See the individual assets in this Summary of Assets for specific instructions for confirming the information for each type of asset.

What are the management concerns for intangible personal property? The Executor must collect all the Decedent's personal property in the possession of others, including intangible personal property. The contents of all safes and safe deposit boxes owned or rented by the Decedent must be examined. The contents of the safe deposit box should be inventoried and placed in a safe deposit box that is held in the name of the estate. The Executor must determine whether there are claims that must be filed to collect the assets, whether a lump-sum payment or continuing benefits are more advantageous, and whether there are special management concerns for the assets. Claim and sale information is available by requesting that information from the company or other administrator who is holding the Decedent's intangible personal property. The Executor may file or assist in filing claims. The Executor must place all intangible personal property in safekeeping until distribution of the estate. See the individual assets in this Summary of Assets for specific instructions for management of each type of asset.

May intangible personal property be sold during the administration of the estate? The Executor must review the Will for instructions concerning the sale or specific bequest of intangible personal property. Intangible personal property may be sold or liquidated to raise cash to pay debts, expenses, or taxes; to prevent losses in value because of a declining market; or to divide the proceeds of an asset among legatees. The Executor may need to consider sale of assets for other reasons as well. For example, certain stock can be sold back to the corporation that issued the stock (redeemed) to obtain a tax-favored distribution from that corporation. See Stocks in this Summary of Assets for a discussion of this provision. There are circumstances in which intangible personal property must be sold even when its sale is prohibited by the Will. See Chapter 9 for a discussion of these circumstances.

The sale of intangible personal property can be accomplished as soon as the Executor has been appointed by the court and has proper authority for the sale. The Executor must review the Will to be sure that it expressly permits the Executor to sell personal property. If the Will does not give express authority to sell personal property, the estate attorney must obtain a court order expressly authorizing the Executor to sell personal property.

In seeking the court order, the petition must state that the sale is necessary to pay debts, expenses, taxes, or legacies; that there is a risk of loss of value in the asset; or that the sale of intangible personal property is in the best interest of the estate for some other reason. When none of these conditions is met, all interested persons can agree in writing that the sale is in the best interest of the estate and the court will give permission for the sale.

The sale price of intangible personal property is controlled by the market price at the time of the sale. See each type of asset for instructions regarding sale price.

For obvious reasons, the sale of estate property to a family member or associate of the Executor is prohibited by state statute even where the Executor has authority to sell property without court supervision. Such a sale is known as self-dealing. See Chapter 8 for a discussion concerning the requirement to avoid self-dealing. This requirement may be overcome if the duty not to self-deal is waived in the Will, or if the court, with full knowledge of the relationship, approves of the buyer and the sale price before the sale.

Whether the court ordered the sale or the Will waived the court's supervision, a complete accounting of the sale must be filed and approved by the court before the estate can be closed and the Executor discharged. The Executor must keep a copy of all documents relating to the sale and a copy of the payment check to support the accounting for the sale or liquidation. All proceeds must be deposited into the estate account until the court orders distribution.

What income is generated by intangible personal property? Most types of intangible assets generate income. For example, stocks generate dividends and capital gains, and bonds, mortgages, and deposit accounts generate interest income. Insurance, however, does not generate income except when the proceeds are left on deposit. See the individual assets in this Summary of Assets for specific information regarding the potential for income from each type of asset.

Additionally, the proceeds of the sale are taxable as a capital gain if the proceeds exceed the basis in the asset and are deductible as a loss if the basis exceeds the proceeds. However, because for most assets basis is stepped up at death to the market value on the date of death, the sale price and the basis are usually the same and there is no gain or loss. A gain can arise when the value of the asset increases between the date of death and the sale date. A loss can occur when the value of the asset decreases between date of death and the sale date. See Chapter 10 for a discussion of basis.

The proceeds of the sale of investments held in IRA, 401(k), and other tax deferred plans are not subject to the basis step-up rule. Instead, because the money used to purchase these investments was not previously taxed as income, when the asset is probate property, the full amount of the proceeds will be included as income of the estate.

On what federal estate tax schedule is intangible personal property reported? Each type of intangible personal property is reported on its own schedule. For example, bonds are reported on Schedule B; stocks on Schedule B; mortgages, notes, and cash on Schedule C; annuities on Schedule I; and insurance on Schedule D. See the individual assets in this Summary of Assets for specific instructions concerning the proper schedule to report each type of asset on the federal estate tax return.

Is intangible personal property reported on the probate inventory? Many types of intangible personal property are the subject of state law provisions that allow the Decedent to name a beneficiary of the asset. That beneficiary will receive the asset directly, and the asset will not be part of the probate estate. However, if the Decedent named the estate as the beneficiary, if the named beneficiary has died before the Decedent and no contingent beneficiary was named, if the named beneficiary chooses to disclaim the asset, or if the asset is not one that is permitted to have a beneficiary, then the estate will be the recipient of the asset and the asset will be reported on the probate inventory. Intangible personal property can be placed into a trust that transfers the property to a beneficiary at Decedent's death. The property is not reported on the probate inventory if it is held in such a trust.

How is intangible personal property transferred out of the estate? Transfer of ownership of all probate property from the estate to the legatee is made by court order. Many types of intangible personal property can be transferred in-kind. In-kind means that the asset remains invested in the same asset and only the name of the owner is changed. An in-kind transfer avoids the costs of sale and the commissions for reinvestment by the recipient. A stock account can be distributed by dividing the shares among separate legatees. Some legatees may prefer to receive their legacy in cash, whereas other legatees may choose to take their legacy in-kind to avoid payment of a second load or sales commission to reinvest their money. See the individual assets in this Summary of Assets for specific instructions for transferring each type of asset.

JEWELRY

What is jewelry? Jewelry is the adornments worn on the person, including rings, earrings, bracelets, necklaces, and hair ornaments, among other things.

What type of asset is jewelry? Jewelry is tangible personal property. The laws of the state where the jewelry is located govern the administration, sale, and distribution of jewelry in the probate estate.

How is jewelry described? The description of jewelry should be very specific and include a detailed statement of the type of piece; type and color of metal or other material; type, size, and shape of stones; size of band and chains; and inscriptions or other distinguishing marks on the piece.

How is jewelry valued? Valuation of jewelry requires that a market for the piece be identified and a comparable market price be established. Appraisal by someone with knowledge and experience with the specific type of jewelry will be required. An independent appraisal is recommended for all jewelry of significant value. Valuation by a jeweler may be sufficient for an estate that is not required to file a federal estate tax return and where appraisal by a licensed appraiser is not required by state statute. If an estate tax return will be filed or state law requires an appraisal, an appraisal by a licensed appraiser is required. If jewelry is sold in an arm's length sale before the estate is ordered to be distributed, the price for which the jewelry sold is the fair market value. If a value different than the sale price was reported to the court on an inventory or to the state and federal governments on any tax return, the inventory and any tax returns may need to be amended to reflect the fair market value.

How is information about jewelry confirmed? The appraiser's or jewelry dealer's written statement will confirm the description and value. The ownership of tangible personal property is usually determined by possession; however, insurance records, receipts, and other records may provide proof of ownership of property that was not in the Decedent's possession at death.

What are the management concerns for jewelry? Jewelry must be safely stored and adequately insured. Early distribution or sale of jewelry will minimize the risk of loss and the costs of storage and insurance. However, the Executor may not distribute tangible personal property without a court order. Moreover, unless sale of assets is authorized by the Will, the Executor must obtain a court order to sell. Jewelry may be the subject of state spousal and minors' allowances. The Executor should consult with the estate attorney to determine whether the jewelry will be considered a part of those allowances.

May jewelry be sold during the administration of the estate? The Executor must review the Will and any personal property memorandum for instructions concerning the distribution or sale of tangible personal property generally and jewelry specifically. Jewelry may be sold to pay debts, expenses, or taxes; to avoid the costs of storage, insurance, and maintenance; to prevent losses in value because of a declining market; or to divide the proceeds of sale among Legatees. There are circumstances in which jewelry must be sold even when its sale is prohibited by the Will. See Chapter 9 for a discussion of these circumstances.

Jewelry that is located in a state other than the state in which the primary probate proceeding is being conducted will be subject to an ancillary, that is, an additional and supplementary, probate proceeding for administration, sale, and distribution of the jewelry. The Executor must consult with the estate attorney to determine how, when, and where to begin the ancillary probate proceedings.

The sale of jewelry can be accomplished as soon as the Executor has been appointed by the court and has proper authority for the sale. The Executor must review the Will to be sure that it expressly permits the Executor to sell tangible personal property. If the Will does not give express authority to sell personal property, the estate attorney must obtain a court order specifically authorizing the Executor to do so.

In seeking the court order, the petition must state that the sale is necessary to pay debts, expenses, taxes, or legacies; that the value of the jewelry may decline during the administration of the estate; or that the sale of the jewelry is in the best interest of the estate for some other reason. When none of these conditions is met, all interested persons can agree in writing that the sale is in the best interest of the estate and the court will give permission for the sale.

For obvious reasons, the sale of estate property to a family member or associate of the Executor is prohibited by state statute even where the Executor has authority to sell property without court supervision. Such a sale is known as self-dealing. See Chapter 8 for a discussion concerning the requirement to avoid self-dealing. This requirement may be overcome if the duty not to self-deal is waived in the Will, or if the court, with full knowledge of the relationship, approves of the buyer and the sale price before the sale.

Within the limits of the state requirement for a minimum price, setting the sale price is the responsibility of the Executor. The advice of the estate attorney or a jeweler will be a helpful guide, but the Executor has the final decision. Although the Executor should attempt to get the best possible price, it is also important to complete the sale within a reasonable time. Storage costs and insurance are expenses that cannot be recovered. A prompt sale removes these expenses from the estate.

State statutes control the minimum sale price for personal property. This required price is usually a percentage, for example, 80 percent, of the value reported in the probate inventory. The estate attorney must be consulted before any asset is sold to ensure that the sale price complies with the required minimum price. If there are no buyers at the required minimum price after the jewelry has been offered for sale for a reasonable length of time, the estate attorney must seek court authority to amend the probate inventory to reflect the lower market value and to reduce the minimum sale price.

Jewelry should be sold "as is," and the buyers must be required to inspect the pieces for themselves or to hire a professional to inspect for them. Whether the sale is accomplished by private sale, estate sale, or by auction, the Executor should make no statements concerning the condition of the property to the buyers. This is an area of potentially serious liability for the Executor personally and for the estate. The statements of the Executor may be considered by the buyer as a warranty or guarantee of the condition of the property. If the Executor's statements prove to be incorrect, the buyers may make a claim for their losses against the estate and against the Executor personally.

Jewelry may be sold by private sale, at an estate sale, or by auction. Sale of tangible personal property by a local professional is highly recommended for the reasons set out in detail in Chapter 8. The Executor should contact several reputable jewelers, estate sale professionals, or auction companies to discuss the timing of the sale, sale costs and commissions, reserved bids, and advertising. These professionals will charge a percentage of the total sale proceeds as their sales commission. The Executor or estate attorney should negotiate and confirm in writing a reasonable commission before the sale. This cost is an expense of the estate and will be paid from estate assets. The professional must provide a detailed receipt for items sold and the amount of the proceeds.

In all cases, an accounting of the sale must be filed and approved by the court before the estate can be closed and the Executor discharged, even when the court ordered the sale or the Will waived the court's supervision. The Executor must keep a copy of all documents relating to the sale and a copy of the payment check to support the accounting. All proceeds must be deposited into the estate account for administration and to await the court's order of distribution.

What income is generated by jewelry? Generally, jewelry does not generate income. However, the proceeds of the sale are taxable as a capital gain if the proceeds exceed the basis in the jewelry and are deductible as a loss if the basis exceeds the proceeds. However, because the basis is stepped up at death to the market value on the date of death, the sale price and the basis are usually the same and there is no gain or loss. A gain can arise when the value of the jewelry increases between the date of death and the sale date. A loss can arise when the value of the jewelry decreases between date of death and the sale date. See Chapter 10 for a discussion of basis.

On what federal estate tax schedule is jewelry reported? Schedule F. Other Miscellaneous Property.

Is jewelry reported on the probate inventory? Generally, yes. Jewelry is usually owned by an individual and is in the possession of the owner. Jewelry generally does not have a title or other document of ownership that would show joint ownership with right of survivorship. Intangible personal property such as jewelry can be placed into a trust that transfers the jewelry to a beneficiary at Decedent's death. The jewelry is not reported on the probate inventory if it is held in such a trust.

How is jewelry transferred out of the estate? The transfer of ownership of jewelry from the estate to the Legatee is made by court order, either as an early distribution during the time the estate is being probated or in the final distribution of the estate. The Executor should obtain a receipt and deliver the asset directly to the Legatee. If the asset must be shipped, then the determination of whether the estate or the recipient will pay the cost of shipping must be part of the court's order for distribution. The Executor must also ensure that the asset is adequately insured until delivery to the legatee. Insurance for the risk of loss or damage to the asset must be purchased as part of the shipping cost. An ancillary, that is, an additional and supplementary, probate proceeding may be necessary to transfer ownership of jewelry located in a state other than the state in which the primary probate proceeding is conducted.

JOINT INTERESTS

What is a joint interest? Joint interest is a mode of owning property, not a separate type of asset. There are two types of joint interests that are commonly used to own property: joint tenancy with right of survivorship (JTROS) and tenancy in common (TC). Both personal and real property can be owned in either manner. In some states, real property can also be held by husband and wife as tenants by the entireties (another type of joint interest). In all types of joint ownership, all joint tenants own the undivided right to occupy and possess the property while the joint tenants are alive. At death, these types of ownership operate differently. Property owned by joint tenants with right of survivorship or tenants by the entireties becomes the property of the surviving joint tenant. The ownership interest of the deceased joint tenant is extinguished. In contrast, the Decedent's share of the property owned as tenants in common belongs to the estate of the deceased tenant.

What type of assets are joint interests? Tangible and intangible personal property and real estate can be owned in joint tenancy. See the specific asset in this Summary of Assets for a discussion about the law that governs the sale and distribution of the underlying asset.

How is a joint interest described? The property owned as joint property is described in the same manner as the underlying asset is described in this Summary of Assets. The names of the joint owners, the percentage of ownership, and the type of joint ownership (tenant with right of survivorship, tenant by the entireties, or tenant in common) is necessary. Consult the specific type of asset in this Summary of Assets for instructions for describing the underlying property.

How is a joint interest valued? Joint property is valued as the underlying asset is valued. See the individual assets in this Summary of Assets for specific instructions regarding valuation.

How is information about a joint interest confirmed? Information about joint property is confirmed as information about the underlying asset is confirmed. See the individual assets in this Summary of Assets for specific instructions regarding confirmation of information.

What are the management concerns for a joint interest? Property owned with a joint tenant as tenants in common is managed as the underlying asset is managed with the exception that the surviving joint owner must be consulted as a co-owner. See the individual assets in this

Summary of Assets for specific instructions. Property owned with a joint tenant with right of survivorship or tenants by the entireties passes to the surviving joint owner at the death of one tenant and is no longer part of the Decedent's estate. The surviving joint tenant has the responsibility and authority for management.

May a jointly owned interest be sold or liquidated during the administration of the estate? The Executor must review the Will for special instructions regarding any property owned as tenants in common. Property held as joint tenants with rights of survivorship is not probate property and is not subject to sale or liquidation by the Executor. See the individual asset in this Summary of Assets for specific information regarding the sale of each type of asset.

What income is generated by a jointly owned interest? Income from joint property is generated by the underlying asset as described in the section for that individual asset in this Summary of Assets. The income from the property owned as joint tenants with right of survivorship or tenants by the entireties is not part of the estate income. Income from the property owned as tenants in common is estate income to the extent the estate is entitled to the income from the property. Sale of property that is part of the probate estate may generate a capital gain if the property is sold for more than its date-of-death value; or it may generate a loss if it is sold for less than its date-of-death value.

On what federal estate tax schedule is a joint interest reported? Property owned as joint tenants with right of survivorship and tenants by the entireties is reported on Schedule E. Supplemental Income and Loss. Property owned as tenants in common is reported on the schedule on which the underlying property is reported with the notation of the proportionate interest of the Decedent in the property. See the individual asset in this Summary of Assets for specific instructions.

Is the joint interest reported on the probate inventory? Assets held by the Decedent as a joint tenant with right of survivorship are not reported on the probate inventory. The Decedent's share of property owned as a tenant in common is reported on the schedule that includes that type of property with the notation that this is an asset owned by the estate as a tenant in common and the Decedent's proportionate share. Any property can be placed into a trust that transfers the interest of a tenant in common to a beneficiary at Decedent's death. The interest of the tenant in common is not reported on the probate inventory if it is held in such a trust. In some states, the Decedent's share of real estate owned as a tenant in common can be transferred to a third party by a Transfer on Death Deed.

How is a joint interest transferred out of the estate? Property owned by the Decedent as a joint tenant with right of survivorship was transferred to the surviving joint tenant at the Decedent's death. For real property, a death certificate should be filed with the register of deeds in the county and state where the real estate is located. For intangible personal property, a death certificate should be filed with the account representative or administrator of any account held as joint tenants with rights of survivorship. The share of property owned by the Decedent as a tenant in common will be transferred by court order or Executor's Deed. See the individual asset in this Summary of Assets for specific transfer instructions for each asset. Any tangible personal property with a title that provides for ownership by joint owners, such as an automobile, will belong to a surviving joint owner with right of survivorship at Decedent's death. In some states, by statute or by custom, joint owners are treated as being joint owners with rights of survivorship although there is no indication on the title of the right of survivorship. The estate attorney or the state department of motor vehicles should be consulted for state laws or department of motor vehicles transfer requirements.

JUDGMENTS

What is a judgment? A judgment is an order by a court directing a debtor to pay money to the creditor. When the Decedent was the creditor, the judgment is a valuable asset and the Executor must enforce the judgment. A judgment can be due to Decedent for past due child support, alimony or a property settlement in a divorce, a decision or settlement of a personal injury suit, or an award for damages.

What type of asset is a judgment? A judgment is intangible personal property. In the probate estate, the administration and distribution of a judgment is governed by the laws of the state of the Decedent's domicile. However, the methods available for collection of the judgment and the interest rate applicable are governed by the law of the state where the judgment was rendered.

How is a judgment described? The description of a judgment will include the name of the parties; the name of the court and its location including city, county, and state; the court case number; the date of the judgment; and the terms of the judgment including amount, the time for payment set out by the court, and the applicable interest rate.

How is a judgment valued? The value of a judgment is set by the court order that grants the judgment. A copy of the court order and any calculations made for interest will be necessary to determine the value. If there is a likelihood that the judgment will not be paid, then the value of the judgment must be discounted for purposes of the probate inventory and the estate tax return. If a judgment is sold in an arm's length sale before the estate is ordered to be distributed, the price for which the judgment sold is its fair market value. If a value different than the sale price was reported to the court on an inventory or to the state and federal governments on any tax return, the inventory and any tax returns may need to be amended to reflect the fair market value.

How is information about a judgment confirmed? The court's order will confirm the parties, the terms of the judgment, and the value. The reasons for any discount from the amount ordered by the court (such as doubt as to collectibility) must be documented. The applicable interest rate payable for delay in payment is determined by the statutes of the state where the judgment was rendered.

What are the management concerns for a judgment? A judgment must be collected by the Executor. Collection of the judgment may be accomplished as soon the Executor is appointed by the court. Collection of the debt does not require authority to sell. A letter to the debtor demanding payment must be sent. If the debtor does not pay promptly, the Executor must act immediately to collect the debt. Failure to make all reasonable efforts to collect may result in a personal liability for the Executor.

May a judgment be sold during the administration of the estate? The Executor must review the Will for instructions concerning any judgment. A debt owed to the Decedent may be sold to prevent loss in value or to divide the proceeds of the judgment among Legatees. The sale of the judgment can be accomplished as soon as the Executor has been appointed by the court and has proper authority for the sale. In order to have proper authority to sell the judgment, the Executor must review the Will to be sure that it permits the Executor to sell the judgment. If the Will does not give express authority to sell personal property, the estate attorney must obtain a court order expressly authorizing the Executor to sell personal property. In seeking the court order, the petition must state that the sale is necessary to pay debts, expenses, taxes, or legacies; that there is a risk of loss of value in the asset; or that the sale of the debt is in the best interest of the estate for some other reason. When none of these conditions is met, all interested persons can agree in writing that the sale is in the best interest of the estate and the court will give permission for the sale.

For obvious reasons, the sale of estate property to a family member or associate of the Executor is prohibited by state statute even where the Executor has authority to sell property without court supervision. Such a sale is known as self-dealing. See Chapter 8 for a discussion concerning the requirement to avoid self-dealing. This requirement may be overcome if the duty not to self-deal is waived in the Will or if the court, with full knowledge of the relationship, approves of the buyer and the sale price before the sale.

Whether the court ordered the sale or the Will waived the court's supervision, a complete accounting of the sale must be filed and approved by the court before the estate can be closed and the Executor discharged. The Executor must keep a copy of all documents relating to the sale and a copy of the payment check to support the accounting for the sale. All proceeds must be deposited into the estate account to await the court's order of distribution.

What income is generated by a judgment? Judgments are subject to statutory interest. That interest is income when paid.

On what federal estate tax schedule is a judgment reported? Schedule F. Other Miscellaneous Property.

Is a judgment reported on the probate inventory? Generally, yes. If the judgment has not yet been collected at the time of the Decedent's death, the Decedent's right to receive that property is owned solely by the Decedent's estate and is part of the Decedent's probate estate. In rare cases, a judgment may have been assigned to a trust before the Decedent's death. After the Decedent's death, the judgment will transfer to the beneficiaries named in the trust. The judgment is not reported on the probate inventory if held in such a trust.

How is a judgment transferred out of the estate? If the judgment has been ordered, but not collected, the right to receive the payments will be transferred by the journal entry of final settlement or other court order to the new owner. The Executor must notify the judgment debtor of the transfer and of the obligation to pay the new owner. If the case has not been fully litigated, the rights under the lawsuit may transfer to the new owner. See Lawsuit in this Summary of Assets.

LAWSUIT

What is a lawsuit? If the Decedent was involved in a lawsuit that makes a claim for recovery of damages, that lawsuit may survive the Decedent and be an asset in the Decedent's estate. The Decedent's death may result in a claim for wrongful death for the Decedent's family or for damages on behalf of the Decedent's estate. The Executor must consult with the estate attorney to determine the obligations of the Executor concerning these lawsuits, including the obligation and authority of the Executor to initiate the lawsuit or to negotiate a settlement for the estate.

What type of asset is a lawsuit? A lawsuit is intangible personal property. In the administration of an asset that is part of the probate estate, the laws of the state of the Decedent's domicile govern the administration and distribution of the rights to a lawsuit. However, the laws of the state where the lawsuit is filed will control the legal proceedings in a lawsuit.

How is a lawsuit described? The description of the lawsuit states the nature of the claim made—for example, a suit for recovery of contract damages, a medical malpractice suit, or an action for damage to property. The description also must include the names of the parties to the lawsuit; the case number; the name of the court; and the city, county, and state where lawsuit is filed.

How is a lawsuit valued? The value of the lawsuit is merely speculative until the lawsuit is settled or decided. The amount asked in the pleading is evidence of the upper limit of possible value, and the amount offered and refused in settlement is evidence of the lower limit of possible value of the suit. It is possible that there will be no damages awarded in a lawsuit. Once settled or fully decided, the value of the lawsuit is finally determined and a judgment is ordered. A copy of the judgment and any calculations made for interest will be necessary to determine the value. The estate attorney and the attorney handling the lawsuit should be consulted in determining the value prior to settlement or court decision.

How is information about a lawsuit confirmed? The pleadings filed in court and settlement offers are evidence of value before the lawsuit is settled or decided. The court's order or the settlement agreement is definitive of the value once the lawsuit is decided or settled.

What are the management concerns for a lawsuit? If the Decedent was a party in a lawsuit in progress before the death of the Decedent, the rights to the lawsuit may belong to the estate. The Executor must consult with the estate attorney for instructions. If the death of the Decedent was caused by the intentional act or by the negligence or malpractice of another, the estate of the Decedent may own the right to initiate a lawsuit and the heirs may also have a right to initiate a suit on their own behalf for wrongful death. The Executor must initiate a lawsuit, if appropriate, on account of the death of the Decedent or other claims the Decedent may have had.

May a lawsuit be sold during the administration of the estate? The state laws control the sale of any lawsuit. The Executor must review the Will for instructions concerning the lawsuit, if any. The sale of the lawsuit can be accomplished as soon as the Executor has been appointed by the court and has proper authority for the sale. In order to have proper authority to sell the lawsuit, the Executor must review the Will to be sure that it expressly permits the Executor to sell personal property. If the Will does not give express authority to sell personal property, the estate attorney must obtain a court order expressly authorizing the Executor to sell the lawsuit. In seeking the court order, the petition must state that the sale is necessary to pay debts, expenses, taxes, or legacies; that there is a risk of loss of value in the asset; or that the sale of the debt is in the best interest of the estate for some other reason. When none of these conditions is met, all interested persons can agree to the sale in writing and the court will give permission for the sale.

For obvious reasons, the sale of estate property to a family member or associate of the Executor is prohibited by state statute even where the Executor has authority to sell property without court supervision. Such a sale is known as self-dealing. See Chapter 8 for a discussion concerning the requirement to avoid self-dealing. This requirement may be overcome if the duty not to self-deal is waived in the Will, or if the court, with full knowledge of the relationship, approves of the buyer and the sale price before the sale.

Whether the court ordered the sale or the Will waived the court's supervision, a complete accounting of the sale must be filed and approved by the court before the estate can be closed and the Executor discharged. The Executor must keep a copy of all documents relating to the sale and a copy of the payment check to support the accounting for the sale. All proceeds must be deposited into the estate account until the court orders distribution.

What income is generated by a lawsuit? The lawsuit itself does not generate income. The settlement or award of compensatory damages is not taxable income. See IRC § 102. Any punitive damages paid are fully taxable as income.[2] Interest paid on a settlement or award is taxable income.

On what federal estate tax schedule is a lawsuit reported? Schedule F. Other Miscellaneous Property.

2 O'Gilvie vs. IRS, 519 US 79 (1996)

Is a lawsuit reported on the probate inventory? Yes, if the Decedent had the right to sue, that right may belong to the estate after the Decedent's death. Wrongful death claims are made directly by the family and are not reported on the probate inventory. Theoretically, it would be possible for the Decedent to have assigned the rights to a lawsuit to a trust that transfers assets to a beneficiary at Decedent's death. If the lawsuit was placed in such a trust, it would not be reported on the probate inventory.

How is a lawsuit transferred out of the estate? The journal entry of final settlement or other court order will transfer the rights in the lawsuit to the new owner, if such a transfer is not prohibited by statute. If the judgment has been ordered, but not collected, the right to receive the payments will be transferred to the new owners by court order. See Judgments in this Summary of Assets.

LIFE INSURANCE

What is life insurance? Life insurance is a contract between the owner of the policy and the insurance company in which the insurance company agrees that for a specified premium the insurance company will pay to a beneficiary a sum of money upon the death of the insured. There are multitudes of types of life insurance policies including whole life, universal life, endowment, and term life insurance. The Decedent may have owned the policy that insured his or her own life. The death benefit of a policy that insured the Decedent's life will be paid to a beneficiary or the Decedent's estate. The Decedent may have owned a policy on the life of another person. That policy is a valuable asset that will be transferred to a new owner. However, the death benefit of the policy that insures the life of another person will not be payable until the death of that other person.

What type of asset is life insurance? Insurance is intangible personal property. The laws of the Decedent's state of domicile govern administration and distribution of life insurance policies owned by the Decedent on the life of another and also govern the administration and distribution of the death benefit of a life insurance policy when the estate is the beneficiary of those proceeds.

How is life insurance described? Life insurance is described by the name of the insurance company, the policy number, the name of the owner, the name of the insured, and the names of the beneficiaries, if any.

How is life insurance valued? When the Decedent was both the owner of the policy and the insured, the amount of the death benefit paid by the insurance company to the estate or a beneficiary is the value of the policy for estate tax purposes. When the estate is the beneficiary, the proceeds are part of the probate estate. Upon a request from the Executor, the insurance company will provide a statement of the death benefit of each life insurance policy on IRS Form 712.

When the Decedent was the owner of the policy, but not the insured, the insurance policy is an asset in the Decedent's estate and the value of that policy at the time of Decedent's death is included in the probate inventory and on the estate tax return. The technical name of the value of a policy for which the insured has not yet died is the "interpolated terminal reserve," an amount similar to its cash value. Upon the request of the Executor, the insurance company will provide a statement of the value of the insurance policy on Decedent's date of death.

When the Decedent was the insured, but not the owner of the policy, the proceeds will be paid to the beneficiary and the value of the proceeds will not be included in Decedent's probate or taxable estate. One exception to this rule is when the Decedent gave ownership of the policy insuring the Decedent's life to another person within the three years prior to Decedent's death. See Gifts Made before Death in this Summary of Assets.

How is information about life insurance confirmed? The insurance company's statement of the value of the proceeds on an IRS Form 712 will confirm the recipient and amount of proceeds of a policy that insured the life of the Decedent. The statement of the interpolated terminal reserve from the insurance company will confirm the value of a policy owned by the Decedent but which did not insure the life of the Decedent.

What are the management concerns for life insurance? The policy and any riders should be found and kept in a safe place. The Executor must notify the insurance company of the death of the Decedent and request claim forms for policies that insured the life of the Decedent and change of ownership forms for policies owned by the Decedent but which insured the life of another person. The Executor may file or assist in filing claims for life insurance policies for which the Decedent was the insured. The policies that insured the life of the Decedent must be sent to the insurance company as part of the claim. Keep a copy of the policy and any riders. The original policies should be mailed by registered mail with return receipt requested to the insurance company or hand delivered to a representative of the insurance company. The Executor should request a receipt for each policy delivered to a representative.

The Executor should also request that IRS Form 712 be provided by the insurance company.

When the Decedent owned policies insuring the lives of others, the Executor must place these policies in safekeeping until the estate is distributed by court order. The Executor should also request instructions from the insurance company for their requirements to transfer ownership.

May life insurance be liquidated during the administration of the estate? The death benefit of a life insurance policy that insured the life of the Decedent and is payable to the estate may be collected when the Executor has been appointed by the court. The proceeds must be deposited into the estate account to await distribution by the court.

If the Decedent owed a policy on the life of another person, the Executor must review the Will for instructions concerning the policy. Unless the policy is specifically bequeathed or the Will prohibits cancellation, the policy may be liquidated for its cash value to raise cash to pay debts, expenses, or taxes or to divide the proceeds of an asset among Legatees. There are circumstances in which the policy must be liquidated even when prohibited by the Will. See Chapter 9 for a discussion of these circumstances.

What income is generated by life insurance? If the Decedent was the insured, the death benefit is not taxable income to the beneficiary. Any interest that is paid because of a delay in distributing the proceeds is interest income to the recipient. If the Decedent owned the policy but was not the insured, then the policy does not generate income. A return of premium, often called a dividend, is not income for tax purposes.

On what federal estate tax schedule is life insurance reported? Insurance on the Decedent's life when the Decedent was also the owner of the policy is reported on Schedule D. Life Insurance on the Decedent's Life. Insurance on the Decedent's life when the Decedent was not the owner of the policy is not reported on any federal estate tax schedule unless the Decedent had given ownership of the policy away during the three years preceding Decedent's death. Gifts given within three years of death are reported on Schedule G. Transfers During Decedent's Life. A life insurance policy owned by the Decedent that insures the life of another person is reported on Schedule F. Other Miscellaneous Property.

Is life insurance reported on the probate inventory? When the insurance was on the life of the Decedent and the Decedent was the owner of the policy, the Decedent usually named a beneficiary of the insurance policy. That beneficiary will receive the death benefit directly and the proceeds are not part of the probate estate. However, if the Decedent named the estate as the beneficiary, if the named beneficiary has died before the Decedent and no contingent beneficiary was named, or if the named beneficiary chooses to disclaim the death benefit, then the estate will be the beneficiary of the insurance policy and the death benefit will be reported on the probate inventory.

When the insurance was on the life of the Decedent and the Decedent was not the owner of the policy, the proceeds of the life insurance policy are not reported as probate property unless the estate was the beneficiary of the policy.

When the insurance was on the life of another person and the Decedent was the owner of the policy, the policy is the property of the Decedent's estate and is reported on the probate inventory.

Intangible personal property such as insurance can be placed into a trust that transfers the insurance to a beneficiary at Decedent's death. The insurance is not reported on the probate inventory if it is held in such a trust.

How is life insurance transferred out of the estate? When the insurance was on the life of the Decedent and the Decedent was the owner of the policy, the Decedent has usually named a beneficiary of the insurance policy. That beneficiary will receive the death benefit directly and the benefit will not be part of the estate. However, if the Decedent named the estate as the beneficiary, if the named beneficiary has died before the Decedent and no contingent beneficiary was named, or if the named beneficiary chooses to disclaim the death benefit, then the estate will receive the death benefit. The Executor must request and complete claim forms provided by the insurance company. The death benefit must be deposited in the estate bank account and will be distributed pursuant to the court's order of distribution.

When the insurance policy insured the life of the Decedent and the Decedent was not the owner of the policy, the death benefit of the life insurance policy is not part of the Decedent's estate unless the estate is the beneficiary. The beneficiary of a policy will receive the death benefit directly.

When the insurance policy insures the life of another person and the Decedent was the owner of the policy, the policy owned by the Decedent on the life of another person is the property of the Decedent's estate and will be distributed pursuant to the court's order of distribution. The estate attorney or the Executor must contact the insurance company to obtain change of ownership forms. Change of ownership forms from the insurance company must be completed and signed by the Executor.

The forms must be mailed to the insurance company with a certified copy of the court's order of distribution and any other documents requested by the insurance company.

MUTUAL FUNDS

What are mutual funds? Ownership of mutual funds is the ownership of shares of a mutual fund company that uses the invested money of its owners to purchase many different stocks or bonds. Professional managers manage this pool of money. Investments in a mutual fund allow investors to own a highly diversified portfolio with a relatively small investment.

What type of assets are mutual funds? Shares of a mutual fund company are intangible personal property. The laws of the Decedent's state of domicile govern the administration and distribution of mutual fund shares in the administration of the estate.

How are mutual funds described? The description of mutual funds includes the full name of the mutual fund company and the specific funds that are owned in that company, the account number, the number of shares owned, the names of all the owners, the mode of ownership, any restrictions on the fund shares, and the names of any Transfer-on-Death beneficiaries.

How are mutual funds valued? The date-of-death value of a mutual fund account is easily determined by contacting the account representative or the mutual fund company for written confirmation of ownership, beneficiaries, the number of shares, and date-of-death value. The price used to value the mutual fund shares is the redemption price, that is, the amount the estate would realize upon the sale of the shares back to the issuing company.

How is information about mutual funds confirmed? The written report from the mutual fund company about the owners, number of shares, the value, and beneficiaries is the best method of confirming the ownership and value information.

What are the management concerns for a mutual fund? The Will must be consulted for specific instructions with regard to sale or distribution of mutual funds. If there are no specific instructions, the Executor must determine whether these funds will be retained for distribution in-kind or sold and distributed in cash. The Executor must consider early sale or transfer of mutual fund holdings to avoid losses. Even a mutual fund balanced between income and growth stocks involves a risk of loss that may not be permissible for investment of estate funds. Within a reasonable period of time the Executor must evaluate the risk involved in holding the mutual funds, the state law regarding retention of assets purchased by the Decedent, and sell the shares and distribute the proceeds "in cash," distribute the mutual fund shares "in-kind," or obtain written approval from legatees for retention of mutual funds. In-kind means that the mutual fund shares remain invested in the mutual fund and only the name of the owner is changed. This in-kind distribution avoids the costs of sale and the commissions for reinvestment by the recipient. In cash means that the mutual fund shares are sold at the current market price and the sales proceeds are distributed to the estate and then to the legatees. A transfer in-kind will require that each recipient either already have or open a new investment account in his or her own name to receive the distribution. The Executor cannot open an account for the recipient; each recipient must open his or her own account and give the account number to the Executor or estate attorney before the mutual fund shares can be transferred. The Executor must obtain instructions from the mutual funds company for the transfer requirements early in preparation for distribution.

Redemption of Mutual Funds. Mutual fund shares owned by the Decedent may qualify for favorable tax treatment. A special provision of the tax code, IRC § 303, permits, in some instances, the redemption of stock owned by the Decedent's estate under tax-favored rules. The value of the stock redeemed under this provision can be up to the amount paid by the estate for death taxes and the amount of funeral and some administration expenses. This redemption of stock for cash is treated as an exchange of the stock for full payment of the stock redeemed. The significance of this redemption is that when certain criteria are met, the exchange of stock for cash avoids treatment as an income taxable dividend. When the estate is comprised of significant amounts of stock, the Executor must take care to determine whether this benefit is available to the estate. Consult with the estate attorney or a CPA to determine whether the estate is eligible for this tax-favored redemption to pay death taxes and funeral and administration expenses.

May mutual funds be sold during administration of the estate? The Will must be consulted for specific instructions with regard to sale or distribution of mutual funds. The Executor must review the Will for instructions concerning the sale of mutual funds. Mutual funds may be sold to raise cash to pay debts, expenses, or taxes; to prevent losses in value because of a declining market; or to divide the proceeds of an asset among legatees. The Executor may need to consider sale of assets for other reasons as well. Certain mutual funds can be sold back to the corporation that issued the mutual funds (redeemed) to obtain a tax-favored distribution from that corporation. There are circumstances in which mutual funds must be sold even when such sale is prohibited by the Will. See Chapter 9 for a discussion of these circumstances.

The sale of mutual funds can be accomplished as soon as the Executor has been appointed by the court and has proper authority for the sale. The Executor must review the Will to be sure that it expressly permits the Executor to sell personal property. If the Will does not give express authority to sell personal property, the estate attorney must obtain a court order expressly authorizing the Executor to sell personal property.

In seeking the court order, the petition must state that the sale is necessary to pay debts, expenses, taxes, or legacies; that there is a risk of loss of value in the asset; that the sale or liquidation of the mutual funds is in the best interest of the estate for some other reason. When none of these conditions is met, all interested persons can agree in writing that the sale is in the best interest of the estate and the court will give permission for the sale or liquidation.

For obvious reasons, the sale of mutual funds to a family member or associate of the Executor is prohibited by state statute even where the Executor has authority to sell property without court supervision. Such a sale is known as self-dealing. See Chapter 8 for a discussion concerning the requirement to avoid self-dealing. This requirement may be overcome if the duty not to self-deal is waived in the Will, or if the court, with full knowledge of the relationship, approves of the buyer and the sale price before the sale.

Whether the court ordered the sale or the Will waived the court's supervision, a complete accounting of the sale must be filed and approved by the court before the estate can be closed and the Executor discharged. The Executor must keep a copy of all documents relating to the sale and a copy of the payment check to support the accounting for the sale or liquidation. All proceeds must be deposited into the estate account until the court orders distribution.

The sale price of mutual funds is controlled by the market price at the time of the sale. Mutual funds held in book-entry form are sold by the brokerage or investment company when the Executor provides a letter of instruction requesting the sale. The Executor should contact the investment company for additional requirements for sale. Liquidation of some funds may require compliance with restrictions on the fund.

What income is generated by a mutual fund? Dividends earned on the stocks and interest on the bonds owned by the mutual funds are income. These dividends and interest are passed on to the owners of the mutual fund shares as income. Capital gains are realized when stocks and bonds are sold by the fund manager for a profit, and capital loss is realized when those securities are sold for a loss. These gains and losses are also passed on to the owners of the mutual fund shares as income. The income from mutual funds will be reported on IRS Form 1099-DIV.

On what federal estate tax schedule are mutual funds reported? Schedule B. Stock and Bonds.

Are mutual funds reported on the probate inventory? Mutual funds may have been owned by the Decedent solely and have no transfer-on-death beneficiary named. These mutual funds are part of the Decedent's probate estate, are reported on the probate inventory, and are subject to probate administration. However, mutual funds often have a co-owner or a pay-on-death beneficiary named. If there is a joint tenant with right of survivorship on the mutual fund, that co-owner will own the fund after the death of the Decedent. If there is a named beneficiary who survives, the fund will be distributed to that beneficiary directly by the mutual fund company. If there is no beneficiary named, if the beneficiary does not survive, or if the beneficiary disclaims the account, and there is no contingent beneficiary, the estate will be the owner of the mutual fund shares and the mutual fund shares must be included in the probate inventory. Intangible personal property such as mutual fund shares can be placed into a trust that transfers the shares to a beneficiary at Decedent's death. The mutual fund shares are not reported on the probate inventory if they are held in such a trust.

How is a mutual fund transferred out of the estate? Mutual fund shares can be transferred in-kind. In-kind means that the mutual fund shares remain invested in the mutual fund company and only the name of the owner is changed. This avoids the costs of sale and the commission for reinvestment for the Legatee. Most mutual fund companies have families of funds that allow transfer among many different funds with different investment goals without incurring new sales commissions. One option for the Executor is to distribute all funds in-kind to allow Legatees to choose whether they want to liquidate or retain the investment in the mutual fund company. In order to accomplish an in-kind transfer, each Legatee must either already have or must open a personal account with the mutual fund company or other investment company to receive the distribution. The legatee's investment account number and the investment company's Depository Transfer Clearing (DTC) number must be provided to the Executor by each Legatee. The account number and the DTC number for each Legatee will be included in the Letter of Instruction that is sent to the holder or transfer agent of the funds. The Executor must sign the Letter of Instruction with the signature Medallion Guaranteed instructing the registered representative of the account to distribute the shares. The estate attorney will prepare this letter for the Executor's signature. All other requirements for transfer must also be completed and returned to the mutual funds company.

OIL, GAS, AND OTHER MINERAL INTERESTS

What are oil, gas, and other mineral interests? Mineral interests are the right to extract oil, gas, or other minerals from real estate. Those who own the surface real estate land also own the minerals on and under the land unless those mineral interests have been severed from the ownership of the surface. The right to extract oil, gas, or minerals can be leased from the landowner when the mineral interests are not severed or from the owner of the severed mineral interest. That lease is also an interest in oil, gas, or other minerals.

What type of assets are oil, gas, and other mineral interests? Ownership of the surface with mineral interests intact, ownership of severed mineral interests, and ownership of the mineral lease are all interests in real estate. The laws of the state where the real estate is located govern the administration, sale, and distribution of mineral interests in the estate.

How are oil, gas and other mineral interests described? Oil, gas, and mineral interests are described by the full legal description of the surface real estate under which the mineral interest is found, the type (royalty, over-riding royalty, or working interest) and percentage of the interest, the mineral being extracted, the names of all owners, and the mode of ownership. The description should also include any Transfer-on-Death deeds, life estates, remainder interests, liens, or other restrictions or conditions that apply to the interest.

How are oil, gas, and other mineral interests valued? Because the value of an interest in oil, gas, and other minerals is an estimate or speculation of what the well or mine will produce in the future and because oil, gas, and other minerals are depleting assets, special techniques are required for valuing these interests. The estate attorney, an oil and gas accountant, or an appraiser will take into account current production, age of wells or mines, and reserve estimates based on formations, among other things, in arriving at an estimated value. If a federal estate tax return is required or if the state law requires an appraisal, the valuation of mineral interests will require appraisal by a licensed appraiser who is experienced in the valuation of oil, gas, and mineral interests. Consult the estate attorney or an oil and gas accountant for information about how these interests are valued under the state law and local custom.

If mineral interests are sold in an arm's length sale before the estate is ordered to be distributed, the price for which the interests are sold is the fair market value. If a value different than the sale price was reported to the court on an inventory or to the state and federal governments on any tax return, the inventory and any tax returns may need to be amended to reflect the fair market value.

How is information about oil, gas, and other mineral interests confirmed? Confirmation of ownership and the legal description of the real estate and the underlying oil, gas, or other mineral interest are obtained in a copy of the deed, the Journal Entry of Final Settlement, the Decree of Descent, or other document of title filed with the Register of Deeds or the Clerk of the Court of the county where the surface land is located. The property tax statement is a guide to locating the deed or other document of title. The documents and correspondence from the individual or company that pays the check for lease or for production from the mine or well are also a guide to locating the deed or other document of title to the oil, gas, or other mineral interests. The statement of an appraiser or oil and gas accountant who specializes in valuing oil, gas, and other minerals will confirm the value of the mineral interest. A statement of a county or state appraisal for property tax is independent, but not conclusive, evidence of the value of the interest.

What are the management concerns for oil, gas and other mineral interests? When the Decedent's estate includes royalties, that is, a share of the profits from the sale of the extracted minerals paid to the owner of the property, the production company that pays the royalties must be given notice of Decedent's death and instructions for payment of royalties to the estate. It may be necessary for the Executor to sign lease agreements. If the Will does not give specific authority to sign lease agreements that extend beyond the time the estate will be open, the Executor should secure court authority to sign these lease agreements. All payments must be deposited into the estate account. Whether the mineral interests will be appraised by a licensed appraiser or informally must be determined. The Executor must consult the Will for specific instructions with regard to sale or distribution of oil, gas, and other mineral interests. If there are no specific instructions, the Executor must determine whether these interests will be retained or sold. The Executor should determine whether real estate taxes are owed on the real estate and request that the real estate tax statements be mailed to the Executor or the estate attorney. Payment of real property taxes and mortgage payments should be made if there are sufficient funds. The Executor must obtain adequate insurance on the property if there are sufficient funds. If the property had been held in joint tenancy with an individual who died before the Decedent, the certified death certificate of that deceased individual must be filed in the deed records of the county where the real estate is located. If the property was received by the Decedent in a probate proceeding, the final order of distribution from the probate court may need to be filed with the deed records. Other clouds on the title, including disputes as to ownership, may also need to be cleared, that is, all legal impediments to a free and clear title removed, with the help of the estate attorney.

If the real estate was on the market before Decedent's death, the Executor must notify the real estate broker who holds the listing contract of Decedent's death and of the appointment of the Executor.

The Executor must determine the obligations of the estate under rent and lease agreements. Notice of termination of leases and other agreements regarding the mineral interests must be sent to the lessees when necessary. New leases on the mineral interests must be signed when necessary. Secure court authority to enter into oil, gas, or mineral leases when necessary. Lessees must be instructed to send payments to the Executor.

Can oil, gas, and other mineral interests be sold during the administration of the estate? The Executor must review the Will for instructions concerning the sale of real estate and mineral interests. Those interests may need to be sold to pay debts, expenses, or taxes of the estate; to avoid the costs of property taxes, insurance, and maintenance on the property; to prevent loss in value because of a declining market; or to divide the proceeds among Devisees. There are circumstances in which mineral interests must be sold even when sale is prohibited by the Will. See Chapter 9 for a discussion of these circumstances.

Oil, gas, and other mineral interests that are located in a state other than the state in which the primary probate proceeding is being conducted will be subject to an ancillary, that is an additional and supplementary, probate proceeding for administration, sale, and distribution. The Executor must consult with the estate attorney to determine how, when, and where to begin the ancillary probate proceedings.

The sale of the these mineral interests can be accomplished as soon as the Executor has been appointed by the court and has proper authority for the sale. The Executor must review the Will to be sure that it expressly permits the Executor to sell real estate. If the Will does not give express authority to sell real estate, the estate attorney must obtain a court order specifically authorizing the Executor to sell real estate.

In seeking the court order, the petition must state that the sale is necessary to pay debts, expenses, or taxes due from the estate; that value of the mineral interests may decline during the administration of the estate; or that the sale of the mineral interests is in the best interest of the estate for some other reason. Even if none of these conditions is met, the court will give permission for the sale if all interested persons agree in writing that the sale is in the best interest of the estate. The Executor must consult the Will for specific instructions with regard to sale or distribution of oil, gas, and other mineral interests. If there are no specific instructions, the Executor must determine whether these interests will be retained or sold. If the property is to be sold, the method of sale must be determined. The mineral interests may be sold directly by the Executor, by a mineral interest broker in a private sale, or by an auctioneer in a public sale. The Executor must obtain court approval for sale if the Will does not expressly provide for sale of real estate without court supervision. The Executor must set the asking price and determine a minimum price that will be considered if an offer is made. The sale price must comply with the statutory requirements for sale price. Consult the estate attorney for the state law requirements for a minimum price and other requirements of sale.

What income is generated by oil, gas, and other mineral interests? Ongoing sale of production of oil, gas, or other mineral interests is ordinary income. The production company will report the income on IRS Form 1099-MISC. Lease payments are also income. The check is the record of a lease payment; make a copy of the check before depositing it. Expenses and depletion are offsetting deductions from income. The sale of any oil, gas, or mineral interest for more than its basis generates an income taxable gain; the sale for less than its basis generates a loss. See Chapter 10 for a discussion of basis and gain in the sale of estate assets.

On what federal estate tax schedule are oil, gas, and mineral interests reported? Schedule A. Real Estate.

Are oil, gas, and mineral interests reported on the probate inventory? Oil, gas, and other mineral interests may have been owned by the Decedent solely and have no Transfer-on-Death beneficiary named. These interests are part of the Decedent's probate estate, are reported on the probate inventory, and are subject to probate administration. If there is a joint tenant with right of survivorship who co-owns an interest with the Decedent, that co-owner will own the property after the death of the Decedent and the property will not be reported on the probate inventory. If no joint tenant survives the Decedent, the interest will be part of the Decedent's probate estate. In some states, a Transfer-On-Death Deed may transfer real estate, including oil, gas, and mineral interests, to a beneficiary at the Decedent's death. If there is a named beneficiary who survives, the interest will belong to that beneficiary directly upon the Decedent's death and the property will not be reported on the probate inventory. If there is no beneficiary named, if no beneficiary survives, or if the beneficiary disclaims the real estate, the Decedent's estate will be the owner of the property and the property must be reported on the probate inventory. Real estate, including oil, gas, and other mineral interests, can be placed into a trust before the Decedent's death that transfers the property to a beneficiary at Decedent's death. The real estate is not reported on the probate inventory if held in such a trust.

How are oil, gas, and other mineral interests transferred out of the estate? Oil, gas, and other mineral interests are transferred to the new owner by the probate court's order of distribution. In addition to being filed in the probate court, the court's order of distribution from the state where the primary probate proceedings are conducted must be filed with the Register of Deeds in the county where the real estate associated with the oil, gas, and other mineral interests is located. No other deed is necessary. The court's order of distribution may be filed in any county (or parish) of the state where the estate is administered. However, the court's order of distribution from one state is not effective to transfer real property, including oil, gas, and other mineral interests, located in another state. An ancillary, that is, an additional and supplementary, probate proceeding will be required to transfer the real estate located in a state other than the one in which the primary probate proceedings are conducted. In addition to filing the court's order with the Register of Deeds, a certified copy of the court's order of distribution must be sent to the production company that had been buying the oil, gas, or other minerals produced. New division orders and instructions for payment of proceeds will be prepared and sent by the production company to the new owners for their signatures.

PERSONAL AND HOUSEHOLD EFFECTS (*See also* FAMILY MEMORABILIA)

What are personal and household effects? Personal and household effects are those items used in daily life including clothing, linens, books, bicycles, china, crystal and silverware, cooking utensils, sports equipment, furniture and furnishings, and all other personal property of a similar nature.

What type of assets are personal and household effects? Personal and household effects are tangible personal property. The laws of the state where the property is located govern the administration, sale, and distribution of tangible personal property in the probate estate.

How are personal and household effects described? Unless an item is specifically mentioned in the Will or is of significant value, personal and household effects can be described in general terms. See the individual assets in this Summary of Assets for specific instructions for the description of each type of asset.

How are personal and household effects valued? An informal valuation by the Executor or by an independent third party, such as a dealer or an auctioneer, may be sufficient for valuing personal and household effects. Keep in mind that a dealer or an auctioneer may value personal and household items below the retail market value if the auctioneer intends to offer to purchase those items for resale. For purposes of the estate tax return, items in the same room can be grouped together if none of the individual items has a value in excess of $100.00. The value is the price a willing buyer would pay a willing seller for the item at an estate sale, not the replacement value or the amount for which the items are insured. Used furniture, other than antiques, will usually be valued below the $100 threshold. Appraisal by a licensed appraiser may be required for any item of significant value. See the individual assets in this Summary of Assets for specific instructions for the valuation of each type of asset.

How is information about personal and household effects confirmed? The inventory of the Executor will be the most common report of the personal and household effects that confirms the description and value of those items. The written appraisal by a licensed appraiser, or the statement of an auctioneer or other dealer will confirm the description and value. Ownership of personal and household effects is most commonly determined by possession. Purchase receipts, insurance coverage for specific assets, and other written documents may be evidence of ownership.

What are the management concerns for personal and household effects? The Executor must ensure safe storage and insurance for personal and household effects such as jewelry, clothing, books, china, crystal, silverware, furniture and furnishings, and art objects. The Executor also must collect the personal property of the Decedent that is in the possession of others. The contents of all safes and safe deposit boxes must be examined and inventoried. Sale or early distribution will minimize the costs of storage and insurance. However, unless the Will authorizes sale of personal property, personal and household effects may not be sold without a court order. The Executor may not distribute any estate asset to any Legatee without a court order of distribution. Personal and household effects are the subject of state spousal and minors' allowances. The Executor must consult with the estate attorney to determine whether the personal and household effects will be part of those allowances.

May personal and household effects be sold during administration of the estate? The Executor must review the Will and any personal property memorandum for instructions concerning the sale or distribution of personal and household effects. The Executor must also consult with the estate attorney to determine whether the personal and household effects are subject to the spousal and minors' claims under the statutes of the state. If not prohibited, the personal and household effects may be sold to pay debts, expenses, or taxes; to avoid the costs of storage, insurance, and maintenance; to prevent losses in value because of a declining market; or to divide the proceeds of sale among legatees. There are circumstances in which assets must be sold even when their sale is prohibited by the Will. See Chapter 9 for a discussion of these circumstances.

Personal and household effects that are located in a state other than the state in which the primary probate proceeding is being conducted will be subject to an ancillary, that is, an additional and supplementary, probate proceeding for administration, sale, and distribution. The Executor must consult with the estate attorney to determine how, when, and where to begin the ancillary probate proceedings.

The sale of personal and household effects can be accomplished as soon as the Executor has been appointed by the court and has proper authority for the sale. The Executor must review the Will to be sure that it expressly permits the Executor to sell personal property. If the Will does not give express authority to sell personal property, the estate attorney must obtain a court order specifically authorizing the Executor to sell personal property.

In seeking the court order, the petition must state that the sale is necessary to pay debts, expenses, taxes or legacies; that the asset is a wasting asset (the value of the asset will be less as time goes by); or that the sale of the personal and household effects is in the best interest of the estate for some other reason. When none of these conditions is met, all interested persons can agree in writing that the sale is in the best interest of the estate and the court will give permission for the sale.

For obvious reasons, the sale of estate property to a family member or associate of the Executor is prohibited by state statute even where the Executor has authority to sell property without court supervision. Such a sale is known as self-dealing. See Chapter 8 for a discussion concerning the requirement to avoid self-dealing. This requirement may be overcome if the duty not to self-deal is waived in the Will, or if the court, with full knowledge of the relationship, approves of the buyer and the sale price before the sale.

Within the limits of the state requirement for a minimum price, setting the sale price is the responsibility of the Executor. The advice of the estate attorney, an auctioneer, or dealer in personal property will be a helpful guide, but the Executor has the final decision. Although the Executor should attempt to get the best possible price, it is also important to complete the sale within a reasonable time. Storage, maintenance, and insurance are expenses that cannot be recovered. A prompt sale removes these expenses from the estate.

State statutes control the minimum sale price for personal property. This required price is usually a percentage, for example, 80 percent, of the value reported in the probate inventory. The estate attorney must be consulted before any asset is sold to ensure that the sale price complies with the required minimum price. If there are no buyers at the required minimum price after the assets have been offered for sale for a reasonable length of time, the estate attorney must seek court approval to amend the probate inventory to reflect the lower market value and to reduce the minimum sale price.

Personal and household effects should be sold "as is," and the buyers must be required to inspect the property for themselves or to hire a professional to inspect for them. Whether the sale is accomplished by private sale, estate sale, or by auction, the Executor should make no statements concerning the condition of the property to the buyers. This is an area of potentially serious liability for the Executor personally and for the estate. The statements of the Executor may be considered by the buyer as a warranty or guarantee of the condition of the property. If the Executor's statements prove to be incorrect, the buyers may make a claim for their losses against the estate and against the Executor personally.

Although personal and household effects can be sold by private sale, sale of tangible personal property at an estate sale or an auction by a professional is highly recommended for the reasons set out in detail in Chapter 8. The Executor should contact several reputable estate sale or auction companies to discuss the timing of the sale, sale costs and commissions, reserved bids, and advertising. These professionals will charge a percentage of the total sale proceeds as their sales commission. The Executor or estate attorney should negotiate and confirm in writing a reasonable commission before the sale. This cost is an expense of the estate and will be paid from estate assets. The professional must provide a detailed receipt for items sold and the amount of the proceeds.

In all cases, an accounting of the sale must be approved by the court before the estate may be closed and the Executor discharged. This is true even when the court ordered the sale or the Will waived the court's supervision. The Executor must keep a copy of all documents relating to the sale and a copy of the payment check to support the accounting. All proceeds of a sale must be deposited into the estate account for administration and to await the court's order of distribution.

What income is generated by personal and household effects? Generally, no ordinary income is generated by personal and household effects. The sale of any asset for more than its basis generates an income taxable gain. The proceeds of the sale are taxable gain if those proceeds exceed the basis in the assets and are deductible as a loss if the basis exceeds the proceeds. However, because the basis is stepped up at death to the market value on the date of death, the sale price and the basis are usually the same and there is no gain or loss. A gain arises when the value of the asset increases between the date of death and the sale date. A loss arises when the value of the asset decreases between date of death and the sale date. See Chapter 10 for a discussion of basis and gain in the sale of estate assets.

On what federal estate tax schedule are personal and household effects reported? Schedule F. Other Miscellaneous Property.

Are personal and household effects reported on the probate inventory? Generally, yes. Personal and household effects are often the subject of state spousal and minors' allowance laws. See Chapter 9 for a discussion of spousal and minors' allowance. Personal and household goods usually do not have a title or other document of ownership that can transfer ownership of the assets at death by a beneficiary designation or show ownership by joint tenants with right of survivorship. Tangible personal property such as personal and household effects can be placed into a trust that transfers the property to a beneficiary at Decedent's death. The personal and household effects are not reported on the probate inventory if they are held in such a trust.

How are personal and household effects transferred out of the estate? The transfer of ownership of the personal and household effects to the legatee is made only after the court's order, either as an early distribution during the time the estate is being probated or in the final distribution of the estate. The transfer is made by actual delivery of possession into the hands or control of the Legatee. The Executor should obtain a receipt from the Legatee and deliver the assets directly to the legatee. If the assets must be shipped, the determination of whether the estate or the recipient will pay the cost of shipping must be part of the court's order for distribution. The Executor must also ensure that the assets are adequately insured until delivery to the Legatee. Insurance for the risk of loss or damage to the assets must be purchased as part of the shipping cost. An ancillary, that is, additional and supplementary, probate proceeding may be necessary to transfer of ownership of personal and household effects located in a state other than the state in which the primary probate proceeding is conducted.

PETS

What are pets? As difficult as it may be to think of pets as property, pets are tangible personal property. In addition to their value as friends and companions, pets are sometimes very valuable monetarily. Any animal kept for personal enjoyment or companionship is a pet. Examples of pets include dogs, cats, birds, fish, turtles, hamsters, gerbils, and horses, as well as goats, ferrets, wolves, foxes, snakes, hedgehogs, and other exotic or wild animals kept in the home.

What type of assets are pets? Pets are tangible personal property. The laws of the state where that property is located govern the administration, sale, and distribution of tangible personal property in the estate.

How are pets described? Pets are described by the type of animal, breed, gender, size, color, markings, and, if registered, by the registering organization and registration number.

How are pets valued? Pets are generally without significant monetary value. Valuation by a veterinarian or a pet dealer may be sufficient. If the animal has significant value, then appraisal by a licensed appraiser who is experienced in the valuation of such animals may be necessary.

If an animal is sold in an arm's length sale before the estate is ordered to be distributed, the price for which the animal sold is its fair market value. If a value different than the sale price was reported to the court on an inventory or to the state and federal governments on any tax return, the inventory and any tax returns may need to be amended to reflect the fair market value.

How is information about pets confirmed? The Executor will usually report the description of the pets. The report of a licensed appraiser, a veterinarian, or animal dealer, if obtained, will confirm the description and value of the pet. Ownership of pets is most commonly determined by possession. However, purchase receipts, insurance coverage, and registration documents may show ownership.

What are the management concerns for pets? The care of a live animal requires that food, water, shelter, and medical care, including immunizations, be provided. The Executor should be mindful of the emotional needs of animals that were dependent upon the Decedent for companionship and security. Pets need to be placed in a secure, nurturing environment for temporary care. A veterinarian should be consulted for specific information. Valuable animals may need to be insured. Early distribution or sale of animals will minimize the trauma to the animal and reduce the risk of loss and cost of maintenance. However, the Executor may not distribute a pet to any Legatee without a court order. The Executor may not sell any pet without a court order unless the Will authorizes sale of personal property. In some instances, euthanasia of pets is appropriate. In circumstances where a pet cannot be properly cared for or where adoption is not feasible because of age, health, or temperament, euthanasia may be appropriate. Contact the local humane society or a veterinarian. A pet may be the subject of state spousal and minors' allowances. Consult with the estate attorney to determine whether any pets will be included as part of those allowances.

May pets be sold during administration of the estate? The Executor must review the Will and any personal property memorandum for instructions concerning pets. Unless prohibited or specifically bequeathed, pets may be sold to pay debts, expenses, or taxes; to avoid the costs of maintenance and insurance, to prevent harm from coming to the animal; or to divide the proceeds of sale among Legatees. There are circumstances in which pets must be sold even when their sale is prohibited by the Will. See Chapter 9 for a discussion of these circumstances.

Pets that are located in a state other than the state in which the primary probate proceeding is being conducted will be subject to an ancillary, that is, an additional and supplementary, probate proceeding for administration, sale, and distribution of the animals. The Executor must consult with the estate attorney to determine how, when, and where to begin the ancillary probate proceedings.

The sale of the pet can be accomplished as soon as the Executor has been appointed by the court and has proper authority for the sale. The Executor must review the Will to be sure that it expressly permits the Executor to sell personal property. If the Will does not give express authority to sell personal property, the estate attorney must obtain a court order specifically authorizing the Executor to sell personal property.

In seeking the court order, the petition must state that the sale is necessary to pay debts, expenses, taxes, or legacies; that the pet may be best cared for by a purchaser; or that the sale of the pet is in the best interest of the estate for some other reason. When none of these conditions is met, all interested persons can agree in writing that the sale is in the best interest of the estate and the court will give permission for the sale.

For obvious reasons, the sale of estate property to a family member or associate of the Executor is prohibited by state statute even where the Executor has authority to sell property without court supervision. Such a sale is known as self-dealing. See Chapter 8 for a discussion concerning the requirement to avoid self-dealing. This requirement may be overcome if the duty not to self-deal is waived in the Will, or if the court, with full knowledge of the relationship, approves of the buyer and the sale price before the sale.

Within the limits of the state requirement for a minimum price, setting the sale price is the responsibility of the Executor. The advice of the estate attorney, a veterinarian, or a pet dealer will be a helpful guide, but the Executor has the final decision. Although the Executor should attempt to get the best possible price, it is also important to complete the sale within a reasonable time. Maintenance costs and insurance are expenses that cannot be recovered. A prompt sale removes these expenses from the estate.

State statutes control the minimum sale price for personal property. This required price is usually a percentage, for example, 80 percent, of the value reported in the probate inventory. The estate attorney must be consulted before any pet is sold to ensure that the sale price complies with the required minimum price. If there are no buyers at the required minimum price after the assets have been offered for sale for a reasonable length of time, the estate attorney must seek court approval to amend the probate inventory to reflect the lower market value and to reduce the minimum sale price.

Pets should be sold "as is," and the buyers must be required to inspect the animals for themselves or to hire a professional to inspect for them. Whether the sale is accomplished by private sale to an individual, by a dealer or by auction, the Executor should make no statements concerning the condition of the animals to the buyers. This is an area of potentially serious liability for the Executor personally and for the estate. The statements of the Executor may be considered as a warranty or guarantee of the condition of the animals by the buyer. If the Executor's statements prove to be incorrect, the buyer may make a claim for losses against the estate and against the Executor personally.

Pets may be sold to a dealer or to an individual. The Executor must keep a detailed receipt of the animals sold and the amount of the proceeds. In all cases, an accounting of the sale must be filed and approved by the court before the estate may be closed and the Executor discharged. This is true even when the court ordered the sale or the Will waived the court's supervision. The Executor must keep a copy of all documents relating to the sale and a copy of the payment check to support the accounting. All proceeds of a sale must be deposited into the estate account to await the court's order of distribution.

What income is generated by pets? Generally, pets do not generate ordinary income. If an animal was leased, the lease payments are income. The proceeds of the sale of any animal are taxable gain if those proceeds exceed the basis in the assets and are deductible as a loss if the basis exceeds the proceeds. However, because the basis is stepped up at death to the market value on the date of death, the sale price and the basis are usually the same and there is no gain or loss. A gain arises when the value of the pet increases between the date of death and the sale date. A loss arises when the value of the pet decreases between date of death and the sale date. See Chapter 10 for a discussion of basis in the sale of estate assets.

On what federal estate tax schedule are pets reported? Schedule F. Other Miscellaneous Property.

Are pets reported on the probate inventory? Generally, yes. Pets usually do not have a title or other document of ownership that can transfer ownership of the pet by a beneficiary designation or show ownership by joint tenants with right of survivorship. Tangible personal property such as pets can be placed into a trust that transfers the property to a beneficiary at Decedent's death. Pets are not reported on the probate inventory if held in such a trust.

How are pets transferred out of the estate? The legal transfer of the ownership of pets from the estate to the Legatee is made upon the court's order, either as a partial distribution during the time the estate is being probated or in the final distribution of the estate. The physical transfer is made by actual delivery of possession of the animal into the hands or control of the Legatee. The Executor should obtain a receipt from the Legatee and deliver the pet directly to the Legatee. If the pet cannot be delivered directly but must be shipped, the determination of whether the estate or the recipient will pay the cost of shipping must be part of the court's order for distribution. The Executor must also ensure that the pet is adequately provided for and insured until delivery to the legatee. Contact a veterinarian, airline, or shipping company for instructions regarding the safety and care of a pet during shipping. Insurance for the risk of loss or injury to the pet must be purchased as part of the shipping cost. An ancillary, that is, an additional and supplemental, probate proceeding may be necessary to transfer ownership of pets located in a state other than the state in which the primary probate proceeding is conducted.

PROMISSORY NOTE

What is a promissory note? A note is a signed written document containing a promise to pay a definite sum of money at a specified time and at a specified rate of interest. Notes include promissory notes, demand notes, installment notes, mortgage notes, secured and unsecured notes. When the Decedent was owed money and the debtor promised to repay the debt by signing a promissory note, that promissory note is evidence of an asset that belongs to the Decedent.

What type of asset is a promissory note? A promissory note is intangible personal property. The laws of the Decedent's state of domicile govern the administration and distribution of a promissory note in the probate estate.

How is a promissory note described? The description of a promissory note (when the Decedent is owed money) includes the name of the debtor, the names of all those to whom money is owed, the mode of ownership, the terms of the note, and a description of any property that secures the note.

How is a promissory note valued? The value of a note is the principal amount due plus interest accrued to date of death. Valuation of a note requires a calculation of the terms of the note reduced by previously made payments.

How is information about a promissory note confirmed? A copy of the promissory note, the record of the date and amount of payments, and the written calculation of interest are the information necessary to confirm the description, ownership, and value of the note.

What are the management concerns for a promissory note? The Executor must write to all persons indebted to Decedent informing them of Decedent's death and demanding payment with instructions for payments to be sent to the Executor. All payments must be deposited into the estate account. If debtor fails to pay the debts owed, the Executor must make all reasonable efforts to collect the debt, even if the Decedent had neglected to do so. Collection may require employing a collection agency or an attorney to collect the debt. Failure to act promptly may create a personal liability for the Executor.

The Executor does not have the authority to forgive a debt owed to the Decedent or to the estate. All interested persons must agree in writing before the Executor may neglect collection of the debt. Be aware that the forgiveness of a debt is deemed income by the IRS and may result in the debtor owing income tax on the forgiven debt. Consult with the estate attorney to determine whether the state has a statute that transforms forgiveness of debt in a Will into a non-taxable gift.

May a promissory note be sold during administration of the estate? The Executor must review the Will for instructions concerning the promissory note. A debt owed to the Decedent may be sold to a third party to prevent loss in value or to divide the proceeds of an asset among Legatees. The sale of the note can be accomplished as soon as the Executor has been appointed by the court and has proper authority for the sale. In order to have proper authority to sell the note, the Executor must review the Will to be sure that it expressly permits the Executor to sell personal property. If the Will does not give express authority to sell personal property, the estate attorney must obtain a court order expressly authorizing the Executor to sell personal property. In seeking the court order, the petition must state that the sale is necessary to pay debts, expenses, taxes, or legacies; that there is a risk of loss of value in the asset; or that the sale of the note is in the best interest of the estate for some other reason. When none of these conditions is met, all interested persons can agree in writing that the sale is in the best interest of the estate and the court will give permission for the sale.

For obvious reasons, the sale of estate property to a family member or associate of the Executor is prohibited by state statute even where the Executor has authority to sell property without court supervision. Such a sale is known as self-dealing. See Chapter 8 for a discussion concerning the requirement to avoid self-dealing. This requirement may be overcome if the duty not to self-deal is waived in the Will, or if the court, with full knowledge of the relationship, approves of the buyer and the sale price before the sale.

Whether the court ordered the sale or the Will waived the court's supervision, a complete accounting of the sale must be filed and approved by the court before the estate can be closed and the Executor discharged. The Executor must keep a copy of all documents relating to the sale including a copy of the payment check, to support the accounting for the sale.

The sale price of a promissory note will take into account the creditworthiness of the debtor, the amount due on the note, the interest rate, and the collateral that secures the note. All proceeds must be deposited into the estate account until the court orders distribution.

What income is generated by a promissory note? The payment on a promissory note owed to the estate generally includes interest as well as principal. That interest is income and is reportable on the estate income tax return. The payment of principal is a return of capital and not reportable as income. Although an institution reports interest paid to the estate on a note on IRS Form 1099-INT, the Executor must account for interest income on a promissory note owed by an individual. The individual debtor seldom makes a report of the payment of interest income to the recipient. This failure of the debtor to report the interest paid does not remove the Executor's obligation to report the income received. A note that is uncollectible is written off (deducted) as a bad debt in the year the note is determined to be uncollectible.

On what federal estate tax schedule is the promissory note reported? Schedule C. Mortgages, Notes, and Cash.

Is a promissory note reported on the probate inventory? Generally, the right to repayment for a loan was owned solely by the Decedent, and there is little opportunity to name a Pay-on-Death beneficiary for the note. Some notes are owned by co-owners as tenants in common. The portion owned by the Decedent is treated as probate property. The portion owned by the surviving co-owner is not affected by the Decedent's death. A promissory note can be owned by joint tenants with right of survivorship. At the death of one joint owner, the right to repayment belongs to the surviving joint tenant and the asset is not part of the probate estate. Intangible personal property such as a promissory note can be placed into a trust that transfers the note to a beneficiary at Decedent's death. The note is not reported on the probate inventory if it is held in such a trust.

How is a promissory note transferred out of the estate? If the note cannot be fully collected during the administration of the estate, the court order of distribution will transfer the right to collect the debt to the new owner or owners. The Executor must notify the debtor of the transfer by court order and of the obligation to pay the new owner or owners. If payments on the note have been deposited into the estate account, the court will order distribution and the Executor will write a check to distribute those funds.

REAL PROPERTY

What is real property? Real property (also called real estate) is land and whatever is affixed to the land, such as a house, or growing on it, such as wheat or timber. Real property includes farmland; raw land; residential, rental, and commercial property; oil, gas, and other mineral rights; timber; and growing crops. Some condominiums and time-shares are real estate; others are not. The deed or contract granting rights in the condominium or time-share will describe the property interest. The Executor should consult the estate attorney when unsure of whether property is real estate or personal property.

What type of asset is real estate? Real estate is land and whatever is attached to it. At death, the law of the state where the real estate is located governs administration, sale, and distribution of real estate in the probate estate.

How is real property described? The description of real estate includes the street address, if there is one, and the legal description used on the deed and the real estate records. The description must include the county and state where the property is located. Legal-description systems vary from state to state. These different systems include metes and bounds, Spanish land grant, county land plat descriptions, and governmental land survey. Perhaps in the future we will describe property by geo-positioning coordinates. The Executor should discuss the description of real estate with the estate attorney if there is any uncertainty. The legal description of real property is found on the deed, the real estate tax statement, in the deed records, or other ownership documents filed in the county (or parish in Louisiana) in which the real estate is located. The description of real estate also includes the names of all the owners, the mode of ownership, any Transfer-on-Death deeds, life estates, remainder interests, mortgages, and other restrictions or conditions that apply to the real estate being described. For the description of oil, gas, and mineral interest, see that section in this Summary of Assets.

How is real property valued? If a federal estate tax return is required to be filed, then appraisal of the real estate by a licensed appraiser is required. Some farms and small business have been or could be valued at a special-use value under the Internal Revenue Code § 2032A to avoid taxation at the full fair market value of the property when that property is used by the survivors who continue the farming or other business operation. This special-use valuation must meet strict IRS requirements. The estate attorney or CPA will provide information regarding these requirements. When a federal estate tax return is not required to be filed, appraisal of the real estate by a licensed appraiser may be required by state statute. The estate attorney will know the federal and state law pertaining to appraisal of real estate.

If a federal estate tax return is not required, in many states, appraisal of real estate by a licensed appraiser is not required unless an interested party demands such an appraisal. If an appraisal is not required, an estimate of the sale price by comparison of the sale prices of comparable property can be obtained from a realtor or a real estate auctioneer. When neither federal nor state law require an appraisal by a licensed appraiser, the Executor and all those who will be affected may simply decide on a reasonable value based on credible evidence. The local real estate property tax appraisals are useful but are not conclusive evidence of value. If appraisal by a licensed appraiser is not mandatory, the Executor should discuss the benefits of a formal appraisal against the cost and other limitations that accompany such an appraisal.

The income tax consequences of valuation of the real estate can be significant when that real estate is later sold. Many times the Executor and family members report a low value of real estate on the death tax return to avoid death taxes only to be surprised by the very expensive income tax on the profit when the property is sold later. The value that is reported on the death tax return and the probate inventory establishes the new, stepped-up basis for the real estate. If the amount reported as the date-of-death value of the real estate is lower than the amount the real estate is sold for at a later date, the difference between the date-of-death value and the sales price is taxed as capital gain income. In many states, the immediate family pays a very low inheritance tax rate. The combined state and federal income tax on the difference between basis and sales price can easily be four or five times that rate, depending upon the Devisee's tax bracket. The optimum value to report for tax and inventory purposes is the price for which the real estate will actually sell. The Executor must be careful not to undervalue real estate.

If real estate is sold in an arm's length sale before the estate is ordered to be distributed, the price for which the real estate sold is its fair market value. If a value different than the sale price was reported to the court on an inventory or to the state and federal governments on any tax return, the inventory and any tax returns may need to be amended to reflect the fair market value.

How is information about real property confirmed? Ownership and the legal description of real estate is confirmed by a copy of the deed, the Journal Entry of Final Settlement or the Decree of Descent if the real property was received from the estate of another person, or other document of title from the Register of Deeds or the Clerk of the Court of the county where the real estate is located. The real estate tax statement and street address are guides to locating the deed or other document of title. The statement of an appraiser or real estate broker will confirm the value of the real estate. If the property value was estimated, the evidence that supports that estimate should be retained. A statement of a county or state appraisal for property tax purposes is independent, but not conclusive, evidence of the value of real estate.

What are the management concerns for real estate? Real estate is the subject of state homestead laws that protect a surviving spouse and surviving minor and disabled children. The Executor must consult with the estate attorney to determine whether the real estate is subject to any homestead rights. The Executor should determine whether real estate taxes are owed on the real estate and request that the real estate tax statements be mailed to the Executor or the estate attorney. Payment of real property taxes and mortgage payments should be made if there are sufficient funds. The Executor also must obtain adequate insurance on the property if there are sufficient funds. If the property had been held in joint tenancy with an individual who died before the Decedent, the certified death certificate of that deceased individual must be filed in the deed records of the county where the real estate is located. If the property was received by the Decedent in a probate proceeding, the final order of distribution from the probate court may need to be filed with the deed records to clear the title. Other clouds on the title, including disputes as to ownership, may also need to be cleared, that is, all legal impediments to a free and clear title removed.

If the real estate was on the market before Decedent's death, the Executor must notify the real estate broker who holds the listing of Decedent's death and of the appointment of the Executor.

The Executor must determine the obligations of the estate under rent and lease agreements. Notice of termination of leases and other agreements regarding the real estate must be sent to the tenants when necessary. New leases on the real estate must be signed when necessary. Secure court authority to lease real property when the Will does not specifically authorize the Executor to sign leases. Lessees and renters of estate property must be instructed to send payments to the Executor.

May real estate be sold during administration of the estate? The Executor must review the Will for instructions concerning the sale of real estate. Real estate may need to be sold to pay debts, expenses, or taxes of the estate; to avoid the costs of property taxes, insurance, utilities, and maintenance on the property; to prevent loss in value because of a declining market; or to divide the proceeds among Devisees. There are circumstances in which real estate must be sold even when sale is prohibited by the Will. See Chapter 9 for a discussion of these circumstances.

Real estate that is located in a state other than the state in which the primary probate proceeding is being conducted will be subject to an ancillary, that is, an additional and supplementary, probate proceeding for administration, sale, and distribution. The Executor must consult with the estate attorney to determine how, when, and where to begin the ancillary probate proceedings.

The sale of the real estate can be accomplished as soon as the Executor has been appointed by the court and has proper authority for the sale. The Executor must review the Will to be sure that it expressly permits the Executor to sell real estate. If the Will does not give express authority to sell real estate, the estate attorney must obtain a court order specifically authorizing the Executor to sell real estate.

In seeking the court order, the petition must state that the sale is necessary to pay debts, expenses, or taxes due from the estate; that value of the real estate may decline during the administration of the estate, or that the sale of the real estate is in the best interest of the estate for some other reason. Even if none of these conditions is met, the court will give permission for the sale if all interested persons agree in writing that the sale is in the best interest of the estate.

For obvious reasons, the sale of real estate to a family member or associate of the Executor is prohibited by state statute even where the Executor has authority to sell property without court supervision. Such a sale is known as self-dealing. See Chapter 8 for a discussion concerning the requirement to avoid self-dealing. This requirement may be overcome if the duty not to self-deal is waived in the Will, or if the court, with full knowledge of the relationship, approves of the buyer and the sale price before the sale.

Even when the court ordered the sale or the Will waived the court's supervision, a complete accounting of the sale must be filed and approved by the court before the estate can be closed and the Executor discharged. The Executor must keep a copy of all documents relating to the sale, including the payment check, to support the accounting of the sale. All proceeds of a sale must be deposited into the estate account to await the court's order of distribution.

Within the limits of the state's requirement for a minimum price, setting the sale price is the responsibility of the Executor. The advice of the estate attorney, a realtor, or a real estate auctioneer will be a helpful guide to a sale price, but the Executor has the final decision. Although the Executor should attempt to get the best possible price, it is also important to complete the sale within a reasonable time to avoid the expenses of taxes, maintenance, utilities, and insurance that cannot be recovered. A prompt sale of real estate removes these expenses from the estate.

State statutes control the minimum sale price for real estate. This required minimum price is usually a percentage, for example, 80 percent, of the value reported in the probate inventory. The estate attorney must be consulted before any asset is sold to ensure that the sale price complies with the minimum price requirement. If there are no buyers at the required minimum price after the property has been offered for sale for a reasonable time, the estate attorney must seek court approval to amend the probate inventory to reflect the lower market value and to reduce the minimum sale price.

Real estate in an estate should be sold "as is," and the buyers must be required to inspect the property for themselves or to hire professionals to inspect for them. Whether the property is sold by private sale, by a realtor, or by auction, the Executor should make no statements concerning the condition of the property to the buyers. This is an area of potentially serious liability for the Executor personally and for the estate. Statements regarding the condition of the property made by the Executor may be considered by the buyer as a warranty of the condition of the property. If the Executor's statements prove to be incorrect, the buyers may make a claim for their losses against the estate and against the Executor personally.

The Executor may sell the real estate by offering the property for sale without the assistance of a realtor or auctioneer. Sale of real estate by the Executor avoids the payment of the sales commission to the realtor or auctioneer. Sale by private sale assures that, within the limits of the law, control of who buys the property remains with the Executor. State law dictates that when real estate is sold to the Executor's family or associate, the court must be informed of the relationship and sale price and must approve the sale prior to the closing.

When real estate is sold by the Executor in a private sale, whether the buyer pays cash or obtains a commercial mortgage, a contract for sale must be prepared and signed by the buyers and the Executor. The contract must state, in detail, the terms of the sale, including purchase price, closing date, provisions for earnest money, and how the condition of the property is to be determined. The estate attorney should prepare this contract for a private sale. Because the sale must be approved by the court, the contract should contain a provision that the sale is contingent upon approval by the court. This contract is necessary to protect the estate, for the buyer to obtain financing, and for the closing company to close the sale.

The Executor may sell real estate by contracting with a realtor. Employing a realtor to sell real estate is often the most reliable way to offer the real estate to the largest number of potential buyers over a reasonably short period of time to obtain the best price. The Executor should contact a well-established and reputable realtor to discuss the sale of the property, the listing price, the realtor's plans to promote the property, the length of time the estate will be under contract with the realtor, and the commission. The Executor should avoid hiring close friends or relatives in the business of real estate because the objectivity that is necessary for the Executor to supervise the realtor can be compromised. The property will be shown by the realtor. The sale will be negotiated with the assistance of the realtor and the closing will be arranged by the realtor.

The real estate can be sold at auction for a quick sale to avoid the continuing costs of maintenance, utilities, property taxes, and insurance. The Executor should contact several reputable auction companies to discuss the timing of the sale, sales cost, reserved bids, and advertising. The auctioneer must provide a receipt for the proceeds.

Regardless of the method the Executor uses to sell the real estate, an Executor's Deed will be prepared by the estate attorney for the Executor's signature. When real estate is sold at a private sale, the company that transacts the closing—that is, the execution of all the terms of the sales contract—will provide a closing statement that sets out all the financial details of the transaction. Ask for this closing statement and review it carefully before the actual closing, and correct any mistakes immediately. At closing, the Executor will receive the proceeds and deliver possession of the property to the buyer.

It is extremely unwise for the Executor to agree that the estate will carry the note for the buyer. Carrying a note is actually loaning the money to the buyer. If the potential buyer does not have sufficient credit worthiness to obtain a loan from an established savings and loan company or a bank, then loaning the buyer money from the estate is not prudent and the Executor would be violating a fiduciary duty to the estate.

What income does real estate generate? Payments made for the rental and lease of real estate are income. Rent or lease expenses and a depreciation deduction are allowable to offset the income. The proceeds of the sale are taxable gain if they exceed the basis in the real estate and deductible as a loss if the basis exceeds the proceeds. However, because the basis is stepped up at death to the market value on the date of death, the sale price and the basis are usually the same and there is neither a gain nor a loss. A gain arises when the value of the asset increases between the date of death and the sale date. A loss occurs when the value of the asset decreases between date of death and the sale date. See Chapter 10 for a discussion of basis and gain in the sale of estate assets. Proceeds from Real Estate Transactions are reported on IRS Form 1099-S. The seller must provide the proof of the basis of the property sold. See Oil, Gas, and Mineral Interests in this Summary of Assets for information regarding royalty income on those specific assets.

On what federal estate tax schedule is real estate reported? Schedule A. Real Estate.

Is real estate reported on the probate inventory? Real estate is reported on the probate inventory if owned by the Decedent solely and no Transfer-on-Death beneficiary was named. If real estate was owned by joint tenants with right of survivorship, upon the death of the Decedent the surviving co-owner will own the property and the real estate will not be reported on the probate inventory. If no joint tenant with right of survivorship survives the Decedent, the real estate will be part of the Decedent's probate estate and will be reported on the probate inventory. In some states, a Transfer-on-Death Deed may transfer real estate to a beneficiary at the Decedent's death. If there is a named beneficiary who survives, the real estate will belong to that beneficiary after the Decedent's death and the property will not be reported on the probate inventory. If there is no beneficiary named, if the beneficiary does not survive and no contingent beneficiary survives or if the beneficiaries disclaim the real estate, the Decedent's estate will be the owner of the property and the property must be reported on the probate inventory. Real estate can be placed into a trust that transfers the property to a beneficiary at Decedent's death. The real estate is not reported on the probate inventory if held in such a trust.

How is real estate transferred out of the estate? Real estate is transferred to the new owner by the journal entry of final settlement or other court order. The court's order of distribution certified by the Clerk of the Court must be filed with the Register of Deeds in the county where the real estate is located. No other deed is necessary. The court's order of distribution from the state where the primary probate proceedings are conducted may be filed in any county (or parish) of the state where the estate is administered. However, the court's order of distribution from one state is not effective to transfer real estate located in another state. An ancillary, that is, an additional and supplementary, probate proceeding will be required to transfer the real estate located in a state other than the one in which to primary probate proceedings are being conducted. Consult with the estate attorney regarding ancillary proceedings in a state other than the state where the primary probate proceedings are conducted.

REFUNDS

What is a refund? Refunds are the return of money owed to the Decedent for unused items or services. Refunds may be due for unused newspaper and magazine subscriptions, club dues, traveler's checks, airline tickets, travel vouchers, income taxes, club memberships, and safe deposit box rental. Refunds may also be due from prepaid deposits for nursing home costs, utilities, rent, and prepaid funeral expenses.

What type of assets are refunds? Refunds are intangible personal property. The laws of the Decedent's state of domicile govern the administration, sale, and distribution of refunds in the administration of the estate.

How is a refund described? The refund is described by the name of the company, organization, or individual paying the refund, the payee, and the reason for the refund.

How is a refund valued? The amount that is refunded is the value.

How is information about a refund confirmed? A copy of the refund check, a check stub, or the letter that accompanies the payment will confirm the source of payment, the recipient, and the value of a refund.

What are the management concerns for a refund? The Executor must make reasonable efforts to cancel newspapers and magazine subscriptions and request refunds. The Executor should also notify all clubs, organizations and activities in which Decedent participated of the Decedent's death. Refunds must be requested where appropriate.

Traveler's checks purchased by the Decedent usually can be redeemed by sending a certified return-receipt-requested letter with the contents insured to the issuing company with the traveler's checks, a death certificate, and a copy of the Letters Testamentary certified by the court clerk with instructions for payment to the estate. However, before sending these documents, the Executor should obtain specific instructions for redemption from the company that issued the travelers checks. All unused airline tickets, travel vouchers, and gift certificates must be redeemed as soon as is reasonably possible. The Executor should contact the company or organization for requirements for redemption. Tax refunds for returns that were filed during the Decedent's life will be sent to the Decedent at Decedent's address of record. The Executor can deposit that refund check into the estate account. When the Executor files the tax return after the Decedent's death, the tax refund will be paid to the estate of the Decedent. The Executor must request any other refunds due. All refunds must be deposited into the estate account to await distribution by court order.

May a refund be liquidated during the administration of the estate? A refund may be collected as soon as the Executor is appointed by the court. The Executor must keep a copy of the check that pays the refund to support the accounting. All refunds must be deposited into the estate account until the court orders distribution.

What income is generated by a refund? Generally, refunds do not generate income. Refunds of taxes when the taxes were deducted in a prior year may be required to be included in taxable income for the year in which the refund is received. The amount of the income is determined from the prior year's tax return.

On what federal estate tax schedule is a refund reported? Schedule F. Other Miscellaneous Property.

Is a refund included in the probate inventory? Generally, yes. A refund is usually owned by the Decedent solely, and there is little opportunity to create a joint tenancy with right of survivorship or to make a beneficiary designation.

How is a refund transferred out of the estate? The Executor must deposit the refund into the estate account. The court will order payment of the refund along with all other funds in the estate account in the order of distribution of the estate, and the Executor will write a check to distribute those funds.

RETIREMENT PLANS

What are retirement plans? The federal tax law encourages individuals to invest money for retirement in programs such as individual retirement accounts (IRAs), 401(k)s, 403(b)s, profit-sharing plans, and stock bonus plans by providing preferential tax treatment for these plans. These retirement plans are held in separate accounts and are subject to special rules of distribution and taxation.

What type of assets are retirement plans? Retirement plans are not a separate type of asset; they are arrangements for holding different types of assets under the special taxation and distribution rules of the federal tax code. Tangible and intangible personal property and real estate may be placed in these retirement plans, but, generally, the plans are funded with stocks, bonds, and mutual funds. Administration and distribution of the retirement plans that are assets in the probate estate are governed by the law of the state of Decedent's domicile.

How are these retirement plans described? The retirement plan is described by the type of program under which the plan is administered, for example, 401(k), 403(b), IRA, KEOGH, etc.; the name of the company that administers the plan; the account number of the plan; the name of the owner; and the names of the beneficiaries.

How is a retirement plan valued? The value of a retirement account is the account balance on the Decedent's date of death and, if necessary, the alternate valuation date (the date exactly six months after the date of death). The retirement plan administrator will provide a statement of the retirement account value to the Executor or a beneficiary upon request.

How is information about a retirement plan confirmed? A written statement from the plan administrator specifically requested by the Executor will confirm the description, ownership, account value, beneficiary designations, and the portion of the retirement account that is subject to income tax.

What are the management concerns for a retirement plan? Assets held in tax deferred retirement plans must be examined to ensure that those assets are properly invested. The Executor should apply for or assist beneficiaries in applying for all retirement and death benefits payable to the Decedent's estate, surviving spouse, minor children, or other beneficiaries. Prior employers, even from many years ago, should be contacted and the potential for benefits, including retirement plan benefits, explored.

May a retirement plan be liquidated during administration of the estate? The Executor must review the Will for instructions concerning any retirement plan. Unless the Will prohibits sale or liquidation, assets in a retirement plan may be sold or liquidated to raise cash to pay debts, expenses, or taxes; to prevent losses in value of the plan's assets because of a declining market; or to divide the proceeds of the plan among Legatees. There are circumstances in which a retirement plan may be liquidated even when its sale is prohibited by the Will. See Chapter 9 for a discussion of these circumstances. However, the income tax consequences of liquidation must be carefully considered by the Executor, estate attorney, and CPA to avoid unnecessary tax cost.

An accounting of the liquidation must be reported to the court. The Executor must keep a copy of all documents, including a copy of the payment check, to support the accounting. All proceeds must be deposited into the estate account until the court orders distribution.

What income is generated by a retirement plan? Distributions of pre-tax dollars from a tax deferred retirement plan are taxable as income. These plans can be a significant source of income tax liability for the estate and beneficiaries. Careful consideration of the withdrawal options is necessary. Careful provisions must be made for payment of all taxes. The plan administrator is required to produce a statement of the taxable portion of the account on IRS form 1099-R and can be required to withhold taxes, if desired.

Generally, the proceeds of the sale of investments held in IRA, 401(k), and other tax deferred plans are not subject to the basis step-up rule. Instead, because the money used to purchase these investments was not previously taxed as income, the full amount of the proceeds will be included as income either to the estate or to the beneficiary of the plan.

On what federal estate tax schedule is the retirement plan reported? Schedule I. Annuities. However, any right to payments that ceases at death is not included in the Decedent's gross estate. Social security and pension benefits are not included in the Decedent's gross estate even if the payments continue for the surviving spouse.

Are retirement plans reported on the probate inventory? Usually the Decedent named a beneficiary of the retirement plan. That beneficiary will receive the benefit directly, and the benefit is not reported on the probate inventory. Retirement plans are subject to special rules regarding the rights of a surviving spouse even when the estate or another person is named as the beneficiary. Discuss the rights of a surviving spouse with the estate attorney before making claims for retirement plan proceeds or requesting a final distribution of the plan. However, if the Decedent named the estate as the beneficiary, if the named beneficiary has died before the Decedent and no contingent beneficiary was named, or if the named beneficiary chooses to disclaim the retirement benefits, then the estate will be the beneficiary of the retirement plan and the plan will be reported on the probate inventory. Intangible personal property such as a retirement plan can be placed into a trust that transfers the retirement plan to a beneficiary at Decedent's death. The retirement plan is not reported on the probate inventory if it is held in such a trust.

How is a retirement plan transferred out of the estate? If the retirement benefits will be paid to the estate, the Executor or the estate attorney must contact the plan administrator to obtain claim forms. The completed forms must be signed and returned to the plan administrator. Money payable to the estate from the plan must be deposited into the estate account. The court will order payment of the funds in the order of distribution of the estate, and the proceeds will be distributed by check. Pay close attention to the rights of a surviving spouse to the proceeds of a retirement plan that is administered under federal tax laws.

If the retirement plan will remain in the plan, the Executor, successor owner, the beneficiary, or the estate attorney must request transfer of ownership forms and instructions for transfer from the retirement plan administrator. There may be alternatives offered for distribution. The consequences of each alternative should be well understood before an election for distribution is made. The forms must be completed, signed as instructed, and returned to the plan administrator.

STOCKS

What are stocks? Stocks represent ownership in a corporation. The shares of a corporation may be publicly traded on a stock exchange or sold over the counter, or the stock may represent ownership in a closely held family business. Stocks include preferred stock, common stock, stock rights, penny stocks, dividends, shadow stock, warrants, and options.

What type of asset are stocks? Stocks are intangible personal property. The laws of the Decedent's state of domicile govern the administration, sale, and distribution of stock in the administration of the probate estate.

How is stock described? Stock is described by the company name, the type of stock (preferred, common, etc.), the number of shares, the stock certificate number or the account number, whether the stock is held in book-entry form, a CUSIP number, the par value, the name of the owner, the mode of ownership, any restrictions shown on the face of the stock, and the names of any beneficiaries. The principal exchange upon which the stock is sold, if the stock is listed, and the abbreviation or symbol used to identify the stock on that exchange are also useful information.

How are stocks valued? The value of stocks traded on an exchange can be determined by reference to market quotations published in the *Wall Street Journal* or other financial newspaper. The value of stock is the mean between the highest and lowest quoted prices on the valuation date. If there were no sales of that stock on the valuation date, then a weighted average of the means between the highest and lowest sales on the nearest date before and the nearest date after the valuation date is taken as the value (Treasury Regulations Section 20.2031-2(b)(1)).

Rather than attempt to calculate this value from the raw data, the Executor may request a statement of the date of death value of stock from the account representative for any stock held in book-entry form in an investment account. The value of stock traded on an exchange that is not held in book entry form may be obtained from an Internet site, such as www.askresearch.com. Ask the estate attorney or an investment account representative for assistance.

Stock of a closely held business or stock that is not actively traded may require appraisal by a licensed appraiser. In order to properly value the underlying company, the appraiser may refer to such factors as earning capacity, net worth, dividend-paying capacity, general economic outlook in that industry, and stock values of similarly situated corporations. The value of stock of closely held businesses may be discounted because of lack of control or lack of marketability; or it may be priced at a premium for a majority or controlling interest. The estate attorney will know of a licensed appraiser who has expertise in valuing such stock.

How is information about stock confirmed? If the stock is traded on a stock exchange or over-the-counter (OTC), the description, ownership, and date-of-death value can be confirmed by requesting the information in writing from the brokerage or investment company where the stock is held. If a brokerage company does not hold the stock, a registered investment representative still can confirm in writing the ownership, the description, and the value. A fee may be charged for this service. The face of the stock confirms the description and ownership of stock held in certificate form. The date-of-death values for stock certificates that are held in certificate form can be obtained from a copy of the *Wall Street Journal* or other financial newspaper, from the public library reference section, or on an Internet site such as www.askresearch.com. Information to confirm the description and ownership of closely held stock can be obtained from the company that issued the stock or from the face of the stock certificate. Appraisal by a CPA or licensed appraiser of closely held stock may be necessary to confirm the value.

What are the management concerns for stock? The Executor must immediately cancel and settle any open orders and accounts with brokers. The Executor must check preferred stock, options, and other securities for expiration of rights and conversion privileges. The Will must be consulted for specific instructions with regard to sale or distribution of stocks. If there are no specific instructions, the Executor must determine whether stock will be retained for distribution in-kind or sold and distributed in cash. For a closely held business, a quick sale must be considered to preserve value where the Decedent was a primary manager of the business and the productiveness of the business rested largely on his or her abilities. Holding stock involves a risk of loss that may not be permissible for investment of estate funds. Within a reasonable period of time the Executor must evaluate the risk involved in holding the stock, consult the state law regarding retention of assets purchased by the Decedent, and either sell or distribute the stock or obtain written approval from Legatees for retention of the stock. In making the decision whether to sell the stock or to distribute in-kind, the legatees should be made aware that if stock is sold, the cost of reinvestment of proceeds of the sale may include a commission to the broker. The Executor is wise to obtain instructions from transfer agents for transfer or sale early in preparation for distribution or sale. In addition, the Executor and the Legatees must determine whether the stocks will be purchased by a family member or an employee or sold by a broker on the over-the-counter market or on an exchange. For a closely held business, the Executor must determine whether a Buy-Sell agreement exists and act according to its terms. The Executor must also determine whether an appraisal will be necessary.

A special provision of the federal tax code (IRC § 303) permits redemption of stock owned by the Decedent's estate of up to the amount of estate and inheritance taxes and the amount of funeral and some administration expenses of the estate when certain requirements are met. This redemption of stock for cash is treated as an exchange of the stock in full payment of the stock redeemed. The significance of this redemption is that the amount redeemed under this provision is not subject to income tax. Without this special provision, the exchange of stock for cash from the corporation is treated as a taxable dividend. The Executor must consult with the estate attorney or CPA regarding this special tax-savings provision when the Decedent's estate has substantial stock holdings.

May stock be sold during the administration of the estate? The Executor must review the Will for instructions concerning the sale of stock. Stock may be sold to raise cash to pay debts, expenses, or taxes; to prevent losses in value because of a declining market; or to divide the proceeds of an asset among legatees. The Executor may need to consider sale of assets for other reasons as well. Certain stock can be sold back to the corporation that issued the stock (redeemed) to obtain a tax-favored distribution from that corporation. There are circumstances in which stock must be sold even when its sale is prohibited by the Will. See Chapter 9 for a discussion of these circumstances.

The sale of stock may be accomplished as soon as the Executor has been appointed by the court and has proper authority for the sale. The Executor must review the Will to be sure that it expressly permits the Executor to sell personal property. If the Will does not give express authority to sell personal property, the estate attorney must obtain a court order expressly authorizing the Executor to sell stock.

In seeking the court order, the petition must state that the sale is necessary to pay debts, expenses, taxes, or legacies; that there is a risk of loss of value in the asset; or that the sale of the stock is in the best interest of the estate for some other reason. When none of these conditions is met, all interested persons can agree in writing to sell the stock and the court will give permission for the sale.

For obvious reasons, the sale of stock to a family member or associate of the Executor is prohibited by state statute even where the Executor has authority to sell property without court supervision. Such a sale is known as "self-dealing." See Chapter 8 for a discussion concerning the requirement to avoid self-dealing. This requirement may be overcome if the duty not to self-deal is waived in the Will, or if the court, with full knowledge of the relationship, approves of the buyer and the sale price before the sale.

Whether the court ordered the sale or the Will waived the court's supervision, a complete accounting of the sale must be filed and approved by the court before the estate can be closed and the Executor discharged. The Executor must keep a copy of all documents relating to the sale and a copy of the payment check to support the accounting. All proceeds must be deposited into the estate account until the court orders distribution.

The sale price of stock is controlled by the market price at the time of the sale. If the stock is held in certificate form, the Executor may deposit it with a brokerage or investment company to have it placed in book-entry form for sale. Stock held in book-entry form is sold by the investment company when the Executor provides a letter of instruction requesting the sale. The Executor should contact the investment company for instructions for sale.

What income is generated by stock? Taxable income is generated on stock in the form of dividends. Dividends are reported on IRS form 1099-Div. When the stock is sold, capital gain or loss is also reportable as income. Proceeds of the sale of stock are reported on IRS Form 1099-Broker's Statement. The seller must provide the proof of the basis of the property sold. See Chapter 10 for a discussion of basis and gain in the sale of estate assets. For income tax purposes, the proceeds of the sale are taxable as a capital gain if they exceed the basis in the asset and deductible as a loss if the basis exceeds the proceeds. However, because the basis is stepped up at death to the market value on the date of death, the sale price and the basis are usually the same and there is no gain or loss. A gain arises when the value of the asset increases between the date of death and the sale date. A loss arises when the value of the asset decreases between the date of death and the sale date.

The proceeds of the sale of investments held in IRA, 401(k), and other tax deferred plans are not subject to the basis step-up rule. Instead, because the money used to purchase these investments was not previously taxed as income, the full amount of the proceeds will be included as income to the estate or to the beneficiary of the plan.

On what federal estate tax schedule is stock reported? Schedule B. Stocks and Bonds. Dividends payable after the Decedent's date of death but declared to the Decedent as a holder of record before the Decedent's date of death are reported separately on Schedule B.

Is stock reported on the probate inventory? Stock may be owned by the Decedent solely and have no Pay-on-Death beneficiary. This stock is part of the Decedent's probate estate, reported on the probate inventory, and subject to probate administration. However, stock often has a co-owner or a Pay-On-Death beneficiary. If there is a joint tenant with right of survivorship on the stock, the surviving co-owner will own the stock after the death of the Decedent and the stock is not reported on the probate inventory. If there is a named beneficiary who survives, that beneficiary will own the stock after the Decedent's death and the stock is not reported on the probate inventory. If there is no beneficiary named, if the named beneficiary does not survive and no contingent beneficiary survives, or if the beneficiaries disclaim the stock, the estate will be the owner of the stock and the stock must be reported on the probate inventory. Intangible personal property such as stock can be placed into a trust that transfers the stock to a beneficiary at Decedent's death. The stock is not reported on the probate inventory if it is held in such a trust.

How is stock transferred out of the estate? Stock can be transferred in-kind. An in-kind distribution means that the stock is transferred directly into the name of the new owner. Shares owned by the estate can be distributed to separate Legatees by dividing shares by a stated value or in percentages. To receive an in-kind distribution of stock, each Legatee must either already have or open a brokerage account in his or her own name before the distribution. The Legatee's investment account number and the investment company's Depository Transfer Clearing (DTC) number must be provided to the Executor by each Legatee. The account number and the DTC number for each Legatee will be included in the Letter of Instruction that is sent to the holder or transfer agent of the stock. The estate attorney or the Executor must request instructions for transfer from each transfer agent or from the registered representative of the account. Usually the transfer agent or the registered representative will require a certified death certificate, a Letter of Instruction signed by the Executor with that signature Medallion guaranteed, a copy of the Letters Testamentary certified by the clerk of the court in the last 30 to 60 days, and a copy of the court's order of distribution certified by the clerk of the court in the last 30 to 60 days. A tax waiver for state death taxes and an Affidavit of Domicile may also be required. The instructions of the transfer agent or the registered representative should be followed carefully. These transactions can take several communications with the transfer agent or registered representative before all the requirements are fulfilled to the transfer agent's satisfaction. Be patient. When stocks are transferred in-kind to a new account, there is no reinvestment fee, but there may be a transaction fee. The Executor should inquire about fees prior to transfer. Transfer of closely held stock may require compliance with restrictions on those stocks. Instructions for transfer will be provided upon request by the company that issued the stocks.

TANGIBLE PERSONAL PROPERTY

What is tangible personal property? Tangible personal property is property that has intrinsic value—that is, its usefulness is not merely representative. The following special categories of tangible personal property are discussed under these titles in this Summary of Assets: Antiques, Art, Automobiles, Family Memorabilia, Goods in Storage, Jewelry, Personal and Household Property, and Pets. Other items of tangible personal property such as gold and silver bullion, precious stones, business equipment, and collections are not discussed specifically. Consult with estate attorney for additional information.

What state's law controls administration of tangible personal property? The laws of the state where tangible personal property is located govern administration, sale, and distribution of tangible personal property in the probate estate.

How is tangible personal property described? The description of tangible personal property includes a description of the physical characteristics of the property and the name of the owner. Tangible personal property customarily has no written or recorded title; possession of the property is primary evidence of ownership. A bill of sale may also be evidence of ownership. It is important that the Executor consult with the estate attorney concerning the status of any untitled property if there is a controversy about ownership.

For purposes of any estate tax return, personal property must be itemized. However, items in the same room that have a value of $100 or less may be grouped together. Individual items or sets of items having a total value in excess of $3,000 must have an appraisal from a licensed appraiser filed with the estate tax return. The Executor must file a written, sworn statement with the federal estate tax return that the list of itemized property is complete and that the appraisers were disinterested and qualified.

For purposes of distribution of the assets to Legatees, a more detailed description may be necessary. Determine with the estate attorney how detailed a description is required. Consult the specific type of asset in this Summary of Assets for instructions for the description of each type of tangible personal property.

How is tangible personal property valued? Determine with the estate attorney the type of valuation that is required. The value of tangible personal property can be determined in a variety of ways, including agreement of the parties, an informal valuation by a dealer or estate sale professional, or a formal, written appraisal by a licensed appraiser. If tangible personal property is sold in an arm's length sale before the estate is ordered to be distributed, the price for which the property sold is its fair market value. If a value different than the sale price was reported to the court on an inventory or to the state and federal governments on any tax return, the inventory and any tax returns may need to be amended to reflect the fair market value. Review the section on the specific type of asset in this Summary of Assets for more specific instructions for the valuation of each type of tangible personal property.

How is information about tangible personal property confirmed? The Executor should record the facts used to determine the value in any informal valuation. A formal written appraisal prepared by a licensed appraiser will confirm the description and value of those items appraised. Consult the Summary of Assets for instructions for the confirmation of information of each specific type of tangible personal property.

What are the management concerns for tangible personal property? The Executor must collect the Decedent's personal property in the possession of others. The contents of all safes and safe deposit boxes must be examined. The contents of the safe deposit box should be inventoried and placed in a safe deposit box in the name of the estate. The Executor must ensure that all tangible personal property is safely stored and adequately insured. Some items are affected by heat, cold, and humidity. Consult with a dealer for special instructions for care of specific assets. Early distribution or sale of these assets will minimize the risk of loss and the costs of storage, maintenance, and insurance. However, property cannot be distributed without a court order. Tangible personal property may be the subject of state spousal and minors' allowance. The Executor must determine with the estate attorney whether the tangible personal property will be included in that allowance. Consult the specific type of asset in this Summary of Assets for instructions for management of each type of tangible personal property.

May tangible personal property be sold during administration of the estate? Tangible personal property is commonly the subject of state spousal and minors' allowance laws. The Executor must consult with the estate attorney to ensure that these laws are followed. The Executor must review the Will and any personal property memorandum for instructions concerning sale of tangible personal property. The Executor must also review any personal property memorandum to be sure that the tangible personal property has not been specifically given (bequeathed) to a Legatee. If the tangible personal property is not part of the spousal and minors' allowance or specifically bequeathed and nothing in the Will prohibits sale, property may be sold to pay debts, expenses, or taxes; to avoid the costs of storage, insurance, and maintenance; to prevent loss in value because of a declining market; or to divide the proceeds of the sale among legatees. There are circumstances in which tangible personal property must be sold even when it is specifically bequeathed or when its sale is prohibited by the Will. See Chapter 9 for a discussion of these circumstances.

Tangible personal property located in a state other than the state in which the primary probate proceeding is being conducted will be subject to an ancillary, that is, an additional and supplementary, probate proceeding for administration, sale, and distribution. The Executor must consult with the estate attorney to determine how, when, and where to begin the ancillary probate proceedings.

The sale of tangible personal property can be accomplished as soon as the Executor has been appointed by the court and has proper authority for the sale. The Executor must review the Will to be sure that it states that the Executor has the authority to sell personal property. If the Will does not give express authority to sell personal property, the estate attorney must obtain a court order specifically authorizing the Executor to sell personal property.

In seeking the court order, the petition must state that the sale is necessary to pay debts, expenses, taxes, or legacies; that the value of the asset will decline as time goes by; or that the sale of the tangible personal property is in the best interest of the estate for some other reason. When none of these conditions is met, all interested persons can agree in writing that the sale is in the best interest of the estate and the court will give permission for the sale.

For obvious reasons, the sale of estate property to a family member or associate of the Executor is prohibited by state statute even where the Executor has authority to sell property without court supervision. Such a sale is known as self-dealing. See Chapter 8 for a discussion concerning the requirement to avoid self-dealing. This requirement may be overcome if the duty not to self-deal is waived in the Will, or if the court, with full knowledge of the relationship, approves of the buyer and the sale price before the sale.

Within the limits of the state requirement for a minimum price, setting the sale price is the responsibility of the Executor. The advice of the estate attorney or a dealer in personal property will be a helpful guide, but the Executor has the final decision. Although the Executor should attempt to get the best possible price, it is also important to complete the sale within a reasonable length of time. Storage and maintenance costs, personal property taxes, and insurance are expenses that cannot be recovered. A prompt sale removes these expenses from the estate.

State statutes control the minimum sale price for tangible personal property. This required price is usually a percentage, for example, 80 percent, of the value reported in the probate inventory. The estate attorney must be consulted before any asset is sold to ensure that the sale price complies with the required minimum price. If there are no buyers at the required minimum price after the assets have been offered for sale for a reasonable length of time, the estate attorney must seek court approval to amend the probate inventory to reflect the lower market value and to reduce the minimum sale price.

Tangible personal property should be sold "as is," and the buyers must be required to inspect the property for themselves or to hire professionals to inspect for them. Whether the sale is accomplished by private sale or by auction, the Executor should make no statements concerning the condition of the property to the buyers. This is an area of potentially serious personal liability for the Executor as well as for the estate. Any statements of the Executor may be considered by the buyer as a warranty or guarantee of the condition of the property. If the Executor's statements prove to be incorrect, the buyers may make a claim for their losses against the estate and against the Executor personally.

Tangible personal property may be sold to an individual in a private sale or at an "estate sale" or by auction in a public sale. Sale of tangible personal property by a professional is highly recommended for the reasons set out in detail in Chapter 8. The Executor should contact several reputable estate sale or auction companies to discuss the timing of the sale, sale costs and commissions, reserved bids, and advertising. Usually these professionals will charge a percentage of the total sale proceeds as a sales commission. The Executor or estate attorney should negotiate and confirm in writing a reasonable commission before the sale. This cost is an expense of the estate and will be paid from estate assets. The professional must be required to provide a detailed receipt for items sold and the amount of the proceeds.

In all cases, an accounting or report of the sale must be filed and approved by the court before the estate may be closed and the Executor discharged. This is true even when the court had previously ordered the sale or the Will waived the court's supervision. The Executor must keep a copy of all documents relating to the sale and a copy of the payment check to support the accounting. All proceeds of a sale must be deposited into the estate account for administration and to await the court's order of distribution.

What income is generated by tangible personal property? Generally, no income is generated by tangible personal property. If property is leased, lease payments are income. The proceeds of the sale of tangible personal property are taxable as gain if those proceeds exceed the basis in the assets and are deductible as a loss if the basis exceeds the proceeds. However, because the basis is stepped up at death to the market value on the date of death, the sale price and the basis are usually the same and there is no gain or loss. A gain occurs when the value of the asset increases between the date of death and the sale date. A loss arises when the value of the asset decreases between the date of death and the sale date. See Chapter 10 for a discussion of basis and gain in the sale of estate assets.

On what federal estate tax schedule is tangible personal property reported? Schedule F. Other Miscellaneous Property.

Is tangible personal property reported on the probate inventory? Usually, yes. Tangible personal property is usually in the possession of the owner and does not have a title or other document of ownership. Because of this, there is little opportunity to transfer tangible personal property to a co-owner or beneficiary. Tangible personal property can be placed into a trust that transfers the tangible personal property to a beneficiary at Decedent's death. The tangible personal property is not reported on the probate inventory if it is held in such a trust.

How is tangible personal property transferred out of the estate? Tangible personal property is commonly the subject of state spousal and minors' allowance laws. The Executor should consult with the estate attorney regarding these spousal and minors' rights before distributing tangible personal property. The transfer of the ownership of tangible personal property from the estate to the Legatee is made by court order, either as a partial distribution during the time the estate is being probated or in the final distribution of the estate. The physical transfer is made by actual delivery of possession of each item into the hands or control of the Legatee. The Executor should obtain a receipt from the Legatee and deliver the item directly to the Legatee. If the item must be shipped, the determination of whether the estate or the recipient will pay the cost of shipping must be part of the court's order for distribution. The Executor must also ensure that the item is adequately insured until delivery to the legatee. Insurance for the risk of loss or damage to the item must be purchased as part of the shipping cost. An ancillary, that is, an additional and supplementary, probate proceeding may be necessary to transfer ownership of tangible personal property located in a state other than the Decedent's domicile at death. Review the section on the specific type of asset in this Summary of Assets for instructions for transfer of each type of tangible personal property.

TRUSTS

What is a trust? A trust is a legal arrangement that vests the legal ownership of property in a trustee and the beneficial ownership of that same property in a beneficiary. The trustee is responsible for management of the trust; the beneficiary is entitled to all the benefits from the trust. There are many types of trusts, including Revocable Living Trusts, Testamentary Trusts, Irrevocable Trusts, Insurance Trusts, and Crummey Trusts. The Executor must consult with the estate attorney to determine the exact nature and terms of the trust. For purposes of administering the Decedent's estate, it must be determined whether the Decedent retained a life interest that would require the trust assets to be reported on the Decedent's estate, inheritance, or income tax returns and whether there is any interest in the trust that must be administered by the Executor as part of the probate estate. A revocable living trust for which the Decedent was the grantor and the lifetime beneficiary that transfers its assets to successor beneficiaries at the Decedent's death is reported on the Decedent's estate tax return but is not part of the probate estate. If the estate is the beneficiary of any trust assets, the Executor must administer those assets as probate property. A trust can contain real estate or tangible or intangible personal property.

What type of asset is a trust? A trust is not a type of asset itself, but like retirement accounts, it is an arrangement whereby all types of assets, including real estate and personal property, can be held in the trust. See the Summary of Assets for a description of each specific type of asset.

How is a trust described? The description of the trust includes the complete name of the trust, the date the trust and any amendments were signed, the name of the trustee, the tax identification number of the trust, a complete description of the assets held in the trust, and the interest that is owned by the Decedent's estate. If the estate is to receive assets from the trust, a complete description of the assets that will be received by the Decedent's estate is necessary. See the specific type of asset in this Summary of Assets for instructions for the description of specific assets.

How is a trust valued? The interest owned by the Decedent's estate must be determined under the terms of the trust. The valuation of a right to a stream of income from a trust will require special valuation techniques. The estate attorney or a CPA familiar with fiduciary accounting should be consulted. Assets that are to be transferred by the trust are valued in the same manner as that type of asset is valued when it is not held in trust. See the specific type of asset in this Summary of Assets for instructions for the valuation of specific assets.

How is information about a trust confirmed? The trust document, the account statements for the assets held in trust, and the documents and calculations used in valuing the interest or trust assets are necessary to confirm the information.

What are the management concerns for a trust? If the Decedent was a beneficiary of a trust, the Executor and estate attorney must examine the trust document to determine whether the Decedent's estate is entitled to benefits from the trust. If the Decedent was the trustee of a trust, the Executor must examine the trust document to determine who is the successor trustee and transfer the necessary documents and information to that successor. When the Decedent was the trustee of a trust, a final accounting must be prepared and presented to those entitled to it. If no one is entitled to an accounting immediately, the accounting must be preserved for the estate's and the Executor's protection. Each asset that is transferred to the Decedent's estate must be managed as that asset would be managed in the absence of the trust.

May a trust be liquidated during the administration of the estate? Generally, a trust is administered according to its own terms. If the probate estate has any interest in trust assets or income, the Executor must review the Will for instructions concerning those trust assets and income. Unless prohibited by the Will or the asset is given as a special bequest, any asset that is transferred from a trust to the probate estate may be sold or liquidated under the same conditions as that asset would be sold if the asset has been an original part of the probate estate. See the individual asset in this Summary of Assets for specific information regarding the sale of that type of asset.

What income is generated by a trust? The interest owned by the estate may include the right to income and that income is taxable. If the assets of the trust are being distributed to the estate free of trust, those assets may include accrued interest, dividends, deferred income, and realized capital gains that are taxable to the estate. A statement of income from the trust should be reported to any beneficiary, including the estate, on a IRS Form K-1 or 1099.

On what federal estate tax schedule is a trust reported? A trust in which the Decedent was the Grantor is reported on Schedule G. Transfers During Decedent's Life. Trust income and assets transferred to the estate when the estate is the beneficiary and the Decedent was not the Grantor are reported on Schedule F. Other Miscellaneous Property.

The federal tax authorities are also interested in whether the Decedent had any rights to appoint another person to take assets from a trust that the Decedent did not own. These rights are reported on Schedule H.

Are trust assets reported on the probate inventory? Trust assets are usually transferred outside of probate according to the terms of the trust. However, some trusts name the estate of the Decedent as the beneficiary or do not name a beneficiary at all—for example, trusts created for the purpose of allowing a bank trust department to administer trust assets during the owner's life. The assets of such a trust revert to the owner at the owner's death or name the owner's estate as the beneficiary. A careful review of the trust documents is essential to identify probate property.

How are trusts transferred out of the estate? Trust assets are usually transferred according to the terms of the trust, not at the direction and order of the probate court. However, when the estate is named as the beneficiary of the trust, the assets received from the trust are transferred free of the trust in the same manner as that type of asset would be transferred if there had been no trust. See the section for each type of asset in this Summary of Assets for further instructions regarding transfer of each type of asset out of the estate.

Appendix VI

Questions to Ask Your Attorney

Throughout the *Executor's Guide*, the notes are used in three distinct ways. First, when a question is raised that each state may answer with a different rule, the note asks: "What is this state's rule?" Second, when a question is a matter of federal law and therefore uniform throughout the United States, the federal law is cited. Third, a few examples and explanations are placed in the notes where those examples or explanations would obstruct the flow of the text.

These notes are collected here as a guide to discussing the administration of the estate with the attorney. All notes are labeled by chapter and number for easy reference in the text. For example, footnote 4.6 is the sixth footnote in Chapter 4.

Each estate is unique. Many of the questions asked here will not pertain to the estate you are administering, but will deal with special situations that may be encountered in some estates. Rely on the judgment and experience of the estate attorney to know what is relevant to this estate.

CHAPTER 1

1.1 How is the probate estate defined by state statute?

1.2 How does the state define the Decedent's taxable estate? The federal law definition of taxable estate is found at IRC § 2051.

1.3 How is the Executor's role defined by this state's statute?

1.4 What are the duties of the Executor under this state's law?

1.5 How is Fiduciary Duty defined by this state's statute?

1.6 Can the duty to avoid self-dealing be waived by a Will?

1.7 Is a Settlement Agreement authorized by this state's statute?

1.8 How much is the surcharge or penalty for breach of fiduciary duty?

1.9 Are the Co-Executors responsible for acts of one another in this state?

1.10 Can the court appoint an Executor who lives out of this state?

1.11 What duties may the Executor delegate?

1.12 What is this state's requirement for the appointment of an in-state agent for an out-of-state Executor?

1.13 Can the Executor decline to serve in this state? Under what circumstances?

1.14 Can the court appoint an Administrator of the Will if no named Executor can serve?

1.15 Are the expenses of the Executor reimbursed as an administrative expense in this state?

1.16 Are Executor's fees authorized by this state's statute? Is the basis of the fees hourly or a percentage of the estate?

1.17 Federal and state income taxes are payable on Executor's fees. IRC § 61(1)

1.18 Durable Power of Attorney terminates at death of Testator! What is this state's statute?

1.19 Who has authority to make funeral arrangements after the death of the Testator?

CHAPTER 2

2.1 What are the legal requirements for a Will under this state's statute?

2.2 How is "domicile" defined by this state's statute?

2.3 Under what circumstances is a Foreign Will valid in this state?

2.4 Is a Holographic Will valid under this state's statute?

2.5 Nuncupative Will
   1. Is an Oral or Nuncupative Will recognized in this state?
   2. What circumstances must exist for the Oral Will to be valid?
   3. What property may be transferred under an Oral Will?
   4. What are the requirements for formalizing the Oral Will?

2.6 How is the Living Will defined by this state's statute?

2.7 How is a Codicil defined by this state's statute?

2.8 Is a Memorandum Distributing Personal Property authorized in this state's statutes?

2.9 Is a self-proving clause authorized in this state's statutes?

2.10 What is this state's requirement for consent of the surviving spouse to the Decedent's Will?

2.11 Does this state's statutes presume that a Will is revoked if that Will cannot be found?

2.12 What are this state's criteria for presenting a copy of a Will, instead of the original, for probate?

2.13 What is the time limit for offering the Will for probate in this state?

2.14 What exceptions are there in this state to the time limit for offering a Will for probate?

2.15 What procedures are available to force someone who is withholding the Will to produce it?

2.16 What are the definitions of ademption, advancement, and extinguishment in this state's statutes?

2.17 How is the payment of the funeral bill and expenses of administration provided for in this state's statutes?

2.18 How does this state's statute provide for succession in a case where the named Legatee predeceases the Testator?

2.19 What is the hierarchy for abatement in this state's statutes? What gifts are used to pay debts and expenses?

CHAPTER 3

3.1 Does this state require that the Will be filed with the court and an estate proceeding opened?

3.2 What are this state's requirements for an Executor to be appointed by the court?

3.3 What is this state's requirement for notice to be sent to all interested persons?

3.4 Does the Executor have some limited powers before appointed by the Court? What specific powers?

3.5 Which state statute authorizes the Executor to act under the Letters Testamentary?

3.6 Do creditors have the right under this state's law to administer the estate?

3.7 Is probate administration required to transfer property in this state?

3.8 How are creditors' claims classified under this state's laws? See Chapter 9 for classification of creditors' claims.

3.9 How are assets allocated among Legatees and Devisees under this state's laws? See Chapter 12 for allocation of assets.

3.10 Does this state's statutes require the Will to be filed with the probate court?

3.11 Is there a procedure in this state to preserve the Will if there are no probate assets?

3.12 Does this state have summary probate procedures or authorize use of an affidavit to transfer small estates? What is the maximum value of the estate to qualify for these procedures?

3.13 May the requirement for bond be waived under this state's statute or at the court's discretion?

3.14 How is the amount of bond calculated?

CHAPTER 4

4.1 How do this state's statutes define "interested persons"?

4.2 What legal notice is required in this state when the estate is opened?

4.3 What legal notice is required in this state of the hearings on creditors' claims?

4.4 What legal notice is required in this state of the hearings on sale of assets?

4.5 What legal notice is required in this state of the hearings on final distribution?

4.6 Is the Executor required to send a copy of the probate inventory to all interested persons?

CHAPTER 5

5.1 What is the legal age or age of majority in this state?

5.2 How is a disabled, impaired, or incompetent adult defined in this state's statutes?

5.3 Is a Power of Attorney for Health Care Decisions authorized in this state?

5.4 What are the requirements for appointment of a Guardian under this state's law?

5.5 Does a minor over age 14 have the right to nominate his or her own Guardian?

5.6 Does the state law prohibit delivery of assets to a minor or disabled person?

5.7 Is there a statutory exception to Conservatorship for small gifts to minors or disabled persons?

5.8 What is the priority of a parent or other relative to be appointed Conservator under state statute?

5.9 May the court appoint a Conservator who lives in another state?

5.10 Must a Conservator post bond?

5.11 Is a Uniform Transfers to Minors Act enacted in this state's law?

CHAPTER 6

6.1 Within what time period does this state require the probate inventory to be filed?

6.2 Federal Estate taxation of Joint Property IRC § 2040.

6.3 Does this state recognize tenancy by the entirety?

6.4 Does this state require that the intent to own property as joint tenants with rights of survivorship be clearly set out in the deed or title?

6.5 Alternate valuation date authorized by federal tax law. IRC § 2032.

6.6 Fair market value defined. IRC Reg. § 20.2031-1(b).

6.7 Regulations require appraisal of specific assets for federal estate tax purposes. IRC Reg. § 20-2031.

CHAPTER 7

7.1 Does this state's statute authorize the Executor to act before court appointment to protect assets?

7.2 What are this state's restrictions on investment of estate assets?

7.3 Does this state's statute give the Executor special authority to retain assets purchased by the Decedent without diversifying those assets?

CHAPTER 8

8.1 Federal tax law authorizes preferential stock redemption at IRC § 303.

8.2 What are the requirements and restrictions for sale of property under this state's statute?

8.3 Do this state's statutes prohibit self-dealing?

8.4 Do this state's statutes set a minimum sale price?

CHAPTER 9

9.1 Written notice to all known creditors is required. *Tulsa Professional Collection Service* v. *Pope*, 485 U.S. 478 (1988).

9.2 What is the nonclaim period in this state?

9.3 What are the homestead rights and spousal and minor children's allowance in this state?

9.4 What is the priority for funeral expense in this state?

9.5 What is the priority for Medicaid reimbursement in this state?

9.6 What is the priority for expenses of last illness in this state?

9.7 What is the priority in this state for expenses of administration of the estate?

9.8 What is the priority in this state for taxes?

9.9 What is the priority in this state for judgments and liens?

9.10 What is the priority in this state for unsecured debts?

9.11 What is the schedule of abatement for this state?

9.12 How are one class of gifts allocated to pay debt when all value of that class is not required to pay debt in full?

CHAPTER 10

10.1 Definition of "Executor" for purposes of the federal tax code. IRC § 2203

10.2 No income tax on inheritances, legacies, or devises. IRC § 102

10.3 Proceeds of tax deferred investment plans such as 401(k), IRA, taxable to beneficiary. IRC § 402

10.4 Income-in-Respect of Decedent taxable as income and included in estate. IRC § 61(14). Also see IRC §1014(c)

10.5 Compensation of Executor is income. IRC § 61(1)

10.6 Original Purchase Price Basis. IRC § 1012

10.7 Carry-Over Gift Basis. IRC § 1015

10.8 Basis Step-Up to Date of Death Value. IRC § 1014

10.9 Basis determined for state death tax return under same rules as for federal estate tax return. IRC § 1014

10.10 Requirements for filing Decedent's final federal income tax return. IRC 6012(a)

10.11 Unified Gift and Estate Tax Credit. IRC § 2010

10.12 Does this state impose a state generation-skipping tax?

10.13 Does this state require an inheritance, succession, or estate tax return?

10.14 State death tax return must be filed by what deadline?

10.15 Deduction of Medical Expenses. Rev. Rul. 77-357, 1977 – 2 Cum.Bull. 328

10.16 Deduction of Estate Administration Expenses. IRC §§ 212, 642(g), and 2053(a)(2)

10.17 Joint return with surviving spouse. IRC § 6013(a)

10.18 Bond Income. IRC § 454

10.19 Gift Splitting. IRC § 2513

10.20 Marital Deduction. IRC §§ 2056(a), 2056(b)(7)

10.21 Date of Death Value or Alternate Valuation Date Value. IRC § 2032, see also IRC §§ 1014, 303, 6166

10.22 Special Use Valuation. IRC § 2032A, see also IRC §§ 1014, 303, 6166

10.23 Installment Payment of Estate Taxes. IRC § 6166

10.24 Distribution in redemption of stock to pay death taxes, funeral, and administration expenses. IRC § 303

10.25 Request by Executor for Tax Audit. IRC §§ 6501(d) & 2204

10.26 When does this state's law require that an estate be opened?

10.27 Whether to keep financial records on calendar or fiscal year basis. IRC § 441

10.28 What investments are permitted under this state's law?

10.29 Are administration expenses allocated to income or principal under this state's law?

10.30 Under this state's law are death tax payments allocated to Residue?

10.31 Charitable remainder trust charitable deduction for estate. IRC § 2055(a). See also IRC § 2518.

10.32 Disclaimer to take advantage of unified gift and estate tax credit and exemptions. IRC § 2518

10.33 Assets must be allocated with respect to likelihood to appreciate or depreciate. See Rev. Proc. 64-19 1964 Cum. Bull. Part I 862.

10.34 Charitable gift. IRC §2055

10.35 *Leigh v. Commissioner,* 72 T. C. No. 91 (1979).

10.36 *Viles v. Commissioner,* 233 F.2d 376 (6th Cir. 1956); John H. Beasley, 42 B.T.A. 275 (1940).

10.37 Request for prompt assessment of income taxes. IRC § 6501(d)

10.38 Request for discharge from liability. IRC §6905.

CHAPTER 11

11.1 What time is allowed to file disclaimers under this state's law? Federal tax law requires that disclaimers be filed within nine months from date of death. IRC §§ 2046, 2518; Treas. Reg. § 20.2055(c)

11.2 What are the provisions under this state's law for Pre- and Post-Marital Agreements?

11.3 Does this state's statutes provide a requirement for survival to avoid double probate and double taxation?

11.4 Has this state adopted the Uniform Simultaneous Death Act?

11.5 What provisions do this state's statutes make for Testamentary Trusts?

CHAPTER 12

12.1 How much time must pass after the Decedent's death before the Petition for Final Settlement may be filed?

12.2 The use of the alternative valuation date of six months after date of death to report the value of the assets on the Federal

Estate Tax Return (706) is an issue that must be addressed when the taxes are reported and paid, not at final settlement. Consult with the estate attorney and the accountant if you have questions concerning the alternative valuation date.

12.3 What is the priority under this state's statutes for homestead rights and spousal and minor children's allowance?

12.4 What is the priority under this state's statutes for funeral expenses?

12.5 What is the priority under this state's statutes for Medicaid reimbursement?

12.6 What is the priority under this state's statutes for expenses of last illness?

12.7 What is the priority under this state's statutes for expenses of administration of the estate?

12.8 What is the priority under this state's statutes and case law for payment of taxes?

12.9 What is the priority under this state's statutes for judgments and liens?

12.10 What is the priority under this state's statutes for payment of Decedent's unsecured debts?

12.11 What is the abatement schedule in this state's statutes?

12.12 For instance, if all the residuary devises and bequests were consumed leaving $5,000 still due to pay the estate expenses and debts, the general devises would be the next class of gifts to be abated. However, abatement is proportional within a class. In an example, the general devises of all Sedgwick County property worth $2,000 to the son and all Kingman County property worth $8,000 to the daughter would be added together. The payment of $5,000 to satisfy the balance of expenses and debts would be made proportionately from all gifts in this class. Here the son's share would be abated and he would receive $1,000 instead of $2,000 and the daughter would receive $4,000 instead of $8,000.

12.13 Do this state's statutes require disinterested parties to witness Wills?

12.14 Do this state's statutes prohibit a convicted murderer from taking assets of the victim's estate?

12.15 In this state, does divorce invalidate gifts in a Will to an ex-spouse?

12.16 Does this state have an anti-lapse statute?

12.17 Do this state's statutes authorize a Settlement Agreement?

12.18 What elections against the Will do this state's statutes provide?

12.19 Does this state have a spousal share that is not an election against the Will?

Glossary

Most of these terms are defined specifically in the text. A few are relevant to intelligent discussion of estate administration, though not specifically addressed in the text.

Accounting—The preparation of financial statements that will give the court, the Legatees and Devisees, and others involved in the estate a clear picture of the property in the estate available for distribution, the income and disbursements of the estate, and a history of the transactions dating back to the time the Executor first took control of the property.

Adeemed by extinction—Property is sold or given by the Testator before death to someone other than the Legatee that removes the property from the Decedent's estate.

Adeemed by satisfaction—Property is given by the Testator before death to a Legatee that satisfies the legacy in the Will.

Administration—The management of the estate of a deceased person. Administration includes collecting the assets; filing necessary reports and returns; selling property; hiring and supervising the estate attorney; paying the debts, expenses, and taxes; and making distribution to the persons entitled to the Decedent's property.

Administrator—The person appointed to manage an estate if the Decedent had no valid Will or if the Will did not nominate a qualified Executor.

Advancement—Money or property given by a parent to a child, in some states, or in other states to a child or other lineal descendant, as an early distribution of the share the child or other descendant would inherit in the parent's estate and intended to be deducted from the estate.

After-born child—A child born after the execution of a parent's Will.

Alternate valuation date—For federal estate-tax purposes, the date six months after the date of death, upon which the estate assets are valued unless property is distributed, sold, exchanged, or otherwise disposed of within those six months. In that case, the value of such property is determined as of the date of disposition.

Attestation clause—The paragraph at the end of a Will indicating by witnesses' signatures that the witnesses have heard the Testator declare the instrument to be his or her Will and have witnessed the signing of the Will.

Beneficiary—The person who receives a beneficial interest under a trust, insurance policy, pay-on-death or transfer-on-death beneficiary designation made by the previous ownder

Bequest—A gift of personal property by Will; also called a legacy. A specific bequest is a gift of specified personal property ("my watch" or "automobile"). A general bequest is one that may be satisfied from the general assets of the estate ("I give $100 to my brother, Sam").

Codicil—A supplement to an existing Will to make some change in the original Will. A Codicil must meet the same requirements regarding execution and validity as a Will.

CUSIP—A 9-digit identification number assigned to a security (*after* Committee on Uniform Security Identification Proceedings).

Death taxes—The taxes imposed by the federal and state governments on the estate of the Decedent at death; include Estate, Inheritance, Succession, and Generation-Skipping Transfer Taxes.

Decedent—The person who dies.

Depository Transfer Clearing (DTC) number—The number that identifies an investment company for the purpose of transferring securities via the Internet.

Devise—A gift of real estate under a Will.

Devisee—The person to whom land or other real property is given by Will.

Disclaimer—The refusal to accept property that has been devised or bequeathed; a renunciation by the beneficiary of his or her right to receive the property. Federal and state tax laws give the requirements for an effective disclaimer. See also **Renunciation**.

Distribution—The formal act of the Executor disposing of the estate's assets to the designated Devisees and Legatees.

Domicile—An individual's true and permanent home; the place to which, regardless of where he or she is living, an individual intends to return. A person may have two or more residences, but only one domicile.

Escheat—In the absence of lawful heirs and subject to the claims of creditors, the property of a person dying intestate is said to escheat, that is, to "return" to the state.

Estate—(1) The property owned by the Decedent at his or her death that becomes subject to the control of the Executor during the period of the estate's administration. (2) The separate taxable entity for federal and state death tax purposes. The estate for federal income tax purposes commences with the death of the Decedent and continues until the probate estate is wound up.

Estate Tax—A tax imposed on the right of a person to transfer property at death. The estate tax is imposed not only by the federal government but also by many state governments.

Executor—The person named by the deceased in his or her Will and appointed by the Court to manage the Decedent's affairs; the Executor under a fiduciary duty to the estate, who stands in the shoes of the Decedent, collects the assets of the estate, pays the debts and taxes, and makes distribution of the remaining property to the Devisees and Legatees. The word Executrix is sometimes used to denote a female Executor, although it is now accepted that the word Executor is used for both male and female persons.

Extinguishment—When a specific gift that is given in a Will is no longer part of the Decedent's estate at the time of death, the gift is inoperative and is extinguished.

Fair market value—The value at which estate property is included in the gross estate for federal estate tax purposes; the price at which property would change hands between a willing buyer and a willing seller, neither being under compulsion to buy or sell and both having knowledge of the relevant facts.

FBO—An abbreviation for the phrase "for the benefit of."

Federal estate tax—A federal excise tax levied on the right to transfer property at death, imposed on and measured by the value of the estate left by the Decedent.

Fiduciary—One occupying a position of trust. Executors, Administrators, Trustees, and Guardians all stand in a fiduciary relationship to the persons whose affairs they are handling. (See Fiduciary Duty in Chapter 1.)

Future interest—A present right, protected by law or equity, to future possession or enjoyment of property. Examples are executory interest, remainders, and reversions. A present interest is one currently in possession or enjoyment, as is typical with a life estate.

Generation-skipping transfer tax (GST)—A flat-rate tax imposed in addition to the gift or estate tax on transfers of more than a certain amount specified by statues (currently a total $1 million) to skip persons (essentially transfers to grandchildren or great grandchildren). The GST tax may be imposed on direct skips (such as when a grandparent writes a check to a grandchild) or where property bypasses one generation in less obvious ways by trust or otherwise.

Gift—A transfer of money or property during the life of the giver that is intended as a gift. For federal gift tax purposes, a gift is an *inter vivos* transfer for no (or insufficient) consideration in money or money's worth. A "gift causa mortis" is a gift of personal property made in the expectation of imminent death, which is automatically revoked if the donor fails to die as anticipated and is revocable by the donor prior to his death.

Grantor—A person who creates a trust; also called a settlor, creator, donor, or trustor.

Gross estate—An amount determined by totaling the value of all property in which the Decedent had an interest at death. (See IRC § 2001 et seq.)

Guardian—There are two classes of guardians: (1) A guardian of the person is appointed by the surviving parent in his or her Will to take care of the personal affairs of minor children. Because each parent is the natural guardian of the minor children, only the surviving parent can effectively nominate the guardian of the child. (2) A guardian of the property, also know as conservator of a minor or incompetent, is a person or institution appointed or named to represent the financial and legal interests of a minor child or incompetent adult. A guardian of the property can be nominated in a Will, nominated by a Ward or Conservatee, or by another person.

Guardian *ad litem*—A lawyer or other qualified individual appointed by the court to represent the interests of a minor or an incompetent in a particular matter before the court.

Heir—A person designated by law to succeed to the estate of a person who dies intestate, that is, without a Will.

Holographic will—A Will entirely in the handwriting of the Testator. In many states, such a Will is not recognized unless it is published, declared, and witnessed as required by statute.

Homestead—The state constitutional or statutory right of a surviving spouse or minor children to retain a house and land as homestead exempt from Decedent's debts (other than mortgage debt), expenses, and taxes.

Income—The income of an estate or trust consists of receipts that are not treated as corpus or principal. The rules, prescribed by state law or the governing instrument, for determining what is income for estate accounting purposes are very similar, but not identical, to those that define taxable income for federal income tax purposes. Thus, dividends and interest are typically income for estate accounting and federal income tax purposes, but capital gains (which are income for federal income tax purposes) are usually added to corpus for estate accounting purposes.

Incompetent—An individual who has been found incapable of managing his or her own affairs by the court. Many states require a finding that an individual is disabled or impaired, instead of incompetent, before appointment of a guardian or conservator. This definition of a disabled person differs from the Social Security and Veterans Administration's definition of a disabled person.

Inheritance—Strictly speaking, refers to the disposition of property, usually real property, at Decedent's death to heirs insofar as it is not controlled by a Will.

Inheritance tax—A tax levied on the rights of the heirs to receive property from a deceased person, measured by the share passing to each heir; sometimes called a succession tax. The federal death tax is an estate tax, as contrasted to an inheritance tax. Some states have state estate taxes and some have inheritance taxes.

Intangible property—Property that has no intrinsic value. The item itself is only the evidence of value. For example, cash, a certificate of stock, a bond, and an insurance policy are all intangible personal property.

Intestate—"Without a Will." A person who dies without a valid Will dies intestate.

Inventory—A schedule of all the assets of an estate, usually prepared by the Executor with the assistance of the estate attorney, submitted to the probate court upon the signature of the Executor.

Issue—All persons descending from a common ancestor.

Joint tenancy with right of survivorship—Concurrent ownership of property by two or more persons, under which ownership passes automatically to the surviving joint tenant(s) upon the death of one by right of survivorship. An interest in a joint tenancy, therefore, does not pass by inheritance or Will. Compare to tenant in common.

Joint Will—A single instrument that is made the Will of two or more persons and is jointly signed by them. (This is not recommended.)

Lapse—The failure of a gift in the Will due to the death of the named recipient during the life of the Testator. Many states have anti-lapse statutes that prevent the failure of the gift in certain circumstances.

Legacy—A gift of personal property by Will; commonly used to include any disposition by Will.

Legatee—A person to whom a legacy is given.

Letters of Administration—A written document signed by the Probate Court and certified by the court clerk authorizing the Administrator to act on behalf of the estate of a person who dies without a valid Will.

Letters Testamentary—A written document signed by the Probate Court Judge and certified by the court clerk authorizing the Executor to act on behalf of the estate.

Lien—An encumbrance on property securing the payment of a debt.

Life estate—The name of the interest owned by a life tenant; an interest in property that terminates at life tenant's death or at the death of another's measuring life.

Life tenant—The person who receives the benefit from a legal life estate or from a trust fund.

Liquid assets—Cash or assets that can be converted readily into cash without any serious loss. Liquid assets include bank accounts, life insurance proceeds, and government bonds.

Living trust—Also called an *inter vivos* trust, created and effective during grantor's life, may be revocable or irrevocable.

Marital deduction—For federal estate-tax purposes, the amount by which the taxable estate is reduced for transfers to a surviving spouse before the tax rate is applied to calculate the estate tax due. Under present federal estate tax law, the marital deduction is unlimited provided that the property passes to the surviving spouse in a qualified manner. The maximum marital deduction is the portion of a Decedent's estate that may be passed to the surviving spouse without the balance of the Decedent's estate being subject to any federal estate tax.

Ministerial acts—Acts of an Executor or Administrator that do not involve major decisions requiring judgment and discretion and whose performance may be delegated to others without breach of fiduciary duty.

Minor—A person who is under the legal age of majority. The legal age of majority can vary from age 18 to 21 depending on the state law.

Next of kin—The person or persons legally related to the Decedent by the nearest degree of kinship. The person or persons who take personal property upon the death of the Decedent without a Will. Also, those persons who are entitled to determine the method of burial, cremation, or other disposal of Decedent's body.

Nonclaim period—The time specified by state statute for creditors to make their demands upon the estate before their claims are barred (not enforceable).

Nonliquid assets—Assets that are not readily convertible into cash without a potentially serious loss.

Nonprobate property—Property that passes outside the administration of the estate, other than by Will or intestacy laws. For example, jointly held property, life insurance proceeds paid to a named beneficiary, or property in an *inter vivos* (living) trust that passes to a beneficiary are non-probate property.

Per capita—"Equally to each individual." In a distribution *per capita*, the recipients share equally without a right of representation. For example, each of five sons would take one-fifth of the estate. In most states, if descendants are related in equal degree to the Decedent, they take *per capita*; if descendants are of unequal degree (such as four sons and a child of a deceased son), a *per stirpes* distribution is made.

Personal effects—This term, often used in Wills, denotes tangible personal property for personal use, such as clothing, shoes, and articles of personal adornment with a personal connection. The term usually is not used to refer to articles of general utilitarian use, such as cars, consumer durables, and furniture.

Personal property—Refers to any property that is not real property. The term "intangible personal property" refers to stocks; bonds; debentures; notes; claims; partnership interests; options; patents; copyrights; beneficial interests in trusts and estates; chooses in action and other rights conferred by law or contract to receive or acquire money, property, or legal protection in carrying on an economically advantageous activity. "Tangible personal property" refers to physical objects that have intrinsic value, such automobiles, art works, home appliances, jewelry, and the like.

Personal representative—The person in charge of administration of an estate; he or she has a fiduciary relationship to the estate beneficiaries. See also **Administrator** and **Executor**.

Per Stirpes—"By stock." A distribution *per stirpes* occurs when issue succeed to the shares of their lineal ascendants by representation. For example, if a person dies survived by three children and by two children of a deceased child (the Decedent's grandchildren), the two grandchildren succeed to their deceased parent's share, so that one-quarter of the estate goes to each of the surviving children and one-eighth to each of the two grandchildren. Whenever a distribution is to be made to the descendants of any person, the property to be distributed shall be divided into as many shares as there are living children of the person and deceased children who left descendants who are then living. Each living child shall take one share and the share of each deceased child shall be divided among the then-living descendants of the deceased child in the same manner.

Posthumous child—A child born after the death of his or her father.

Pour-Over—The transfer of property from an estate or trust to another estate or trust upon the occurrence of an event specified in the instrument. For example, a Will can provide that at Testator's death certain property be paid (poured over) to an existing trust. This is called a pour-over Will.

Power of appointment—A right given to a person to dispose of property that he or she does not own. There are two types of powers of appointment. A general power of appointment is a power over the distribution of property to any person the holder of the power may select—including himself, his estate, his creditors, or the creditors of his estate. A limited power of appointment, sometimes called a special power, is a power over the distribution of property to only specified persons. An example of a limited power is the power to distribute his sister's assets in trust property at his death to any of his sister's children that he designates.

Power of attorney—A written document that enables an individual, the "principal," to designate another person or persons as his or her attorney-in-fact, the "agent" (agent). The attorney-in-fact must act on the principal's behalf. The scope of the power can be severely limited or quite broad. A "durable power" is the power granted to the attorney-in-fact in the document that survives the mental or physical incapacity of the principal. This power ends at death.

Present interest—A present right to use or enjoy property.

Pretermitted heir—A child or other descendant omitted from a Testator's Will. When a Testator fails to make provisions for a child, either living at the time the will is signed or born thereafter, state statutes often provide that such child or the issue of that child, if deceased, takes an intestate share of the Testator's estate.

Principal—(1) The property comprising the estate or fund that has been set aside in trust or from which income is expected to accrue. The trust principal is also known as the trust corpus or res. (2) One who has directed an agent or attorney in fact to act for the principal's benefits and subject to the principal's direction and control.

Probate—The process of proving the validity of the Will and executing its provisions under the guidance of the court. When a person dies, the Will must be filed with the proper court; this is called filing the Will for probate. When the Will has been filed and accepted, it is said to be admitted to probate. The process of probating the will involves accepting the Will as valid and appointing the Executor named in the Will (or appointing an Administrator C. T. A. if no Executor has been named).

Probate property—Property that can be passed under the terms of the Will or (if there is no Will) under the intestacy laws of the state. Also, property held in the individual name of the Decedent or in which the Decedent had an interest at death, such as property held as tenants in common.

Prudent person rule—The duty of an Executor to invest estate assets in such investments as an ordinary, prudent man or woman of intelligence and integrity would purchase in the exercise of reasonable care, judgment, and diligence under the circumstances existing at the time of purchase when dealing with the property of another.

Publication—(1) A declaration by the Testator to the witnesses of the signing of his or her Will that the instrument is his or her Will. (2) Formal notice in a legal newspaper of the commencement of the probate proceeding to administer the estate.

Real property (real estate)—Land, buildings, fixtures, and interests therein. For some purposes and in some jurisdictions, leases, terms for years, and rights to extract or exploit minerals may be classified as realty.

Remainder—A future interest in property that comes into possession or enjoyment upon the expiration of a prior interest such as a life estate.

Remainderman—The person(s) entitled to receive property after the termination of the prior holder's interest. For example, a mother might set up a trust that pays her daughter all the trust income for the daughter's life, but at her daughter's death the principal in the trust would pass to her son, the remainderman.

Renunciation—An unqualified refusal to accept property or an interest in property. It is the abandonment of a right without the direct transfer to someone else. See also **Disclaimer.**

Residue—The remaining part of the Decedent's estate after payment of debts, expenses, devises, and bequests. Wills usually contain a clause disposing of the Residue of the estate that the Decedent has not otherwise bequeathed or devised.

Revocable trust—A trust that can be changed or terminated during the grantor's lifetime.

Rule against perpetuities—A rule of law invalidating interests in property that will vest too far in the future or by which the Devisee is restricted in disposing of the property for too long a time. The common-law rule, which has been changed in many states, holds that "no interest in property is valid unless it must vest, within lives-in-being plus twenty-one years."

Sole ownership—The holding of property by one person so that only that person has the right to sell or give that property during his or her lifetime and at his or her death.

Surcharge—The amount awarded by the court and payable personally by an Executor, Administrator, or Trustee who has negligently performed his or her duty and who has caused a beneficiary any loss due to that negligence.

Tangible personal property—Property that has physical substance—may be touched, seen, or felt—and itself has intrinsic value (such as a car or furniture).

Taxable estate—An amount determined by subtracting the allowable deductions from the gross estate.

Tenancy by the entirety—The holding of property by husband and wife in such a manner that, except with the consent of the other, neither party has a disposable interest in the property during the lifetime of the other. Upon the death of either, the property is owned solely by the survivor.

Tenancy in common—The holding of property by two or more persons in such a manner that each has an undivided interest, which upon death does not pass to the surviving tenant(s).

Testamentary—"By Will." A testamentary document is an instrument disposing of property at the death of the testator.

Testamentary trust—A trust of certain property passing under a Will and created by the terms of the Will.

Testate—Having left a Will or disposed of the estate by Will.

Testator—A person who leaves a Will in force at death.

Trust—A fiduciary arrangement whereby the legal title of the property is held and the property managed by a person or institution for the benefit of another.

Trustee—The holder of legal title to property for the use or benefit of another; an individual responsible under fiduciary standards for the management and investment of trust assets.

Unified tax credit—For federal gift-tax and estate-tax purposes, a dollar-for-dollar reduction against the federal estate and gift tax.

Year	Sheltered Amount	Credit Amount	Maximum Tax Rate
2001	675,000	220,550	55%
2002	1,000,000	345,800	50%
2003	1,000,000	345,800	49%
2004	1,500,000	555,800	48%
2005	1,500,000	555,800	47%
2006	2,000,000	780,800	46%
2007	2,000,000	780,800	45%
2008	2,000,000	780,800	45%
2009	3,500,000	1,565,800	45%
2010	Estate tax repeal	Estate tax repeal	0% estate tax/ 35% gift tax
2011	1,000,000	345,800	

Uniform Transfers to Minors Act (UTMA)—This act is similar to the Uniform Gifts to Minors Act (UGMA) in purpose but allows any kind of property, real or personal, tangible or intangible, to be the subject of a custodial gift. Most states have replaced their UGMA laws with much broader and more flexible UTMA statutes.

Ward—A minor or disabled person who is the subject of a legal guardianship.

Will—The legal expression of what the Testator wants to happen to his or her property when he or she dies. Formal statutory requirements vary, but usually, at a minimum, a Will must be in writing, express testamentary intent, and be signed at the end. Requirements for witnesses vary from state to state.

Index

Bold terms indicate main headings in Appendix V, *Summary of Assets*.

About the Author

LINDA D. KIRBY is an attorney in Wichita, Kansas, who, since 1988, has focused her practice on probate administration, estate planning, premarital agreements, wills, and trusts. Formerly professor of law at the University of Richmond, she has taught at Newman University, Wichita State University, and in continuing education programs for the Wichita Bar Association, certified Financial Planners, and Certified Life Underwriters.